THE CASE FOR POLARIZED POLITICS

THE
CASE *for*
POLARIZED
POLITICS

*Why America Needs Social
Conservatism*

Jeffrey Bell

ENCOUNTER BOOKS · NEW YORK · LONDON

First American edition published in 2012 by Encounter Books,
an activity of Encounter for Culture and Education, Inc.,
a nonprofit, tax exempt corporation.
Encounter Books website address: www.encounterbooks.com

Manufactured in the United States and printed on
acid-free paper. The paper used in this publication meets
the minimum requirements of ANSI/NISO Z39.48 1992
(R 1997) (*Permanence of Paper*).

FIRST AMERICAN EDITION

LIBRARY OF CONGRESS CATALOGING-IN-PUBLICATION DATA

Bell, Jeffrey, 1943–
The case for polarized politics: why America needs social conservatism/by Jeffrey Bell.
p. cm.
Includes bibliographical references and index.
ISBN-13: 978-1-59403-578-4 (hardcover: alk. paper)
ISBN-10: 1-59403-578-4 (hardcover: alk. paper) 1. Conservatism—United States—
History. 2. United States—Politics and government—Philosophy. I. Title.
JC573.2.U6M349 2011
320.520973—dc23
2011025535

10 9 8 7 6 5 4 3 2 1

CONTENTS

CONTENTS

INTRODUCTION

Toward the end of a long and favorable profile by Andrew Ferguson in the June 14, 2010, issue of the conservative magazine *Weekly Standard*, Indiana Governor Mitch Daniels told his interviewer that the next President "would have to call a truce on the so-called social issues," no matter who is elected. "We're going to just have to agree to get along for a little while," he said, so we can deal with the economic and financial crisis that erupted late in the second term of President George W. Bush. This crisis, politically speaking, remained the first order of business well into the second year of the Democratic presidency of Barack Obama.

A day or two after the article's appearance, another *Standard* reporter, John McCormack, attempted to pin Daniels down on what a truce on social issues might mean: "To clarify whether Daniels simply wants to de-emphasize these issues or actually not act on them, I asked if, as president, he would issue an executive order to reinstate Reagan's 'Mexico City Policy' his first week in office. (Obama revoked the policy during his first week in office.) Daniels replied, 'I don't know.'"*

Among the policy objectives of American social conservatives, reissuing of the Mexico City–related executive order by newly elected Republican presidents is one of the least risky in terms of potential political cost. First issued by President Ronald Reagan more than a quarter-century ago, it prohibits U.S. foreign-aid funds from being used for abortion services. In fact, according to a Gallup poll taken in early 2009, Obama's retraction of the Mexico City executive order in his first week in office was the only policy in the beginning stages of his administration to face majority opposition (58 percent to 35 percent) among American voters.[†]

Daniels, who in a long career in appointive as well as elective office had always been known as pro-life, later "clarified" his position, saying he would in fact sign the executive order if he were to become president. But as an instance of the coolness of top Republican leaders toward the social-conservative agenda, at a time when polls showed the GOP riding high in the 2010 midterm elections due to the continuing weak economy and the perceived ineffectuality of the Obama administration and the Democratic Congress in responding to it, the Daniels episode did not prove anomalous or isolated.

Later in the summer of 2010, popular conservative TV talk show host Glenn Beck said in an interview that when it came to social issues: "Honestly, I think we have bigger fish to fry. You can argue about abortion or gay marriage all you want. The country is burning down." And when Federal district judge Vaughn Walker ruled on August 4, 2010, that the voters of California

---

* WeeklyStandard.com, June 8, 2010, "More on Mitch Daniels' Proposed 'Truce' on Social Issues."

† Gallup.com, February 2, 2009, "Americans Approve of Most Obama Actions to Date."

violated the U. S. Constitution by voting in 2008 to reaffirm their state's traditional definition of marriage, hardly any Republican elected officials offered even a word of criticism for the judge or his decision, which (among other holdings) stated that religious-based disapproval of homosexual conduct was by its nature a form of bigotry—by implication, the equivalent of a hate crime.

Then, at the end of summer, in early September, Mississippi Governor Haley Barbour, for decades one of the most influential GOP strategists and fund-raisers in national politics, weighed in. At an on-the-record press breakfast in Washington, Barbour said: "I think what Mitch said is very similar to what I have responded to today. The voters have on their mind the economy, jobs, spending, debt, and taxes. And good campaigns are about the issues that are on the people's minds. . . . I'll put my bona fides up against anybody's as a social conservative. . . . But that ain't going to change anybody's vote this year because people are concerned about jobs, the economy, growth, and taxes. . . . You are using up valuable time and resources that can be used to talk to people about what they care about."

Shortly after Barbour's advice on leaving social issues out of his party's election-year agenda, Republican congressional sources notified social-conservative activists that social issues would be systematically excluded from House Republicans' "Pledge to America" statement to be issued in late September 2010, following the final round of primaries and less than six weeks from Election Day.

Some striking things were true about this series of events, which were themselves part of a larger question concerning the status of social conservatism. First, the palpable discomfort and disdain directed at social conservatives and their issues were expressed not by social liberals—who in recent decades have almost completely disappeared from the ranks of Republican elected officials—but by members of the conservative and Republican elite whom most

3

social-conservative activists consider to be fellow adherents of social conservatism.

The second striking aspect of the 2010 events is that the impulse of conservative and Republican elites to jettison or marginalize the social-conservative agenda was neither new nor surprising. It was the latest in a series of such efforts dating back at least to 1989; more often than not, these efforts came in response to social-conservative gains or its high visibility in the politics of the immediately preceding period.

The third striking feature is that, at least in the short run, the high-level, semi-orchestrated campaign to remove social issues from the party's 2010 agenda came to nothing. Social issues were included in the "Pledge to America" manifesto issued by House Republicans on September 23, 2010. Moreover, in high-profile 2010 Republican primaries, memorable for a spirit of antiestablishment insurgency fostered by the pro-limited-government Tea Party movement, such well-financed social liberals as Tom Campbell in California, Michael Castle in Delaware, and Bill Binnie in New Hampshire went down to resounding defeat at the hands of less well-known U.S. Senate candidates who were socially conservative. In one of the races, the Senate primary in New Hampshire, the standing of the free-spending socially liberal candidate collapsed into a distant third, while the front-running candidates fought down to the wire arguing which of the two was more authentically pro-life.

These are seemingly contradictory events that I believe have a rational explanation, which this book will attempt to offer. In recent decades, social conservatism has become not only a core component of Republican election victories, but also a defining characteristic by which Republicans know themselves and are known to others. Yet in the same era in which this was happening, much of elite Republican and conservative opinion has remained hostile to a political role for social issues, preferring they be paid no more than lip service and removed completely from political debate whenever this can be managed.

Such tension would not be possible in any other affluent democracy, because in those democracies nothing remotely resembling social conservatism exists. Its absence is the main reason the politics of Western Europe and Japan have not become polarized, and the continued presence and strength of social conservatism is the central reason politics is polarized here. Understanding why this is so, and why it is likely to continue well into the future, goes a long way toward explaining why American politics has such a different feel from the politics of other affluent democracies, as well as where our very different politics may lead.

If the analysis of social conservatism in this book is wrong, conservative Republican elites who dislike social issues will be able to safely remove such issues from their agenda without suffering serious or permanent consequences. If, on the other hand, this book's analysis approximates reality, they are apt to keep reliving their multiple past experiences of finding this a more difficult separation than they expected. If, given their continued hostility, they nonetheless succeed in sidelining social conservatism, it is likely both to survive as a mass-based movement and to inflict devastating, perhaps fatal, damage to a Republican party that has cast it out.

Social conservatism is a relatively new phenomenon in American politics. Fifty years ago, the term was seldom used. Americans with conservative moral and social values were plentiful, then as now, but there was no such thing as a mass political movement or political philosophy built around such values.

This was in part, of course, because social institutions such as conjugal marriage and moral ideas like the sanctity of unborn human life had not yet come under broad-based political attack, and they therefore had not become a factor in the national political debate. As recently as the 1950s, the divide between liberals and conservatives had nothing to do with whether marriage should be redefined or abortion should be treated as a constitutional right. Beginning in the 1960s, when politics did begin to call moral and social values into question, it generated dismay and protests among holders of traditional values.

But simple reaction does not explain why social conservatism as a political movement came into being and continued to grow. Contemporaneous with the rise of legalized abortion and no-fault (unilateral) divorce in the United States, similar changes elicited similar dismay in Western Europe. But nowhere did this dismay lead to anything remotely resembling the social-conservative political movement of the United States. Conservative parties in Europe largely capitulated to social liberalism and continued to base their critique of the left on economic and foreign-policy issues.

What was true in Western Europe also proved true or is starting to prove true of other affluent democracies, varying mainly in the timing. In Japan, for example, abortion was legalized a generation earlier than it was in Europe, in 1948, and the social and moral revolution in newly affluent Ireland is even now playing itself out. But the bottom line is the same: The United States is the only established First World democracy to have a social-conservative political movement of any consequence. And in the prevailing metaphors of social evolution, this America-only movement is often assumed to be a kind of lagging indicator, soon to wither and disappear.

Yet arguably, its weight in American politics has been on the rise. The national election victories of Bill Clinton in 1992 and 1996 were undeniable setbacks, but the presidential elections of 2000 and 2004 saw social conservatives not only back on the winning side, but also with a higher profile in George W. Bush's coalition than during the GOP presidential victories of the 1980s.

Is all this an anomaly, soon to be eroded or erased by the inexorable march of secular values in modern times? Are the Democratic election victories of 2006 and 2008, and the revival of the left-right economic debate that followed, a harbinger of growing irrelevance for American social conservatism? Many, including not a few social-conservative sympathizers, suspect so. It's a rare social-conservative setback that is not accompanied by predictions of the movement's coming collapse.

The central contention of this book is that social conservatism is not only unlikely to collapse, but that it is becoming increasingly unified and coherent. It is already driving much of the national debate, and its issues are playing a steadily greater role in voters' decisions on whether to vote Republican or Democratic.

This is happening in America, and America only, for a reason. Social conservatism has been, in recent decades, the only mass-based political persuasion that fully believes in and defends the core ideas of the American founding. It has taken over that role from the parties, professions, and institutions that used to perform it, and as a result, it is touching a deep chord in millions of American voters.

Most social conservatives believe that the central principle asserted in the Declaration of Independence is true: "We hold these truths to be self-evident, that all men are created equal, that they are endowed by their Creator with certain unalienable Rights, that among these are Life, Liberty, and the pursuit of Happiness."

It is true that many, perhaps most, Americans feel a certain warmth toward these words. They are not controversial as a sentiment, a metaphor, or even as a summation of the positive idea that the United States represents in the world, to Americans and non-Americans alike.

What divides social conservatives from social liberals is this: Most—not all—social conservatives believe the words in that sentence are literally true. Most—not all—opponents of social conservatism do not believe those words are literally true.

INTRODUCTION

The key words of contention in the sentence are: "truths,"
"self-evident," "created equal," "Creator," and "unalienable
Rights." In other words, social conservatives believe we have
equal political rights that God gave us as part of his creation.
By definition, such rights are not subject to political approval or
review, and they cannot justly be taken away, temporarily or permanently, by a government or by anyone else.

By definition, they have an absolute standing they would
not necessarily have if they were privileges or immunities that
governments or other non-divine sources conferred on people.
The Declaration asserts, and most social conservatives believe,
that rights given by God as creator are given irrevocably to all of
humanity. They are not the peculiar property of any particular
race, class, or category of human beings, nor could they be exclusively American rights.

The sentence just quoted in full from the Declaration is, I
believe, the pivotal one in defining today's social conservatism. It
is the Declaration's second sentence. The document's first sentence is almost as important, because it states the authority under
which the founders are writing the Declaration, the right of the
13 colonies to "dissolve the political bands" connecting them
with Great Britain. The authority given—the *only* authority given
anywhere in the founding document—is "the Laws of Nature and
of Nature's God." So according to our founders, this God-given
Natural Law is what entitles them "to assume among the powers
of the earth, the separate and equal station" that they pledge (in
the Declaration's climactic sentence) "our Lives, our Fortunes,
and our sacred Honor" to obtain.

While in America most social conservatives and most social
liberals believe in equality and the human rights that logically
flow from it, their disagreement over the origin of these rights
has enormous consequences and implications. Most social conservatives believe, with the Declaration, that our rights would

not exist if not for the theistic God who gave them. Most social conservatives believe that this God is the God of the Bible—that is, the God of Christians and Jews. Some others believe our rights originate, if not with the God of the Bible, then with a universal God capable of shaping human affairs—that is, divine providence. Almost all of America's founders believed the rights they were proclaiming and fighting for were God-given in one of these senses.

Most social liberals today believe that equality and human rights are the product of human enlightenment—of progressive self-illumination. Whatever their belief about the existence of God, many if not most social liberals believe biblical religion and other versions of theism are, on balance, profoundly negative forces when it comes to political freedom. Their picture of liberation is often a picture of an intellectually evolving human race fighting free not only from political tyrants but also from traditional religion—particularly monotheistic religions.

This gulf between social conservatives and liberals concerning the role of God and natural law has enormous and intensely controversial implications on a wide range of unsettled issues. But the change this debate has already brought to American presidential politics is seismic.

In 1944 and 1948, the more affluent you were, the more likely you were to vote for Republican presidential nominee Thomas E. Dewey. This was broadly similar to the pattern of the previous presidential elections since 1932, the election that began the New Deal era.

Now, in the early years of the 21st century, affluence is no longer the main predictor. Rather, the more frequently you attended religious services, the more likely you were to vote for Republican nominee George W. Bush in 2000 and 2004. The centrality of economic issues in 2008 and the overall decline in Republican support did not make a significant dent in this pattern.

The transition from one kind of political framework to a very different one took decades, and vestiges of the old alignment are still detectable today (e.g., union members remain heavily Democratic). But it is, at the very least, interesting that the earlier, affluence-based politics, broadly prevalent from 1932 to 1964, was marked by Democratic dominance (7 of 9 presidential elections) and that the rise of social issues, which began to be noticeable in 1968, has been marked by a shift toward Republican preeminence (7 of the past 11 presidential elections).

In addition to the shift toward an era of Republican presidencies, the rise of social issues also coincided with a marked increase in political polarization. As the 1960s unfolded, Americans divided not only over Vietnam and civil rights but also over how to react to violence at home, which skyrocketed by almost every measurement: ghetto riots, campus riots, and a surge in violent crime.

A particularly striking snapshot of the kind of social polarization that ended the New Deal era of Democratic presidencies occurred during the 1968 Democratic National Convention. The three American television networks made a decision to downplay coverage of the convention itself, instead choosing to cover extended fighting on the streets of Chicago between antiwar student protesters and the police. The assumption of network executives and reporters, as well as millions of other Americans who enjoyed elite status, was that the typical viewer would be appalled by the behavior of nightstick-wielding policemen and would sympathize overwhelmingly with the demonstrators.

Within days the networks knew how wrong they were. The vast majority of Americans sided with the police; even more striking was the demographic pattern of this reaction. In the 1950s, a time of relatively low social polarization, it was taken for granted that wealthier people tended to be more politically conservative than middle-class and working-class people. In their reaction to the battle between the student demonstrators and the Chicago police, by contrast, the "have-nots" were far more conservative than the "haves." The vast majority of nonelite Americans firmly supported the Chicago police.

The same reversal persisted in subsequent decades. In fact, it was the one constant in a kaleidoscopically changing series of social issues: abortion, school busing, welfare rights, racial preferences, capital punishment, gun control, the equal rights amendment, school prayer, same-sex marriage, and many others. The most predictable element in each of these widely disparate debates was this: The higher your level of wealth and education—the clearer your elite status—the greater your tendency to support the liberal position on that social issue.

This tendency acted like an acid, gradually eating away at the superstructure of American politics' predictable, textbook divisions: business vs. labor, cities vs. suburbs, haves vs. have-nots. At first, many tended to see these new social issues as temporary factors, products of this crisis or that. Political and other elites preferred to operate in a framework they understood and had mastered, and they did their best to marginalize the new players these issues were bringing into politics.

To these elites, social issues appeared a sideshow, a diversion from the economic and international challenges thought to be the true raw material on which government needed to work its will. But by the late 1980s, Ronald Reagan's unexpected success in economics and foreign policy had temporarily stunned Republican as well as Democratic elites, and social issues suddenly flowed in to take center stage (particularly in the 1988 presidential race).

Later, when economics and foreign policy reappeared in the front lines of America's partisan combat, social issues not only didn't disappear; they began to interact with foreign and economic issues in unexpected ways.

In democratic Europe, the left-of-center social revolution that exploded in the 1960s met little resistance because European conservatives had no framework to mount political resistance outside the familiar arena of economics and foreign policy. On moral-values issues, they sometimes paid lip service to cultural resistance, but a purely cultural critique provided no tools to resist the left's political agenda of relentless cultural and social transformation.

Things took a different course in the United States not because political conservatism was stronger here—as noted earlier, the Republican Party from 1932 to 1964 was extraordinarily feeble by every measure of elective competition—but because America's founding documents rested on God-made natural law, which gave newly active American social conservatives a popular legitimacy, and in time a mass base, that economic conservatives lacked. This helped transform American politics; and under the leadership of Ronald Reagan, American conservatives dealt the left a series of setbacks, at home and abroad, that it had never before experienced in its 200-year history.

Most of Reagan's Republican successors saw social issues not as transformative, but as an occasionally useful, usually unwelcome sideshow. Social conservatives continued to work effectively, however, at the grass roots of politics, building strength and adding depth even as the agenda of social liberals advanced from legalized abortion to the redefinition of marriage to government-funded production of disposable human embryos for use in biomedical research.

In Europe, where conservative political leaders have scored impressive victories over a once powerful Marxist economic agenda, the left's social revolution still shows little sign of meeting political resistance. As for cultural resistance, the churches of Western Europe are largely empty, few babies are born to native Europeans, and work forces continue to age into senescence.

In the United States, by contrast, polarization reigns because social conservatives have proven much harder to marginalize. They are very far from prevailing, but the battle between social conservatives and the left constitutes a sizable portion of the unfinished business of American politics. If social conservatism survives this test, its agenda has a chance to alter the trajectory of world history. This book will attempt to explain why.

I

THE RISE OF SOCIAL CONSERVATISM

1

SOCIAL AND RELIGIOUS REALIGNMENT

For about a decade and a half of the post–New Deal, Republican-leaning era that began in 1968, social issues shared the stage with high-profile economic and foreign-policy crises. The Nixon, Ford, and Carter presidencies grappled with "stagflation," an unexpected toxic mix of very high inflation and stagnant growth. In foreign policy, the fall of the three non-Communist states of Indochina in 1975 was the first wave in a series of Communist takeovers in such Third World countries as Angola, Mozambique, Guinea-Bissau, Ethiopia, Grenada, Nicaragua, and Afghanistan. Even in affluent Western Europe, Euro-Communism was a rising force in parliamentary elections (Italy's Communists lost by only 38 to 34 percent to the ruling Christian Democrats in 1976); and leftist military officers ousted a long-ruling civilian dictatorship and came within an eyelash of imposing a Marxist-Leninist government on Portugal, a charter member of NATO. On top of all this, 1979 brought both the Iranian hostage crisis and the Soviet invasion of Afghanistan, history's first projection of the Red Army outside the Warsaw Pact.

Ronald Reagan was elected president in 1980, along with a Republican Senate and a far more conservative (but still Democratic) House. Reagan's first two years saw a continuation of stagflation, a deep recession accompanied by nearly 11 percent unemployment, and a defiant response by Soviet leaders Leonid Brezhnev and Yuri Andropov to the military buildup begun by Reagan in 1981. This meant that in the election of 1984, the rise of social issues (which continued in the first half of the 1980s) was somewhat obscured by the continuation of partisan disagreement on economics and foreign policy: Democratic nominee Walter Mondale called for at least a partial reversal of the Reagan tax-cut policy and military buildup (singling out for special ridicule Reagan's 1983 commitment to missile defense). Reagan's 49-state victory, followed by the increasing success of his economic and Cold War policies in his second term, meant that the level of partisan conflict on economic and international issues was far lower by 1988.

In the short run, this helped the Democrats. Their candidate for President, Governor Michael Dukakis of Massachusetts, made clear he had no intention of repeating Mondale's pledge to roll back Reagan's tax cuts and Cold War policy. Although known as a thoroughgoing liberal even in the context of liberal southern New England, Dukakis touted the "Massachusetts Miracle" of high-tech economic growth and in his Atlanta acceptance speech declared the central issue of 1988 to be "competence, not ideology." In another departure from Mondale, he picked not a liberal but a centrist Democrat, Texas's Senator Lloyd Bentsen, as his vice presidential running mate.

Electorates, perhaps especially the American electorate, tend to be forward-looking. If voters could be persuaded that Democrats had learned their lesson on economics and foreign policy, they would be open to other factors, such as Dukakis's widely praised record as governor and (on the negative side) charges that Vice President Bush, the Republican candidate, was a "wimp" or (in the withering words of conservative columnist George Will) a "lap dog." By midyear, Dukakis had taken a strong lead in the polls (as much as 17 points) over Bush.

Social Issues Turn the 1988 Election

Given the forward-looking character of the U.S. electorate, the Bush campaign would have been mistaken in trying to revive economics and foreign policy, which were the areas where the Reagan-Bush administration had achieved high credibility—and against which the Dukakis-Bentsen campaign had fairly successfully inoculated itself. Instead, Bush campaign manager Lee Atwater persuaded Bush to highlight his disagreement on a series of social issues on which Dukakis was perceived as vulnerable. These included Dukakis's membership in the American Civil Liberties Union, his veto of a bill mandating the saying of the Pledge of Allegiance in the public schools of Massachusetts, and his opposition to the death penalty.

Above all, Bush (picking up on a charge raised during the Democratic primaries by a 40-year-old candidate from Tennessee, Senator Al Gore) harped on a Dukakis-backed program that awarded extended furloughs to prisoners convicted of serious crimes, including one named Willie Horton who used his leave to commit rape and kidnapping in another state.

The social issues had impact, and the election turned. Bush overtook Dukakis and wound up winning by 8 points in the popular vote, carrying the electoral votes of 40 of the 50 states.

The significance of 1988 for social conservatives is that for the first time, their issues were the main factor in determining a presidential election. In elections between 1968 and 1984, social issues had steadily risen in salience, but never before had they played a central role (in the context of Dukakis's strategy of neutralizing economics and foreign policy) as issues of the first rank in driving the outcome of a national election.

In the internal dynamics of the Republican Party, the growing prominence of social issues was by no means universally welcomed. More than a few affluent Republicans, including many who had risen to party leadership, found social issues distasteful. If this was true even of Richard Nixon's "law and order" themes of 1968 and 1972, it was far truer of the Atwater-injected social issues of 1988.

Moreover, the two Nixon victories were quickly followed in January 1973 by *Roe v. Wade*, the Supreme Court decision that struck down as unconstitutional virtually all serious legal restrictions on abortion. In the wake of this decision, the ratio of abortions to total number of pregnancies quickly shot up to more than 20 percent, making legal abortion a fact of American life that left few voters untouched or indifferent. Affluent Republicans, like analogous conservative elites in Western Europe, were among the quickest to accept this sea change in social policy.

Roe also elevated the already simmering issue of judicial activism to new heights, at the same time making it of central concern to social conservatives. Judicial activism had long been seen by American conservatives as a labored effort by federal and (increasingly) state judges to find constitutional mandates for the latest progressive or liberal fashion, short-circuiting the inconvenience of democratic debate and decision-making.

The classic example of judicial activism was the U.S. Supreme Court's 1857 *Dred Scott* decision throwing out as unconstitutional federal laws prohibiting slavery in the U.S. territories. This was clearly a victory for advocates of slavery in the biggest social issue of the 19th century, ultimately leaving no recourse but civil war to overturn it.

The *Dred Scott* decision went so far as to say that even free blacks could not be citizens of the United States and had no rights that the white majority was bound to respect. Many pro-life critics of *Roe v. Wade* saw it as the recrudescence of *Dred Scott*, an egregious act of judicial elitism that denied fundamental rights to an entire category of human beings.

Religion and the Public Square

Abortion was by no means the only, or even the first, move by judicial elites into the kinds of social issues that marked the latter decades of the 20th century. A series of rulings dating back to the 1940s began to set sharp limits on the role of religion in public life. A particular shock was the Supreme Court's near unanimous 1962 decision banning all school-sponsored prayers, including blandly written nonsectarian ones, from America's public schools.

Liberal-backed judicial curbs on public prayer and other symbols and expressions of faith were making believers more and more uneasy. The year 1988, such an important milestone in the trajectory of social issues at the national level, proved also to be a year in which traditional religion intersected in new and important ways with presidential politics.

In the Republican nomination fight, television evangelist Pat Robertson, son of a long-serving Democratic U.S. senator from Virginia but himself a newcomer to politics, finished second in the Iowa caucuses, ahead of the presumed national front-runner, Vice President Bush, for a time endangering Bush's survival as a candidate. Although Bush recovered to win the nomination and election, Robertson's ability to mobilize previously uninvolved Christian activists began a new era in GOP presidential politics.

In post-1988 cycles, securing religious-conservative backing in early states such as Iowa and South Carolina became an integral part of Republican nomination strategy.

For conservative Protestants—evangelicals, fundamentalists, and Pentecostals—the contrast with just two decades or so earlier was enormous. Since agnostic attorney Clarence Darrow's humiliation of former Democratic presidential nominee William Jennings Bryan in the 1924 Scopes trial over the teaching of Darwinian natural selection in Tennessee's public schools, conservative Protestants had for the most part retreated from the public square, ceding cultural dominance to religious liberals and outright secularists.

From the 1930s to well into the 1960s, religious conservatives seemed content with keeping to their private space. Issues relating to faith and sexual morals were peripheral in politics in these decades, and most conservative Protestants were conservative only in a doctrinal sense. The Democratic Party was not seen as more religious or less religious than the Republican Party, and most conservative Protestants voted on other issues. On balance they were economically and socially downscale, so they tended to be somewhat more Democratic than the national average.

The rise of social issues began to change this. Judicially mandated legalization of abortion at first seemed to inflame a mainly Catholic constituency, but it became clear within a few years that traditional Protestants had become at least as hostile as Catholics were to abortion on demand. The increased power of the New Left in the Democratic Party in 1968 and 1972 was also disturbing. The Chicago convention riots of 1968 and the left-dominated Democratic convention of 1972 came across not only as antiwar but also countercultural, with overtones of free sex and rampant drugs. The most memorable epithet attached to the 1972 campaign of Senator George McGovern of South Dakota described Democrats as the party of "acid, amnesty, and abortion."

The collapse of the Nixon presidency in 1974 seemed for a time to derail the impulse toward social and religious realignment. Nixon's successor, Gerald Ford, picked a prominent liberal, well known as an advocate of legal abortion, Governor Nelson Rockefeller of New York, as his vice president. The following year, Ford chose Federal Judge John Paul Stevens to fill a vacancy on the Supreme Court. Originally seen as a centrist, Stevens soon joined the Court's then overwhelming social-liberal majority.

Meanwhile Democratic primary voters appeared to push back at the countercultural left by picking former Georgia governor Jimmy Carter as the party's standard-bearer in 1976. As a candidate, Carter came across as a typical Southern moderate, but he also was the first presidential nominee of either party in many cycles to talk unapologetically about his religious faith, which he described as "born again." On high-profile social issues such as abortion and busing to achieve racial balance in public schools, the Republican and Democratic nominees in 1976 were virtually indistinguishable.

The result was a close Democratic victory and an electoral map that was more regional than ideological—a throwback to elections won by Democrats Grover Cleveland and Woodrow Wilson in the decades following the Civil War. Carter, the first Southern politician since the 1840s to win the presidency exclusively at the ballot box (that is, without first ascending from the vice presidency), carried all but 2 of the 16 states regarded as Southern or Border. Ford won 25 of the 34 states of the Northeast, Midwest, and West, yet narrowly lost the presidency he had inherited from Nixon.

A major benefit of Carter's faith-friendly, Southern-centered strategy was a strong Democratic showing among theologically conservative Protestants. Exit polling by religion was not as specific as it later became, but most analysts believe Carter won between 60 and 65 percent of Bible-believing white Protestant voters.

Religious Realignment, 1976–1984

In the next two cycles, Democratic strength among conservative white Protestants not only collapsed; it nearly disappeared. In 1980, the Carter-Mondale showing among these voters went from the low 60s to the high 30s; the Democrats' Mondale-Ferraro ticket of 1984 contracted to the high teens (19 percent in the national exit poll). The Democrats had shrunk from roughly a 25-point margin of victory among conservative white Protestants to a deficit of 60 points or more—a cumulative decline of 85 points, in terms of margin. The comparable anti-Democratic swing among the electorate as a whole between 1976 and 1984 was a far smaller 20 points—a result of Carter-Mondale's 2-point popular-vote win over Ford-Dole turning into the 18-point drubbing that Reagan-Bush gave Mondale-Ferraro.

What had happened to cause such a colossal shift among conservative white Protestants in only eight years? Did the novel political appeal of Carter's piety and religious style wear off? Were social issues (as opposed to style) becoming more central for these voters? Were the Democrats again coming off as anti-religious in the vein of the countercultural left of the late 1960s and early 1970s? There is a measure of truth in each of these explanations.

The overarching development was partisan polarization of the abortion issue, most dramatically in presidential politics. When Ronald Reagan won the Republican nomination in 1980, the party platform for the first time endorsed a proposed constitutional amendment banning abortion. When Reagan picked his leading adversary in the primaries, George H. W. Bush, to be his running mate, it was on the understanding that Bush would switch his position from pro-choice to pro-life. He promptly did exactly that.

In both 1976 and 1980, the Democrats carefully paired Carter, widely seen as a straddler on the abortion issue, with the unequivocally pro-choice Walter Mondale. Yet by the time Mondale, running as the former vice president, won a multi-candidate struggle for the nomination in 1984, not one of his principal Democratic opponents was pro-life and all the pressure among the liberal activists who had come to dominate his party's elite was on the pro-choice side.

Mondale picked as his running mate a candidate urged on him by influential liberal feminists: Congresswoman Geraldine Ferraro of New York. At first it seemed an adroit choice. Ferraro was the first woman selected for a national ticket, and her Catholicism was widely believed to be a countermeasure to Reagan's unexpected strength among Catholics four years earlier. (Reagan in 1980 carried Massachusetts, a majority-Catholic state that the Democrats had won handily even with George McGovern as their nominee in 1972.)

But on social issues, particularly abortion, Ferraro proved anything but an asset. Like most Catholic Democratic legislators in the Northeast in the decade or so after *Roe*, Ferraro had opted for a down-the-line pro-choice position on abortion. Almost as soon as she was nominated, she found her position under public and repeated challenge by a number of Catholic bishops, most prominently Archbishop John O'Connor of New York. O'Connor, by background and demeanor the very image of an urban ethnic Democrat, did not accept the view that a Catholic elected official could legitimately be merely "personally opposed" to abortion while supporting its legalization and public funding. The controversy made headlines for some weeks, sharpened by a simultaneous war of words on the same subject between Archbishop O'Connor and New York's liberal governor, Mario Cuomo. This was a vivid, dramatic debate, largely unintended by either party, which brought together the preeminent social issue of the day and the perennial question of religion's role in politics—and did so with a decidedly Catholic flavor.

On another track, Mondale, with what seemed somewhat greater deliberateness and at about the same time, ignited a controversy that called into question the legitimacy of political activism by socially conservative Protestant clergymen. In the context of 1984, activism by men of the cloth did seem like a new phenomenon. Many conservative Protestants saw it as a reluctant move to defend the right to be publicly religious at all.

In 1978, the second year of the Carter presidency, the Internal Revenue Service announced that it would look into revoking the tax exemption of schools known as Christian "academies." These were high schools and elementary schools, many of which had sprung up in the South in reaction to integration of the public schools. The IRS made clear it was willing to effectively close such schools if it found they were functioning as thinly disguised instruments of white separatism. Many believers saw the IRS's move as an attempt by Washington to put private Bible schools out of business, thereby breaking the tacit truce between government and church that had more or less obtained since the Scopes trial.

It was not the first perceived breach of this truce, but for a surprising number of voters, the IRS's announcement seemed a final straw. That it could happen with the acquiescence of their seeming soul mate, President Jimmy Carter, added a poignant flavor of personal betrayal to the affair. National advocacy groups led by prominent evangelicals such as Ed McAteer and television evangelists like Jerry Falwell and Pat Robertson soon sprang up, and by 1984, their momentum had led them into issues far removed from the tax-exempt status of Bible schools. By and large, among evangelicals and other conservative white Protestants, the controversy over race had given way in intensity to abortion and other nonracial issues.

Reagan the Ayatollah

It was in this context that Ronald Reagan, at the conclusion of the 1984 Republican convention in Dallas where he won renomination, addressed a luncheon of Protestant clergymen. He argued in this address that people of faith should unapologetically defend their values in the public square.

It was a speech, at least that portion of it, that Barack Obama could easily have delivered two decades later without anyone raising an eyebrow. In 1984 it caused a political explosion. Walter Mondale, the freshly picked Democratic nominee, castigated Reagan for encouraging a dangerous religious invasion of political life. At one point, Mondale compared Reagan to an "ayatollah," an allusion to Iranian Ayatollah Ruhollah Khomeini, a man Americans knew mainly as an advocate of theocracy and a taker of American hostages who regarded us as the "Great Satan."

Mondale, himself the son of a politically active Lutheran pastor—but one who was committed to the liberal "social gospel" articulated in an earlier era by Walter Rauschenbusch—found himself unexpectedly on the defensive in Middle America. Perhaps encouraged by a wave of media praise, Mondale persisted in driving home his point for some weeks, at precisely the same time his pro-choice running mate was under disapproving scrutiny from Catholic bishops.

During several crucial weeks, from roughly July to September, the double-barreled "religion in politics" issue—religion's public role and abortion—dominated the presidential campaign, although it appeared to have little or no role in the strategic planning of either party. At the beginning of the summer, after the

Democratic convention, the Mondale-Ferraro campaign had closed in some polls to within a few points of Reagan-Bush. In the next two months, the peak of the religion-in-politics debate, Reagan took a huge lead he never relinquished.

The GOP gains were far from evenly distributed. In July, most polls showed Reagan with a significant lead in the South, the Northeast, and the Far West—the three areas that had benefited most from the early phase of Reaganomics. The Midwest, in those years often called the Rust Belt, was the one region that in 1984 had benefited only minimally from the Reagan economic recovery. Moreover, it had long been the least internationalist area of the country, and thus the most likely to have qualms about Reagan's forward strategy in the Cold War at a time when this had not yet led to any U.S.–Soviet summits. The Midwest in July was widely considered a dead heat between the two tickets.

In the Northeast and Far West, the least religious areas of the country, Mondale scored slight gains during the religion-in-politics phase of the campaign, but not enough to threaten Reagan's solid lead along the two economically booming coasts. In the South, the most religious region of the country, Reagan's solid lead turned into a huge landslide.

In the Midwest, the most dovish and most recessionary part of the country, but also the second most religious, the Mondale-Ferraro ticket fell far behind, never to recover. Big urban states such as Illinois and Michigan jumped to the Reagan column and remained there by solid margins, even when Midwesterner Mondale performed well in the first of two presidential debates.

There was another noteworthy departure from past voting patterns. In previous presidential elections when the demographics of religion played a measurable role, Protestant and Catholic voters often seemed to move in opposite directions. When Al Smith and John Kennedy energized the Catholic vote in 1928 and 1960, Republicans Herbert Hoover and Richard Nixon over-performed among Protestants, particularly in the theologically conservative Bible Belt. Even in 1976, Carter's strength among Southern Protestants seemed to trigger a smaller but noticeable countermovement to Gerald Ford among Northern Catholics.

In 1984, by contrast, huge shifts to the Republicans occurred among both Protestants and Catholics, concentrated among the theologically conservative elements within each faith: Bible-believing Protestants and orthodox Catholics. There were features of that year's religion-in-politics debate that almost certainly would have impeded these movements even a few elections earlier. Try to imagine the uneasiness of religious Protestants if, in 1960, New York's Cardinal Spellman had issued a detailed analysis of John F. Kennedy's domestic platform; or, conversely, the reaction of Northern Catholics if Billy Graham had barnstormed from state to state extolling the election of Vice President Richard Nixon as crucial to the survival of Bible-believing Protestantism. Analogous events in 1984 caused barely a ripple against Reagan, indeed they may have even enhanced his appeal to the more observant members of both faiths.

Still, in 1984 social and religious issues were not elbowing economics and foreign policy out of the way. (That was arguably the case in 1988, but it wasn't happening in 1984.) If the economy and foreign policy had looked as unsuccessful in 1984 as they had in 1980, the shifts that year to the Reagan-Bush ticket among conservative believers wouldn't have been possible.

Social Issues in American History

The importance of social issues was nothing new in American politics, as eminent historians Richard Hofstadter, Lee Benson, and Robert Kelley demonstrated in the second half of the 20th century, in opposition to Charles Beard and his school of economic determinism. In *The Cultural Pattern in American Politics*,

Kelley summarized their findings: "It has become clear that we can no longer describe the conflict of economic interest groups and assume that the story is complete. Cultural politics is not a side show that occasionally attracts our attention with odd issues like temperance and Sabbatarianism; it is as pervasive and powerful in shaping public life as is the impact of economic politics."[*]

But the ethno-religious dimension of previous sociocultural issues tended to pit relatively unified denominations against one another. The fight over Prohibition, for example, was in part a battle of most British-descended Protestants against most Catholics and most Lutherans. Even when the U.S. electorate consisted mainly of white Protestant males in the early 19th century, knowing a voter's ethnic and religious identity proved a fairly accurate predictor of his politics. If in 1805 you knew that a Massachusetts voter was a Congregationalist of English ancestry, you could be fairly certain he was a Federalist who favored a state church, temperance, blue laws, opposition to slavery, and a foreign policy that sided with Britain rather than France in the Napoleonic Wars.

The religion-in-politics debates of 1984, by contrast, tended to pit traditional believers of all faiths against the liberals of all faiths, as well as atheists. Social issues such as abortion and "public square" issues like prayer in the schools found Bible-believing Protestants and orthodox Catholics making common cause to a far greater degree than in previous cultural battles. The colossal shift of conservative white Protestants to the GOP column between 1976 and 1984, together with the more gradual shift of Mass-attending Catholics from strong Democratic to mild Republican leanings, underlined a growing political affinity among religious conservatives of all faiths.

---

[*] Robert Kelley, *The Cultural Pattern in American Politics: The First Century* (New York, N.Y.: Alfred A. Knopf, 1979), 265–266.

By the same token, theological liberals and the nonreligious often found themselves pushed away from previous Republican allegiances. In parts of the country such as the Northeast, where main-line Protestants far outnumber evangelicals, and along the northern Pacific Coast, where religious observance is comparatively low, Democrats were net beneficiaries of the rise of social issues.

The regional disparity in reaction was at least equaled by the gulf in status between traditionalists and liberals. In a country where religious commitment splits into two levels, the equivalent of a Scandinavian elite sitting atop a populace from India (as sociologist Peter Berger famously described America's religious culture), it's perhaps not surprising that elites tended to be open to Walter Mondale's view of Reagan as an "ayatollah."

Atwater and Ailes

Four years later, elite opinion was dumbfounded by Pat Robertson's strong showing in Iowa, and repelled by Vice President Bush's dissection of the Dukakis campaign by means of emotion-packed social issues such as prison furloughs, the Pledge of Allegiance, and ACLU membership. Bush campaign manager Lee Atwater and media consultant Roger Ailes, producer of the Bush campaign ads on prison furloughs, became objects of some of the most venomous press coverage ever experienced by architects of a winning presidential campaign. (Their only real rival in this regard is 2000 and 2004 Bush strategist Karl Rove, who helped the next-generation Bush presidency benefit from social issues.)

After the election, Ailes announced he would no longer be involved in political campaigns. More than two decades later, he has kept that vow, although he went on to help transform two different electronic media—syndicated AM talk radio and cable-TV news—into conservative strongholds.

31

Atwater did not leave politics. But only a year after 1988, the year he became the political strategist most identified with the successful deployment of social issues in presidential politics, he emerged as the leading advocate of downgrading social issues in the Republican agenda. His change of emphasis was only the most dramatic of a series of developments that greatly increased the tension between GOP elites and social conservatives. When these tensions coincided with a high-profile series of political setbacks for social conservatives, a movement that had seemed steadily on the rise in the 1980s began to look more and more precarious as the 1990s got under way.

2

THE BIG TENT

President-elect Bush elevated Atwater to the chairmanship of the Republican National Committee. By the 1992 political cycle, he was dead of brain cancer, but his best-remembered moment as Republican chairman saw him declare in 1989 that the GOP should think of itself as a "big tent" to include supporters as well as opponents of abortion rights. Coming from Atwater, a South Carolinian who had cut his political teeth in the campaigns of Strom Thurmond and Ronald Reagan, it was interpreted as a surprising and stinging rebuke to social-conservative voters, many of them only recently recruited into Republican ranks.

Another Republican rebuff to social conservatives occurred in the wake of the June 1989 *Webster v. Reproductive Services* decision by the U.S. Supreme Court. This 5–4 decision upheld some modest state restrictions on abortion. Joined in by all three of Ronald Reagan's appointees to the Court, as well as by William

Rehnquist (whom Reagan had elevated from Associate Justice to Chief Justice three years earlier), it looked at the time like a down payment on a social-conservative judicial realignment in response to the conservative election gains of the 1980s.

But far from occasioning applause from Republican officials, *Webster* generated mainly fear and flight. The two Republican gubernatorial nominees in the 1989 elections found themselves on the defensive. One of them, J. Marshall Coleman in Virginia, defended the pro-life cause weakly and apologetically against aggressive Democratic attacks by Lieutenant Governor Douglas Wilder and narrowly lost his election. The other, Congressman Jim Courter in New Jersey, immediately switched his position from pro-life to pro-choice rather than defend *Webster* and the limited pro-life legislating it made possible. He lost overwhelmingly to the pro-choice Democratic nominee, Congressman Jim Florio, in a state whose electoral votes Republicans had carried in all six of the presidential elections from 1968 to 1988.

These defeats made an already wary Republican establishment even more reluctant to advocate social-conservative positions as public talking points. Few GOP consultants wanted their candidates to follow Courter's example and openly renounce pro-life and other conservative social positions, as this could put the allegiance of millions of Republican-leaning voters in doubt. Many more candidates would resemble Marshall Coleman in mentioning social-conservative issues only when forced by an opponent to do so. The lion's share of Republican elites adhered to Atwater's "big tent" formula, which effectively denied that pro-life views had become a defining characteristic of Republicans.

As president, George H. W. Bush remained loyal to the pro-life commitment he had made to Reagan in 1980, vetoing numerous pro-choice bills that the Democratic-controlled congresses of 1989–1992 had passed. But he was far less apt than Reagan had been to articulate pro-life and social-conservative views, even when occasion seemed to demand it. When asked by reporters about the *Webster* decision while on a golf course, the president responded so tersely that he did not feel compelled to remove the golf tee clenched between his teeth.

1992: Setbacks for Social Conservatives

When Patrick Buchanan challenged Bush from the right in the 1992 primaries, his main line of attack was on economic issues rather than core social issues such as abortion. But when Buchanan, a social conservative, was asked to address the GOP convention in Houston for the sake of party unity, he delivered a rip-roaring speech declaring the country to be in the midst of a "culture war." The most dramatic portion of the speech was a description of the California National Guard's suppression of the Rodney King race riots in Los Angeles earlier that summer— by no means what most social conservatives in 1992 would have selected to characterize current debate on social issues.

The Bush campaign was horrified. James Baker, who had resigned his position as Secretary of State to become White House chief of staff and Bush's chief campaign strategist, let it be known that the general election against Democratic nominee Bill Clinton would be about peace and prosperity—not at all about the social issues.

The problem was that for Bush, economic and foreign-policy issues had been neutralized no less thoroughly than in his 1988 race against Dukakis. The recession of 1990–1991, and the sluggish recovery from it, had made economics a net Democratic asset. And although voters overwhelmingly regarded Bush as more qualified than Clinton to handle foreign policy, the collapse of the Soviet Union in the second half of 1991 had marked a definitive end to the Cold War, and the number of voters listing foreign policy as a major concern predictably shrank to a nearly invisible level.

It could thus be argued that social issues were Bush's one available path to victory in 1992 no less than in 1988. For social conservatives, it's tempting to believe that if Atwater had lived and had remained a major force in the Bush political team, the Bush campaign would have attempted exactly that—perhaps successfully, given the potential vulnerability of Bill and Hillary Clinton on social issues.

But conventional wisdom, certainly among GOP elites led by Atwater himself but even among many social conservatives, was turning more and more pessimistic on the utility of social issues as an overt component of Republican campaign strategy. In 1992, social conservatives sustained a series of demoralizing setbacks that made their issues look like the wave of the past.

In June 1992, just weeks before the Houston GOP convention, social conservatives suffered their most discouraging defeat of all: The Supreme Court in *Planned Parenthood v. Casey* reaffirmed the constitutional right to abortion it had discovered in *Roe v. Wade*. The vote was 5–4 rather than the 7–2 margin 19 years earlier in *Roe*, but it came by way of a court on which eight of nine justices had been appointed by Republican presidents. Adding insult to injury, two Reagan appointees who had been with the pro-life majority only three years earlier in *Webster*, Sandra Day O'Connor and Anthony Kennedy, switched sides to vote with the pro-choice majority. Bush's first nominee, David Souter, confirmed in 1990, switched from an earlier pro-life vote to join them.

In November 1992, not only did Arkansas's Governor Bill Clinton win election as the first socially liberal president in the post-*Roe* era, but pro-choice feminist candidates Barbara Boxer, Dianne Feinstein, Patty Murray, and Carol Mosely-Braun won high-profile U.S. Senate races in California, Washington, and

Illinois. The 1992 election was widely celebrated as the "Year of the Woman."

The national Democratic Party had become so intensely committed to protecting abortion that one of its top vote-getters, Pennsylvania's Governor Robert Casey, was denied the right to speak at the party convention in New York City because of his pro-life advocacy. Following the election, Democratic congressional leaders announced plans to "lock in" *Roe v. Wade* by passing the Freedom of Choice Act in 1993.

Social conservatives also felt beleaguered on the issue of public policy concerning homosexual behavior and relationships. During the campaign, Clinton had endorsed permitting gays to serve openly in the military, something many expected he would accomplish by executive order. During the transition between the Bush and Clinton presidencies, the president-elect indicated that he intended to issue this executive order as one of his first acts in the White House.

Social Issues Bite the Democrats

Instead, the issue exploded. The incoming administration found itself under withering attack from the active-duty military, led by its highest-ranking officer, General Colin Powell, chairman of the Joint Chiefs of Staff and (according to polls) the nation's most admired African American.

It quickly became evident that if Clinton went through with the executive order, he would be choosing to begin his new administration with a high-profile battle against a Democratic-controlled Congress, and he would be standing with a distinct minority of the electorate. Much to the chagrin of his numerous backers in the gay-rights movement, he compromised by accepting a congressional policy of "Don't Ask, Don't Tell" regarding current members of the armed forces. The bottom line was that if a soldier came out of the closet, he or she would be automatically subject to (honorable) discharge from the service.

Similar disappointment came to social liberals with the Freedom of Choice Act, the attempt to lock in *Roe*'s right to abortion on demand by means of federal legislation. After a few hearings, Democratic leaders concluded the bill had no chance to clear the relevant committees in either house, and FOCA was permitted to die a quiet death.

Meanwhile, President Clinton elevated a long-standing friend and ally from his Arkansas days, Dr. Joycelyn Elders, to national prominence. Once confirmed as Surgeon General, Dr. Elders very quickly became the most quoted member of the administration on social issues. An advocate of abortion on demand, Dr. Elders stated that her preferred method of combating unwanted pregnancy was mass distribution of condoms in the public schools. In 1993, she informed Catholic Church leaders that they "must stop this love affair with the fetus." She frequently raised the prospect of decriminalizing narcotics. And in 1994, invited to speak at a United Nations conference on AIDS, she was asked whether it would be appropriate to promote masturbation as a means of steering young people away from riskier forms of sex. She replied, "I think that it is part of human sexuality, and perhaps it should be taught."

The Republican congressional campaign of 1994, which featured Newt Gingrich's "Contract with America," was faithful to Republican conventional wisdom in playing down social issues, confining itself mainly to endorsement of a proposed ban on partial-birth abortion. But social issues, particularly gays in the military and the ever-recurring advocacy of Dr. Elders, made for some of the highest-profile instances of the public's dissatisfaction with the first two Clinton years.

One who may have shared this analysis was Bill Clinton. After the Democrats lost the House and Senate, one of the president's very first acts was to call Dr. Elders into his office to demand her resignation, effective immediately. The administration changed none of its existing social-liberal positions. But never again would any of its spokesmen publicly emulate Dr. Joycelyn Elders's in-your-face assault on traditional morals.

1990s: Gridlock and Eclipse

On the issue of abortion, the politics of the 1990s was character-ized by a kind of trench warfare. Pro-lifers, lacking the votes to ban abortion nationally and somewhat handcuffed by their loss in *Planned Parenthood v. Casey* in the states, turned to an incremen-talist strategy. They pushed parental notification and mandatory waiting periods in state legislatures. They passed bans on partial-birth abortion at the federal level and in many states but were stopped by Clinton's vetoes and by federal and state courts that suspended enforcement of the state bans, pending appeal.

In a secondary ruling of *Casey*, a 7–2 majority of the Supreme Court held out the possibility of greater scope for incremental restrictions than *Roe* or even *Webster* had allowed; but in a 2000 decision, *Stenberg v. Nebraska*, the Supreme Court ruled that state partial-birth laws were unconstitutional. This 5–4 defeat for pro-life forces was made possible by two of the three Reagan- and Bush-appointed justices: In 1992, these two justices voted to uphold *Roe* but raised the possibility of limited restrictions by the states; in 2000, these same two justices ruled that state-level partial-birth abortion bans did *not* constitute such a limited restriction.

For supporters of abortion rights, the 1993 congressional defeat of FOCA deflated the euphoria many had felt following the pro-choice victories of 1989–1992, culminating in the "Year of the Woman." In those years, it seemed plausible that feminist-driven social liberalism would sweep all before it; pro-lifers in the post-*Webster* environment did their best to mount legislative resistance, but Republican politicians were either laconic in the manner of the first President Bush or more than willing to change the subject to some other issue, anxiously reassuring critics that their pro-life identity was a relatively minor facet of their ideological profile.

Defeat of FOCA, passage of "Don't Ask, Don't Tell," and the rise and abrupt fall of Dr. Elders brought social liberals back down to earth. After 1994, the Clinton presidency and Republican Congress found themselves in a kind of armed stalemate on social issues. The Clinton team tolerated no new Elders-style in-your-face social liberalism and (led by First Lady Hillary Clinton) found new relevance in their faith experiences.

While Republicans in Congress became more and more monolithic in their socially conservative voting records, GOP presidential strategy continued the distant stance of the Baker-run 1992 Bush campaign. Republican presidential nominee Bob Dole, a pro-lifer of more than three decades' standing in his congressional voting record, made a bow in the direction of the "big tent" by trying to force a "tolerance clause" into the pro-life section of the 1996 GOP platform. Delegates in San Diego quickly rejected the idea. But (in a pattern that was to hold firm in the conventions of 2000 and 2004) Republican convention managers allowed no pro-life speeches during the convention's prime-time hours on national television.

A similar dichotomy became more and more prevalent in congressional election strategy. Conventional wisdom among Republican campaign officials and consultants was that pro-life and other social issues were on balance helpful in general elections, as long as they were used "below the radar screen" to increase social-conservative turnout. This meant conservative social issues could play a role in targeted voter mail, but seldom in television commercials that went to the electorate as a whole.

This reticence remained the rule even when it came to the centerpiece of pro-life political strategy in the Clinton years: the attempt to pass a federal ban on partial-birth abortion. Twice congressional Republicans passed a ban on the procedure. Twice President Clinton vetoed the ban, and Republicans were unable to muster the two-thirds majority in the Senate needed to override Clinton's veto. Polls showed a solid majority of voters siding with the Republicans on the partial-birth procedure, described even by Daniel Patrick Moynihan, a pro-choice Democratic senator from New York, as "too close to infanticide."

During the election cycles from 1994 to 2000, the Republicans' powerful, well-funded Senate Campaign Committee was presided over by Senators Al D'Amato of New York and Mitch McConnell of Kentucky, both impeccably pro-life in their own voting records. Both had an unwritten rule that denied funding to Republican Senate nominees who put up television commercials supporting the ban. With a single exception, competitive Republican Senate nominees in the 1990s and 2000 complied with the Senate GOP rule and dropped their partial-birth ads.

The one exception was Congressman Mark Neumann, the Republican Senate nominee in Wisconsin in 1998. For reasons widely believed to relate to the Senate's acrimonious debate over campaign-finance reform, McConnell allowed Neumann to put up partial-birth ads against Senator Russell Feingold without depriving Neumann of his Senate Campaign Committee funding.

Neumann, considered to have little chance, ran an unexpectedly close race, losing to Feingold 51–48. The networks' exit poll showed an unusually high 20 percent of Wisconsin voters making abortion their central issue. Within these 20 percentage points, Neumann bested Feingold 17–3. So he led by 14 points among the voters focused, pro or con, on the abortion issue. However, among voters whose primary focus was something other than abortion, Neumann lost in a 17-point landslide to Feingold, 48 to 31. The 20 percent of voters focusing on abortion marked a higher level of interest in the issue than did voters in the year's other Senate races, none of which had elevated the partial-birth issue to the level of TV ads. Yet in 2000, a year when the GOP suffered a net loss of four Senate seats, the unwritten no-abortion-on-TV rule was back in force.

Somewhat surprisingly, Democrats also showed less and less willingness to engage on abortion as the 1990s wore on. From a strategic point of view, perhaps they didn't have to, because abortion on demand was the law of the land and Republican leaders showed little or no inclination to challenge the status quo. But in contrast to the period immediately after the 1989 *Webster* ruling, when elevating the party's pro-choice stance seemed like a magic bullet in Democratic campaigns, the tendency was now to downplay abortion and (echoing President Clinton) emphasize a desire to make abortion "safe, legal, and rare" when the subject did come up. In 1992, the "Year of the Woman," a typical Democratic candidate for the U.S. Senate outside the South frequently and eagerly brought up his or her commitment to preserving abortion rights. By the late 1990s and early 2000s, Democrats mainly talked about it reluctantly and largely in response to questions.

Even with abortion in a policy stalemate at the national level, it almost always appeared as a defining issue in candidates' press biographies and in accounts of contested races. Beginning with the party polarization on abortion that appeared with the 1980 GOP and Democratic platforms, and continuing to the present day, it is typical for a candidate's position on abortion—whether pro or con—to be included in press accounts of races for federal office. Similarly, in presidential elections, the upholding or overturning of *Roe v. Wade* became the main subtext of the increasingly acrimonious issue of federal judicial selection.

By the end of the 1990s, the role of social issues in American politics was notably paradoxical. For different reasons, elites in both parties wanted to downplay them rhetorically. Yet to an ever greater extent, social issues were at the core of the differences between the two parties: Republicans in Congress had become almost uniformly pro-life, Democrats in Congress a little more divided but increasingly pro-choice.

Simultaneously, religious observance had unmistakably emerged and was widely acknowledged as the single best predictor of how Americans were likely to vote in national elections. Political elites, had they been asked, would have been hard-pressed to explain why matters they believed extraneous to politics, and which are extraneous to political self-definition in all other affluent democracies, had become defining and even predictive here. But they were seldom asked such questions.

3

THE RED AND
THE BLUE

In the election cycles of 1998 and 2000, the impeachment of Bill Clinton in the Monica Lewinsky scandal and its aftermath became the emotional center of American politics. On the surface the protracted battle between Clinton and the Republican Congress kept social issues on the back burner, but on the psychic level it implanted moral polarization more deeply than ever into the self-definitions of the two national parties.

The strategic landscape of the 2000 election cycle posed agonizing decisions for that year's presidential nominees, Vice President Al Gore and Governor George W. Bush of Texas. Clinton's impeachment on a near party-line vote by the House and speedy acquittal (on a 50–50 vote) by the Senate left the president with remarkably high job-performance ratings. The economy had performed well during his presidency, and crime rates and welfare rolls joined unemployment in heading down. The U.S. had intervened in several Balkan wars against Serbian strongman Slobodan Milosevic, but American casualties were minuscule. Despite widespread disapproval of Clinton's personal conduct, most Americans did not favor removing the president from office, a fact that hurt Republicans in the 1998 elections and led to the resignation of House Speaker Newt Gingrich in the wake of the GOP's unexpected net loss of five House seats.

However, Clinton and his party emerged from the Lewinsky and other scandals by no means unscathed. As the scandals gained political traction in early 1998, Clinton's personal-approval rating began to diverge significantly from his high job-approval rating. Somewhat surprisingly, the two ratings remained widely apart throughout 1999, even as the immediacy of the impeachment and trial faded.

Clinton Bifurcation and the Rise of Bush

The bifurcation in the electorate's view of Clinton was paralleled by the emergence of George W. Bush as the overwhelming favorite for the GOP nomination. In early 1998, Republican polling showed Bush as just one of several plausible candidates for the nomination. By late 1998, he was the overwhelming front-runner, a status that in 1999 helped him far outpace his rivals in fund-raising and VIP endorsements. Yet during 1998, the year of his sharp rise in national polls, Bush was running for reelection in Texas and remained faithful to a pledge to make no appearances involving national coverage.

Why, in the year 1998 when by his own choice he made little or no national news, did Bush become a dominant GOP front-runner and a modest leader in general-election trial heats against Vice President Gore? What else was happening—what was the central political drama—that began to dominate news cycles as the year 1998 progressed?

It's hard to avoid the thought that Clinton's decline in personal approval during 1998, the year of his impeachment, could well have been matched by buyer's remorse in large portions of the electorate for having retired President George H. W. Bush in 1992. (Interestingly, polls in the same time frame—late 1998 and early 1999—suggested that if voters had the 1992 election to do over, they would vote for the older Bush, but not—in a hypothetical redo of 1996—for that year's GOP nominee, Bob Dole.)

Whatever the merits of the public's conflicted view of President Clinton or the causes of Governor Bush's rise, they were unarguable components of the public opinion that Vice President Gore and his strategists had to deal with at the start of 1999, and indeed for the remainder of the 2000 presidential election cycle. In theory, Gore could have run as a straightforward heir of Clinton—a "new politics" centrist on economic issues such as growth, federal spending, and international trade, liberal but nonconfrontational (post-1994, post-Elders) on abortion, homosexuality, prayer in public places, and other social issues.

But if all the electorate wanted was a Democratic president who would extend the policies of the Clinton years without Clinton, it was puzzling that George W. Bush was leading the scandal-free Gore in most 1999 polling. Ultimately, Gore chose to run on more conventional, un-Clintonian Democratic themes: mildly anticorporate, pro–working class, more skeptical of globalization. When it came time to select his running mate, Gore put forward Senator Joseph Lieberman of Connecticut, the most prominent Democratic critic of Clinton's behavior in the Lewinsky scandal.

By the time of the back-to-back national party conventions and their aftermath, this strategy seemed to be working. Gore gave a well-received acceptance speech, the Lieberman pick was widely applauded as an appropriate gesture of separation from Clinton, and the Gore-Lieberman ticket pulled ahead of Bush-Cheney in the closely watched post-convention polls that so often have proved predictive of the November presidential outcome.

The Bush-Rove 2000 Strategy

Bush's comeback in September and October and eventual victory in the electoral college was at least partly due to Gore's unexpectedly weak performance in the fall presidential debates. But a measure of credit should also go to the campaign strategy devised by Bush and his chief political adviser, Karl Rove.

Bush's strategy was designed to operate on both levels of the phenomenon of Clinton bifurcation—satisfaction with the president's policies and with the overall state of the nation on the one hand, moral disapproval of the way Bill Clinton conducted himself in office on the other.

Bush knew that the last thing voters wanted to hear was denigration of Clinton's successes in bringing the federal budget from deficit to surplus, and in reducing unemployment, welfare, and crime. Equally doomed to failure would be starting an argument over who deserved more credit for these results, the Democratic president or the GOP-controlled Congress. Whatever an objective balance sheet might say, American voters always give credit to the President when things they care about go well. (Benign trends have also been known to help congressional incumbents, including incumbents of the non-presidential party, and 2000 did prove a pro-incumbent year in races for Congress for Republicans as well as Democrats. But for Bush and Rove, this tendency ran counter to their task of persuading voters to *change* parties at the presidential level.)

So the Republican campaign made no attempt to deconstruct Clinton's policies or quibble about their results. Bush's own policy proposals tended to be incremental—e.g., tax cuts rather than radical tax reform—and his self-description as a "compassionate conservative" also implied a mildness of agenda.

Bush did sound different from Clinton in the personal moral dimension, sometimes known as the "character issue." Without mentioning the incumbent, Bush talked frequently of the need to bring dignity to the White House (consistently his strongest applause line) and advocated mobilizing faith-based organizations to attack social problems. Bush's personal story of religious conversion accompanied by the overcoming of a drinking problem underlined his belief that faith can have an impact on personal behavior.

Vice President Gore was conscious of his party's ethical vulnerability, as his selection of Lieberman indicated. It also led him to distance himself from Clinton in his fall campaigning. This caused considerable tension within the administration, but considerably less in most of the closely contested battleground states. In Ohio, Michigan, and Pennsylvania, where voters who were economically liberal but socially conservative held the balance of power, many Democratic officials and strategists shared the Gore campaign's view of Clinton as at best a problematic blessing.

Although explicit social issues were a limited element in the strategy of the Bush-Cheney campaign in the fall of 2000, 29 of the 30 states the ticket carried could be described as socially conservative. (The one socially liberal exception, New Hampshire, also proved to be the sole Bush-Cheney 2000 state that shifted to the Democratic Kerry-Edwards ticket four years later.) Even more than in the Republican presidential victories of the 1980s, self-defined social conservatives found themselves overwhelmingly on the Republican side and social liberals overwhelmingly with the Democrats.

Two Americas

The perception of two value systems, two Americas, each aligned with a major party, contributed to the coining of the terms "Red State" (Republican) and "Blue State" (Democratic). The accelerating sense of moral and ideological polarization was, as argued earlier, in part an outgrowth of the intense and complex voter reaction to impeachment. Undoubtedly the closeness of the 2000 election, with its nearly 40 days of recounts and legal maneuvering, left a bitter residue among Democratic activists who believed, at least tacitly, that winning the national popular vote by a half million votes should have overruled the antique institution of the electoral college, whatever the razor-thin outcome in Florida.

But the Red State/Blue State polarization was also a culmination of decades-long trends in American politics. These included the rise of social issues beginning in the 1960s, the South's capture by the Republicans together with the dwindling of the GOP's Northeastern wing in Congress, and the gradual marginalization of socially liberal Republicans and socially conservative Democrats as viable players in national and (depending on the region) state and local politics.

In the early 1990s, the collapse of the Soviet Union and the dramatic end of the Cold War removed foreign policy as a central voter concern in the elections of 1992, 1996, and 2000. This minimization of foreign policy had not happened in three straight presidential elections since the years 1924 to 1932.

Strategically, the end of the Cold War neutralized issues where Republicans had held a consistent advantage since the 1950s (except for 1964). Moreover, it was arguably a necessary precondition of the election of Bill Clinton, one of the least foreign-policy-credentialed presidential nominees of the 20th century. Clinton's success on domestic issues coupled with his controversial moral behavior helped keep much of the political debate on a social and moral track during the eight years of his presidency, despite wishes to the contrary by key elites in both major parties.

But when the international dimension returned stronger than ever on September 11, 2001, the upshot was not the decline in social-issue polarization that one might have expected, but its accentuation. After a few months of patriotic fervor, national unity, and overwhelming public approval of the Bush administration and its war plans, the conduct of the war on terrorism polarized along roughly conservative-liberal, Republican-Democratic lines. The return to Red-Blue polarization predated the March 2003 invasion of Iraq: It was a widely remarked feature of the congressional elections of 2002. Rather than eclipse domestic political issues as the two World Wars had done, 9/11 turned up the intensity of the cleavage between social conservatism and social liberalism that has increasingly defined American political allegiance since the 1960s.

Why? From the perspective of the social debate in this country, the war on terrorism did not really change the subject. It was a throwback war in the same sense that the social-conservative movement is a throwback movement, at least in the context of the other affluent democracies. The war the United States and its allies are fighting against Islamic jihadists erupted in the midst of a worldwide resurgence of religion, and the war's main *content* is a renewed, intensified dispute about religion and its proper role (if it has a proper role) in politics.

Decline of the Economic-Centered Left

By September 2001, the center of gravity for the American left had shifted decisively away from economics and toward sexual freedom and secularism.

In the first decades of the 20th century, government owner-ship of the means of production and its partner, national economic planning, were seen by Western elites as the cutting-edge path to modernization. This was due in part to the rise of Marxism, and was in part an outgrowth of frequent 19th-century financial pan-ics accompanied by short but sharp depressions, followed by the Great Depression of the 1930s, when industrial capitalism seem-ingly broke down amid chronically high unemployment and mass pauperism in the United States and Europe.

The charisma of the Marxist left began to fade during the West's post–World War II economic recovery juxtaposed against the stagnation of Stalinism; but by the 1960s, Marxism's mild-mannered nephew, Keynesianism, had taken nearly complete control of elite economics, especially in the English-speaking world. Keynesianism tolerated private enterprise but argued that deficit spending and the creation of excess money were far more reliable drivers of large-scale ("macro") economic growth. These two stimulants had one thing in common: They are achievable only through the actions of governmental elites.

A central premise of Keynesianism was that inflation and recession were opposite, almost mutually exclusive evils. Policy elites in the 1960s "knew" that the solution to recession was a temporary dose of inflationary stimulus, and that the solution to inflation was to put a temporary brake on growth. The eco-nomic crisis that hit the West in the 1970s was so unexpected that a new word—"stagflation"—had to be invented to describe it. It was this decisive breakdown of left-of-center economics that opened the way to election victories by Ronald Reagan and Mar-garet Thatcher in the United States and Britain, the strongholds of Keynesianism, and to the supply-side policy revolution that followed.

For a time the economic left in both countries tried for an electoral comeback, not so much by advocating a revival of socialism or Keynesianism as by attacks on budget deficits and a frontal assault on the deep cuts in income tax rates that were the keystone of Reagan-Thatcher supply-side policy. This was more or less true of Walter Mondale in the U.S. election of 1984, and Labour Party candidates Michael Foot, Neal Kinnock, and John Smith in the British elections of 1983, 1987, and 1992.

Rebuffed in all four of these elections, the left-of-center parties in the two countries instead returned to power only after choosing "new politics" centrists Bill Clinton in 1992 and Tony Blair in 1997. Their nomination and election (and reelections) meant that socialist and Keynesian economics began to fade from the political menu not only in the U.S. and Britain, but before long just about everywhere else. If the collapse of the Warsaw Pact in 1989 and the dissolution of the Soviet Union in 1991 ended the dream of top-down Marxism, the U.S. election of 1992 and the British election of 1997 seemed effectively to signal the collapse of democratic socialism at the very end of a century in which it had on more than one occasion been proclaimed unstoppable.

But after a brief period of licking its wounds, the international left found itself far from devastated. The truth is that old-fashioned, state-administered socialism had become something of an albatross for the left, impeding rather than advancing its ability to benefit from the worldwide political and social upheaval of the 1960s.

Indeed, not long after these upheavals peaked in 1968, it became obvious that the enduring, truly revolutionary impact of the 1960s was moral and cultural, not economic. By the end of the 1970s, a new and adversarial form of politically engaged feminism not only became all but unassailable among North American and European elites, but also took a central political role almost everywhere the left was strong.

The quick recovery of the left from the collapse of socialist economics could not but be surprising to analysts, perhaps especially to conservative American ones, who had long *defined* the left in terms of its push for bigger and bigger government that would inevitably culminate in socialism or something very like it. And it's undeniable that this push had been a key feature of the left (and of world politics) since the middle of the 19th century.

Origin and Essence of the Left

But when it first arose in recognizable form in Europe in the closing decades of the 18th century, the left was primarily about other things. These included putting an end to monarchy, eliminating or at least circumscribing the role of traditional religion in society, and liberating humanity from what it saw as repressive institutions. Often included among such institutions was the traditional family, anchored by the Christian ideal of monogamous marriage.

From its beginning, the left was opposed not only by defenders of the old monarchical order but also by significant thinkers within the vast ocean of the European Enlightenment of the 17th and 18th centuries. What we could call the conservative enlightenment was especially strong in the British Isles and the United States, but it included outliers such as Montesquieu and Schiller on the continent.

These two wings of the Enlightenment shared a rejection of ruling monarchy and its view of people as "subjects," or part of a "realm" over which the rulers (royalty and nobility) claimed a measure of ownership. The Enlightenment as a whole affirmed human equality as a moral imperative. But the two wings disagreed vehemently about human nature, and thus about the origin and definition of equality.

Adherents of the conservative enlightenment believed that people, by their nature as rational beings possessing free will—

creatures made "in the image and likeness" of their divine Creator, to put it in biblical language—have equal fundamental rights, rights that the state did not confer and therefore cannot justly take away. They also have obligations, duties they owe to themselves, to others, and to God. People's moral duties together with their moral rights constitute a self-evident law that binds men's consciences even in a "state of nature"—a hypothetical pre-political condition. The laws and institutions of government must therefore be judged by whether they are in accord with a preexisting law—the natural law—that is shaped by human nature and grasped by reason, and that includes God-given equality. The left, as inspired above all by Jean-Jacques Rousseau, held that people in the state of nature are completely free, bound by no laws, and that institutions and laws erected by civilization are inherently a force for repression.

The conservative enlightenment's view of equality as the equal dignity of all human beings dictated a fierce commitment to self-government and constitutional democracy—that is, to the permissible *means*, rather than to a particular end, of politics. The left enlightenment's radical view of nature as a pre-legal state of absolute freedom (and corresponding lawlessness) dictated a suspicion of institutions, including brand-new institutions of the Enlightenment itself, and a relentless drive for liberation from the institutional repression of "natural man."

The left developed a view of equality as an organic accompaniment of pure freedom in the state of nature, but it believes people are far from equal in the present. Power, a necessary evil during the struggle toward pure freedom, must be seized from corrupt persons and institutions—in recent years often referred to as "structures"—and redistributed among the less privileged. The irreplaceable instrument of doing so in the real world is an enlightened vanguard or elite. Such an elite in the revolutionary manifestations of the left is unapologetically coercive. Even in a democratic framework, though, this elite is at the very least highly judgmental, in the spirit of campus speech codes, ever-lengthening lists of "hate crimes," and demands for massive extensions of state and transnational power to deal with alleged global emergencies such as climate change, which the elite declares to be no longer within the bounds of meaningful democratic debate.

Many of the first-wave leaders of the French Revolution were admirers of the two most celebrated conservative revolutions of the modern age, the Glorious Revolution of 1688–1689 in Great Britain and the American Revolution that had just unfolded in the 1770s and 1780s. But in the 1790s, the left concluded that early attempts to erect representative assemblies in France were corrupt; and, led by Maximilien Robespierre, the left took dictatorial power and began the series of arrests and executions known as the Terror.

Who or what was the left? The term was invented precisely in these years, in the 1790s prior to Robespierre's coup d'état, to specify the side of the National Assembly chamber in Paris on which radicals—the Jacobins and their allies—sat. Rousseau died in 1778 and thus did not live to see that his ideas gained the upper hand, defined the French Revolution, and went on to achieve preeminence in setting the world's political agenda for the next two centuries. But that is what happened.

In analyzing the history of the left, it is important to distinguish sharply between ends and means. What is striking is both the variety of means and the singleness of vision of the ultimate goal. The goal of the left is the liberation of mankind from traditional institutions and codes of behavior, especially moral codes. It seeks a restoration (or achievement of) the state of nature, which in this vision is a state of absolute individual liberty—universal happiness without the need for laws.

The proposed political way stations chosen by the left in its drive toward this goal have varied greatly. To name a few: abolition of private property (socialism); prohibition of Christianity or erection by the political elite of a new civil religion to replace it; confiscatory taxation; regulation of political speech to limit the ability of old-line privileged classes to affect politics; the reshaping of education to instill new values and moral habits in the population; confiscation of privately held firearms; gradual phasing out of the nation-state; displacement of the traditional family in favor of child-rearing by an enlightened governmental elite; and the inversion of sexual morality to elevate recreational sex and reduce the prestige of procreative sex. This is, it must be emphasized, a partial list.

Increasingly, people on the left have come to support democracy, rather than the oligarchic preferences of Robespierre, Marx, and Lenin. But democracy as an achievement is far less interesting and far less compelling to the left than is its central goal of guiding humanity toward the vision of total freedom originally described by Rousseau.

It has long been a temptation of those of us who do not share this vision to question the sincerity of the left's commitment to freedom. For example, George Orwell, a disillusioned man of the left who remained a democratic socialist until his death in 1950, came to believe that Marxism's commitment to the withering away of the state was mere cover for a devotion to power for the sake of power.

It's possible nonetheless to distinguish between the practical impossibility of a goal and the sincerity of those who pursue that goal. Indeed, it would seem difficult for a movement to avow and pursue a goal for more than two centuries without actually favoring it and believing it to be achievable.

Karl Marx once described freedom in the Communist utopia as "to do one thing today, another tomorrow, to go shooting in the morning and fishing in the afternoon and in the evening look after the cattle, to indulge in criticism after dinner, just as the fancy takes me."* There is in this vision a deeply desired individual freedom, with no room for coercion—or for the institutional and family constraints that limit most people's autonomy in the lives they find themselves leading.

For the last several decades of its political vitality, from roughly the 1950s to the 1980s, Marxism had lost its belief in itself as the modern world's logical path to economic efficiency. Faith in Marxism was sustained by its continued credibility as a means to achieve social equality through redistribution, even at the expense of an overall decrease in society's wealth. In a sense, Marxism survived on the plane of social values rather than economics.

The "Frankfurt School" of Marxist intellectuals and their ally Antonio Gramsci, an Italian Communist Party leader who died after an extended stay in Mussolini's prisons in the 1930s, sensed the economic weakness of socialism and tried to reorient the left toward "cultural Marxism"—the deconstruction of traditional institutions such as church and family and the transfer of power to people oppressed or underprivileged due to their class, race, or gender. But this tendency of the left long predated Marxism. It would have been instantly recognizable to the visionary founder and first successful politicians of the left, Rousseau and the Jacobins of Paris.

So by 2001, the global left was deeply engaged in social and cultural transformation, just as it had been at its founding. In Western European countries and Japan, there is no equivalent of the American Declaration of Independence; its deference to the Creator and its explicit invocation of natural law and natural rights are not part of the historical record there or of contemporary consciousness. In these countries in particular, the left had

---

* Karl Marx, *The German Ideology* (Marx-Engels Institute, Moscow, ISBN 978-1-57392-258-6, 1845).

won the day so thoroughly on non-economic issues that the right as well as the left felt little or no sympathy, or even comprehension, of American social conservatism.

The question remains: Why did the *American* left, which had been in close contact and combat with social conservatism at least since the 1970s, turn so quickly and vehemently against George W. Bush and his conduct of the war on terrorism? Was the renewed polarization so soon after 9/11 a consequence exclusively of administration missteps? Or did these missteps play into a deeper ideological tension that made renewed polarization a matter not of whether, but when?

4

GEORGE W. BUSH:
Faith-Based Presidency

A televised debate in Iowa in December 1999 among Republican candidates for president is still remembered for one of the most startling answers of any presidential debate. Asked (as were each of his opponents) to name his favorite political philosopher, George W. Bush named Jesus Christ, adding: "He changed my heart."

The Texas governor's answer came in the context of a struggle among several candidates for the pivotal social-conservative vote in the upcoming January 2000 Iowa caucuses.

Although it was not immediately apparent, Bush's answer proved to be a major factor in why his opponents failed to unite Iowa's huge social-conservative vote against him.

Bush went on to win Iowa over his closest competitor, publisher Steve Forbes, 41 to 30 percent. His victory in the caucuses proved crucial in enabling him to survive a landslide loss eight days later to Senator John McCain in socially liberal New Hampshire. After a hard-fought primary victory over McCain in socially conservative South Carolina, Bush was on his way to nomination and election as 43rd president of the United States.

Bush's 2000 presidential campaign strategy, as described in Chapter 3, involved playing down programmatic differences with the Clinton-Gore administration, including on social issues. On abortion, for instance, Bush campaigned as a pro-lifer, preaching the need for a "culture of life" in which every child would be "welcomed in life and protected by law." But according to Bush's political biographer Fred Barnes, probably no more than once in the entire 2000 political cycle did Bush say directly, in response to a question, that he believed *Roe v. Wade* was wrongly decided.

Bush and Social Issues

Rather than a programmatic approach to social issues, Bush emphasized the importance of religion in several dimensions. Like Ronald Reagan 16 years earlier, he praised political involvement by people of faith. He advocated a greater role for religion in partnering with government to help solve social problems such as alcoholism, drug addiction, and crime. And he talked about the importance of religion in his own life in helping him give up drinking and thereby stabilize his marriage.

None of these things, in the context of 2000, were seen as particularly controversial or as an easy target in the primaries or even in the general election. In fact, his Democratic opponent, Vice President Gore, echoed him on the need for a faith-based initiative and began speaking about the importance of Christian faith in his own life. One or more of his opponents may have cringed when Bush praised Jesus Christ as a philosopher, but none ventured any criticism aloud. What would have been the line of attack to put Bush on the defensive, with no risk to the attacker?

The Bush-Rove strategy to get social-conservative support was threefold. First, the candidate held extensive private meetings with social-conservative leaders. Second, he embraced the social-conservative agenda as it existed at the time in national politics: a federal partial-birth abortion ban, opposition to key aspects of the gay-rights agenda, opposition to embryonic stem cell research, elevation to the Supreme Court of judicial conservatives in the mold of Justices Antonin Scalia and Clarence Thomas, restoration by executive order of President Reagan's "Mexico City Policy" prohibiting the use of government funds for the promotion of abortion abroad. Third, Bush emphasized the need for a greater role for religion in public life, up to and including a greater role in government programs via the faith-based initiative.

There was an unspoken trade-off between the modest content of Bush's social-issue agenda and his emphasis on the importance of religion. On social issues, Bush was checking the right boxes but not attempting to advance the goals of social conservatism in a distinctive personal way. On religion, Bush wanted to sound more adventurous and more sympathetic to the role of faith in public life than his opponents did. He succeeded in this without putting forward his own aggressive, cutting-edge agenda. Such an agenda would have violated Bush's strategy of avoiding programmatic specificity at a time when most Americans viewed Clinton-Gore policies favorably.

The emphasis on religion was also well designed to score points on the character issue—"returning dignity to the White House"—which was key to persuading voters ambivalent about Clinton and his legacy to change party control of the executive branch. It all came together credibly, both in the private meetings with social-conservative opinion leaders and in public appearances, because Bush's interest in faith-based initiatives seemed consistent with who he was. Nearly everyone who heard him speak about his faith, privately or in public, judged him to be sincere. This helped minimize suspicions that his elevation of religion was a campaign theme and nothing more.

The early months of the Bush presidency were consistent with his campaign stance. His faith-based initiative was modified and expanded by the House Republican leadership, and it eventually passed the House in June 2001. The president's first policy speech carried on prime-time television (in August 2001) modified a ban on federal medical research funds going to stem cell research that destroyed embryos.

In the speech, Bush told the nation he was opposed to any research that required the killing of a human being, at whatever stage of development, no matter how worthy the aims of the research. But he permitted federal money to go to research on stem cell lines derived by embryo-destructive means prior to the date of his speech. Most in the pro-life movement found this stance acceptable but hardly inspiring. In Bush's early months, the administration's major domestic emphasis was on tax reduction and expanded student testing as a condition of federal aid to education.

As noted in Chapter 3, the 2000 election was the third consecutive presidential cycle in which foreign policy played only a minor role. The Bush-Cheney team promised to begin deployment of a limited defense against ballistic missiles, whereas Democrats favored only continued research on this technology. Deploying the system would require opting out of the ABM Treaty negotiated decades earlier with the Soviet Union, an entity no longer in existence. In his first months as president, Bush carried out his pledge by opting out of the treaty and ordering deployment to begin.

In the campaign, Bush endorsed Clinton's series of interventions to contain and eventually overthrow Serbia's Milosevic, but he made clear that his administration wanted no part of "nation building." He called for greater "humility" in U.S. foreign policy.

9/11 Transforms Bush

The shocking success of Al Qaeda's attacks on September 11, 2001, convinced millions of Americans, including the president, that when it came to our foreign policy, we had a lot to be humble about. In particular, the minimal response to earlier attacks by Al Qaeda and its allies on American embassies in Africa, American residents in the Khobar Towers of Saudi Arabia, and the U.S.S. *Cole* in Yemen in 2000 seemed like an underreaction that all but invited the act of mass murder America had just suffered.

In the midst of the vulnerability and anger most Americans felt in the aftermath of 9/11, there was little chance the president would underreact, and even less chance the Democrats would directly challenge any moves he did make. Analysts mainly on the left, in America and Europe, were ready with explanations for 9/11 that focused on our support for Israel and our alleged insensitivity to Muslim aspirations. But this carried little weight with Americans who turned on their televisions and saw Palestinian crowds celebrating 9/11 in the streets of the West Bank and Gaza. The only other jurisdiction where such quasi-official celebrations were reported was Saddam Hussein's Iraq.

National unity continued during the swift U.S.–led overthrow of Afghanistan's theocratic Taliban regime, Osama bin Laden's unrepentant host government. In these early months of global conflict, very few Democrats objected to the idea of regime change, given the obvious symbiosis, actual or potential, between rogue states and Islamic terrorists. On nearly everyone's list of rogue states was Saddam's Iraq, with its documented record of developing weapons of mass destruction and its willingness to use poison gas in its war against Iran and against Kurdish villages in Iraq itself. Most Democrats in Congress, after all, had voted in 1998 in favor of a resolution advocating the overthrow of Saddam and his Baathist regime. Regime change in Iraq thus became national policy not under Bush in 2001, but in 1998 when President Clinton signed a bipartisan congressional resolution into law, with surprisingly little controversy in a year when the president was in the process of being impeached.

In early 2002, two things happened that began to break the spell of bipartisan unity. Bush strategist Karl Rove gave a talk to Republican candidates planning to run in the upcoming midyear elections; in this talk, he recommended they use President Bush's widely supported conduct of the war on terrorism as a talking point on the campaign trail. Many Democrats and more than a few pundits and editorial writers attacked this as inappropriate. Far more important was the president's reference to an "axis of evil" in his January 2002 State of the Union speech. Singling out Iraq, Iran, and North Korea, Bush vowed to prevent rogue states from obtaining nuclear and other weapons that they could either use or clandestinely hand to Osama bin Laden or other terrorists.

It was not so much the idea of moving against rogue states as the description of them as "evil" that caused a wave of disquiet, and not only on the left. Some Republican alumni of his father's administration began to feel personally aggrieved.

Most members of George H. W. Bush's foreign policy team still defended their decision to refuse aid to the Shiite and Kurdish rebels when they were attempting, unsuccessfully, to overthrow Saddam after the first Gulf War in 1991. Including Saddam in the "axis of evil" implied that it may have been a big mistake to leave him in power for an additional decade. Even less welcome was the admission by Dick Cheney, the secretary of defense for

Bush's father and now vice president, that in the light of 9/11, the U.S. had indeed erred in allowing Saddam to remain in power after the first Gulf War.

Moralists vs. Realists

More broadly, the "axis of evil" formulation put Bush unmistakably in the camp of Reagan-style "moralists" rather than the Nixon-style "realists" that encompassed his own father and most of his father's top foreign-policy advisers, including his secretary of state, James Baker, and his national security adviser, Brent Scowcroft.

This was an argument that had endured in both parties for decades. On the Democratic side, at least rhetorically, John F. Kennedy and Jimmy Carter leaned to the moralist side, Bill Clinton to the realists. For the Republicans, Dwight Eisenhower was seen as a realist, but his own secretary of state, John Foster Dulles, often sounded like a moralist. The Nixon of 1960 ran as a realist, checkmating Nelson Rockefeller who that year sounded more like a moralist. Barry Goldwater was a moralist, succeeded as nominee in 1968 by Richard Nixon who, along with his key adviser Henry Kissinger, took realism to new levels during his presidency.

A pivotal breakthrough for the moralist side occurred at the 1976 Republican convention in Kansas City. Ronald Reagan, on the brink of elimination in that year's early primaries, revived his campaign with a series of speeches attacking the policy of détente widely identified with Secretary of State Kissinger, who under unelected President Gerald Ford was seen as dominating foreign policy. Reagan blamed Kissinger for a series of Communist takeovers that had followed the fall of South Vietnam in 1975, for engineering the takeover of the Panama Canal by Panama, and for President Ford's refusal to meet with Aleksandr Solzhenitsyn, the Nobel Prize–winning Soviet author expelled from his home-land for his advocacy of human rights.

Ford entered the convention with a lead of several dozen del-egates over Reagan, but most delegates (including Ford's own) were strongly conservative, and his lead was precarious. Prob-ably the biggest threat to Ford's nomination was a proposed Rea-ganite amendment to the foreign-policy section of the platform. Its prime author: a key Reagan backer, Senator Jesse Helms of North Carolina. Its title: "Morality in Foreign Policy."

Ford's campaign manager—none other than the future secretary of state under the elder Bush, James Baker—made a judgment that if the Ford forces fought the Reaganite plank, the amendment would pass anyway and the convention would then be in danger of bolting to Reagan. Over Kissinger's vehe-ment objections, Baker ordered the Ford delegates to support the anti-Kissinger plank. By voice vote, delegates added a new sec-tion titled "Morality in Foreign Policy" to the GOP platform. Although Ford kept his grip on the nomination, it was a key turn-ing point in the Reagan revolution and all that followed, in this nation and in the world.

The prominent role of Jesse Helms, better remembered today as his era's most outspoken social conservative than as its lead-ing anti-Soviet hawk, is worth underlining. In the GOP, political prosperity for social conservatives has often coincided with polit-ical prosperity for advocates of morality in foreign policy. Both prospered in the Reagan era, beginning in Kansas City in 1976, never more so than in the Reagan lame-duck year of 1988. That year saw the success of the Atwater-Ailes injection of social issues into the Bush-Dukakis campaign, as well as President Reagan's landmark speech advocating democracy to the applause of the student body at Moscow State University in the final and most successful of the four Reagan-Gorbachev summits.

Beginning in 1989, with the Atwater proclamation of the "big tent" and the GOP flight from the *Webster* decision, a decade-long eclipse began for social conservatives. On the foreign-policy side, George H. W. Bush and his team were dominated by the realists, as became clear in the aftermath of the first Gulf War when the president decided to deny aid to the Iraqi rebels attempting to overthrow Saddam Hussein. Even in the end game of the Cold War, Bush, Scowcroft, and Baker attempted to prevent the breakup of the Soviet Union on the classic realist grounds that stability outweighed other concerns. *New York Times* columnist William Safire memorably dubbed one such Bush effort in Ukraine the "Chicken Kiev" speech. Unlike the Persian Gulf aftermath, on the stage of the late Cold War, worldwide momentum was so much against the realists that their efforts on behalf of Soviet stability came to nothing.

In the 2000 campaign, the third post–Cold War presidential race, Governor Bush ran as a mild realist, seemingly far more an heir to his father than to Ronald Reagan. But the events of 9/11 ended America's vacation from foreign policy. It made millions of Americans reflect on our role in the world—what it had recently been and what it needed to become. President Bush was one such American.

By early 2002, in his State of the Union speech that identified the "axis of evil," it was clear the president had switched to the moralist side of the argument. He now believed that for America to be safe, the Islamic world—and particularly the Arab world—needed to open itself to democracy, and that the United States needed to move aggressively to help make that happen.

Even more important is the way in which Bush's strong religious faith informed his post-9/11 position on the importance of democracy. As 2002 went on, the gulf between Bush and the left widened and deepened. It seems likely that this happened, at least in large part, because Bush had joined a succession of moralist presidents as different from each other as Jefferson and Lincoln, Wilson and Reagan.

He appeared to believe, although he did not say it in so many words, that the United States has a providential role to play on the world stage—that our nation has a destiny, even a vocation, to spread throughout the world the idea that all men are created equal and endowed by their Creator with unalienable rights. Bush seems deeply to believe, as do a great many Americans, that what some name American "exceptionalism" vitally includes a national calling to spread ideals of political morality that are *universal*, in their nature as both divinely ordained precepts and principles of natural law. As the president repeatedly put it, this idea is "not America's gift to the world, it is God's gift to humanity."

The Left vs. American Moralism

The left, which arose in the 18th century as a revolt against the church and other established institutions, had become even more secular after World War II. After seeing the churches emptied in a Europe that was once called Christendom, the last thing the left wanted to see at the start of the 21st century was a social-conservative revival putting the Judeo-Christian God at the center of the worldwide fight for human rights and political equality. To the left, this is far more troubling than Islamic jihadists pressing to make Sharia law universal—jihadists placing God at the center of the fight *against* political equality and human rights. The modern left despises both of these assertive versions of theism, but it seems to feel less threatened by the brand of theism it regards as more primitive—namely the Islamic kind.

It is possible, of course, to take much leftist rhetoric at face value and conclude that its hatred of Bush is based on his image as a warmonger. But if antiwar sentiment is truly at the heart of the left's hatred of Bush, then the left would be equally vehement against a hypothetical President Al Gore, if Gore had won the presidency and conducted the exact same military campaigns against the Taliban and our enemies in Iraq—minus Bush's belief that democracy is God-given.

This is hard to imagine, just as it is hard to imagine rising hatred of Bill Clinton stemming from his decision, without the support of the United Nations, to bomb Kosovo week after week. This is hard to imagine because Bill Clinton did exactly that, and no leftist antiwar movement materialized.

All this would be sufficient to explain increased left-right polarization in the midst of a global war against jihadism. But in 2004 and 2005, still another factor contributed to American polarization. And this factor is consistent with the tendency of foreign-policy moralism and social conservatism to go hand in hand.

In 2004, when severe setbacks in Iraq caused Bush to lose his solid 2001–2003 political advantage from the conduct of the war on terrorism, social issues pushed back toward center stage during a presidential election for the first time since 1988. The gay-rights movement overplayed its hand on its multinational drive to elevate same-sex marriage. In considerable part thanks to that issue, President Bush pulled out another close election and by the end of 2005 had made two appointments that pushed the U.S. Supreme Court significantly to the right.

5

THE AGE OF POLARIZATION

In the first few months after 9/11, President Bush's job approval rating was consistently above 80 percent. A little more than a year later, by the time of the fall election campaign of 2002, it was still at 60 per cent or so. The president's initial tax-cut package passed in 2001, but to spread out its budgetary impact, Congress had resorted to phasing it in only gradually. As a result, not very much of it had taken effect and the recovery from the 2001 recession was at best sluggish. Still, as is usually the case in wartime, public sentiment about the president's handling of the war on terrorism (at this stage positive) trumped everything else combined.

Given this, the last thing Democrats probably wanted the 2002 midterm election to turn on would be issues related to 9/11. In fact a number of influential congressional Democrats, notably House Minority Leader Richard Gephardt, pushed colleagues to strike a bipartisan stance on war issues and change the subject to domestic issues such as health reform where Democrats still enjoyed higher ratings than Republicans.

The most important war-related congressional vote of 2002 was the resolution giving the president authority to take military action against the Saddam Hussein regime in Iraq. Gephardt endorsed the resolution, as did a majority of Democratic senators. But a majority of House Democrats voted against granting the president this power. Coming in the wake of the Taliban's overthrow, and at a time when public confidence in Bush as a war leader was high, Gephardt's inability to carry his caucus was a warning signal that partisan polarization was surprisingly durable and also capable of rising up to dominate politics again.

That it did so in the climactic phase of the 2002 election, and not over Iraq but on what appeared to be a peripheral issue, is the best proof that polarization was beyond the control of either party to stop. The debate at hand was whether to create a new Department of Homeland Security. Influential Democrats wanted to do it; Bush and the Republicans resisted. In the fall, Bush gave in and endorsed the new department. Note that the polarization intensified despite this seeming willingness of George W. Bush to meet the Democrats more than halfway. But Congress, closely divided at this point between a Republican House and a Democratic Senate, deadlocked over whether large-scale new hires of airport security personnel would be unionized.

In the closing days of the campaign, Republicans accused Democrats of holding up an important measure to protect the American people in wartime due to petty politics, namely their subservience to organized labor. The Democrats, who had insisted on the urgency of creating the new department, had no real answer. They strode indignantly into a trap they had largely constructed themselves.

In a stunning outcome predicted by almost no one, Republicans regained the Senate and scored small gains in the House.

It was the first time since 1934 that a second-year election under a newly elected president had seen gains in both houses for the president's party. Even more worrisome for the Democrats, Republican gains reached down into local races, giving Republicans their first national lead in state legislative seats in more than 50 years. By coming across as small-minded and partisan in a time of war, Democrats appeared to have lost small but measurable ground at every electoral level.

Polarization by the Democratic Base

As presidential politics got under way in early 2003, Democratic elites appeared to have learned their lesson. All the major presidential candidates serving in Congress—Gephardt, John Kerry, John Edwards, Joseph Lieberman—had voted to give Bush authority to attack Saddam and also backed the U.S.–led invasion when it began in March 2003.

But a minor candidate, former Governor Howard Dean of Vermont, did not. And the more he turned up the volume against Bush and the occupation of Iraq, the more positive feedback he got from his liberal audiences and the more money flowed in via his tech-savvy internet campaign. Suddenly this "minor" campaign boasted the largest bank account and the most encouraging polls, both nationally and in the critical early states of Iowa and New Hampshire. Dean soon added endorsements from his party's most recent nominee, former Vice President Gore, as well from the principal challenger to Gore in 2000, former Senator Bill Bradley of New Jersey.

This was a clarifying moment in the resurgence of the left. The willingness of many Democrats to polarize the 2002 election around the issue of unionizing Homeland Security workers was widely attributed to truculent liberal legislators in Washington. This was undoubtedly true, but it leaves a more interesting question unanswered. Were the legislators acting more or less on their own, or was a growing anti-Bush wave in the Democratic base beginning to pressure them into across-the-board opposition to the administration?

The Dean phenomenon of 2003 provided a much better test case. The highest-ranking members of the Democratic Party—the front-runners for the Democratic nomination for President—were unanimous in wanting to downplay Bush's conduct of the war as an issue. They had seen the party burned in 2002 and did not want a repeat performance. But the Democratic "netroots," in responding so favorably to Howard Dean, made it clear to Democratic elites that for them, playing down any disagreement with George W. Bush would be highly risky.

Dean crashed and burned in Iowa, but by then the surviving Democratic candidates had taken his lead and become far more critical of Bush's handling of the war. This was underlined by the fact that the presidential candidates seen as insufficiently critical, Gephardt and Lieberman, were quickly eliminated. The surviving candidate who was perhaps the most disdainful of the administration, Senator John Kerry of Massachusetts, won in Iowa and New Hampshire and by March had clinched the nomination.

Bush's performance ratings remained at 60 percent or above with the initial success of the invasion of Iraq. As the insurgency flared up and persisted, though, he fell to the 50s in the second half of 2003; and when chief U.S. weapons inspector David Kay announced in early 2004 that no Iraqi weapons of mass destruction could be found, Bush's rating as a war leader, and the performance rating of his presidency as a whole, quickly dipped to the 50–50 neighborhood, where it more or less remained until the November 2004 general election.

Polls still gave Bush high marks on his conduct of the war on terror, but his negatives on the war in Iraq were such that they neutralized his high rating on the overall war. This division of the two conflicts was itself an issue between the parties. The Republicans argued that overthrowing Saddam's regime was a logical second campaign in the war on terror, while Democrats began arguing that Iraq had become a diversion from the war against al Qaeda and the effort to track down Osama bin Laden. As the news from Iraq became more and more troubling during 2004, Bush began to lose his aura of competence under either strategic premise.

Moreover, at this stage of the Iraq debate, the Democrats were careful to minimize their differences with Bush on the *future* of Iraq. As the nominating conventions approached, Kerry designated as his running mate a rival from the primaries, Senator John Edwards of North Carolina, who like Kerry had voted to authorize Bush to use force against Iraq. Prior to the invasion, Edwards had been, if anything, more hawkish than most Democrats, and neither senator repudiated his vote to authorize war. Both agreed that the U.S. should help Prime Minister Ayud Allawi's interim government go through with the national elections scheduled for January 2005, and that the American military should maintain a presence for as long as our troops were needed for Iraq's democratic transition.

Instead of issuing a direct policy challenge, much of the liberal left converted Bush's handling of Iraq into a character issue, summed up in the slogan, "Bush lied, people died." On the rational level, this accusation made no sense. When asked directly, prominent Democrats nearly always admitted that their vote to overthrow Saddam was based on the same faulty prewar intelligence concerning Iraq's weapons of mass destruction (WMDs) that had influenced Bush—domestic intelligence that agreed with the intelligence conclusions of invasion opponents France, Germany, and Russia. Besides, why would it be in the administration's self-interest to propagate deceptions about WMDs that the invasion's immediate aftermath would so quickly and irrefutably reveal to American voters?

The question had a psychic rather than logical answer. In a time of partisan polarization, conspiracy theories quickly become plausible, even when they make little or no sense. The emergence of the Internet, the cutting-edge medium of political exchange, with its capacity for instant partisan and ideological gratification, helps the tendency along.

The Plame Investigation

A related phenomenon of polarization is the temptation to criminalize political differences. Many Democrats understandably trace this to the nearly pure party-line vote in 1998 to impeach Bill Clinton. Republicans are more inclined to see its origin in Watergate. Few have maintained that Richard Nixon was innocent, but many believe the charisma that subsequently attached to Woodward-Bernstein-style investigations led to career-driven prosecutorial abuses and media distortions, as in the Iran-Contra investigation that cast a pall over Ronald Reagan's last two years in office and that, some believe, doomed George H. W. Bush's race for a second term in 1992 by way of the last-minute, pre-election indictments filed by long-serving independent counsel Lawrence Walsh.

The investigation into the leaking of the identity of CIA official Valerie Plame that began in 2003 seemed to Republicans to fit this pattern. Independent prosecutor Patrick Fitzgerald's investigation resulted in the indictment and conviction of Vice President Cheney's chief of staff, Lewis ("Scooter") Libby and tied up Bush strategist Karl Rove in protracted legal self-defense for nearly three years. Libby's indictment and conviction came despite the fact that Fitzgerald knew from the time of his appointment that neither Libby nor Rove was involved in the original leak; it was Deputy Secretary of State Richard Armitage who originally leaked Plame's identity to columnist Robert Novak. (Rove did confirm to Novak the accuracy of Armitage's leak.)

Because Libby and Rove were among the most powerful advocates and defenders of the Iraq invasion, and because Plame's outing was related to the intelligence that led Bush to invade, the administration was placed far more on the defensive than it otherwise would have been. The proposition that "Bush lied, people died" made no more sense after the Plame leak than before, but an aura of wrongdoing and dirty tricks hung over the Bush White House, inhibiting the defense of the war and further unraveling Bush's 2001–2003 image as a successful wartime president.

From the time Kerry clinched the nomination in March 2004, the Bush-Kerry matchup was dead even, give or take a few points depending on the month. Many analysts noted that Bush had trouble reaching the 50 percent mark even in the polls he was leading, and Bush's defeat, though far from conceded by the Bush-Cheney campaign team, was widely predicted by Democrats and privately feared by Republicans.

The economy had noticeably picked up since summer 2003, when a big portion of the two Bush tax cuts took effect, but the administration received little or no benefit in polling on its economic performance. Democrats had regained a strong overall lead in the polls when domestic nonsocial issues such as health care and education were thrown in with handling of the economy; at the same time, they had pulled roughly even on overall foreign policy. The Democratic advantage on economic and nonsocial domestic issues remained intact through Election Day, despite continued economic improvement under Bush, suggesting that this advantage was driven at least in part by the public's declining overall view of the president's war leadership.

The Marriage Issue and 2004

As to social issues, in the mind of the electorate the president was firmly located on the conservative side. Coupled with his emphasis on the public role of religion and his affirmation of his own faith, socially conservative voters gave Bush a clear edge over Kerry on those issues. But it did not follow that socially conservative voters would be driven mainly or exclusively by social issues at a time when nonsocial issues, particularly foreign policy, had gained visibility.

Regarding the 2000 election, which took place at a time of peace and prosperity when foreign policy played a minimal role, I argued in Chapters 3 and 4 that what we might call the presidential-dignity issue was central in Bush's victory. It proved to be a way of mobilizing social-conservative voters without bringing up the specific issues that increasingly divided and defined the two parties. But in 2004, foreign policy had become central and the Clinton bifurcation factor (low personal approval and high job approval) was no more. If the social-conservative vote was to be activated and maximized, the Bush reelection campaign would have to find some other way to do it.

Like his GOP predecessors in the general elections of 1992 and 1996, the president looked uncomfortable talking about social issues (as distinct from the public role of religion, on which he spoke with confidence). The abortion issue remained static, while both sides waited for the federal courts to resolve the issue of a Bush-signed bill for a national ban on partial-birth abortion. An emerging social issue, embryo-destructive stem cell research, had benefited from an intense campaign by social liberals and biomedical elites touting potential cures for chronic and even terminal diseases, and supporting such research had become a Democratic talking point. Judicial appointments continued as a high-profile polarizing issue between the parties, but the fact that no Supreme Court vacancies had so far opened during the Bush presidency served to limit this issue in 2004.

As for the growing issue of same-sex marriage, Democratic strategists were virtually unanimous. Nearly without exception, they believed a court-driven, universally binding redefinition of marriage was inevitable—assuming it continued to be a peripheral issue in the 2004 elections. For the most part, they hoped and believed it would remain peripheral.

The Supreme Court's June 2003 decision in *Lawrence v. Texas* began to change the probabilities. By a 6–3 vote, the court threw out state antisodomy laws, overturning its 5–4 vote upholding them in 1986 in *Bowers v. Hardwick*. The majority ruled that it is unconstitutional to subject homosexuals to "discrimination both in the public and in the private spheres" and that banning sodomy "invited" such discrimination. It was, according to Professor Gerard Bradley of Notre Dame Law School, the first time the Supreme Court had ever recognized a constitutional right to engage in *any* sexual behavior outside marriage.

The majority opinion denied that *Lawrence* committed the Court to mandating same-sex marriage in some future case. But speaking for the three-member minority including Chief Justice Rehnquist, a skeptical Justice Scalia wrote, "Do not believe it."

All during 2003, including the months before *Lawrence*, it was rumored that high courts in several Blue states were torn between the desire to be the first in the nation to mandate same-sex marriage and the worry that a high-profile decision on the eve of a national election carried risks for the durability of any such decision.

On November 18, 2003, the Supreme Judicial Court of Massachusetts found by a 4–3 majority in *Goodridge v. Department of Public Health* that the 200-year-old Massachusetts Constitution mandated same-sex marriage. It reasoned that because civil marriage has been defined as a civil right, the civil rights of a citizen wishing to marry someone of his or her own sex were violated by continuing to define marriage as between a man and a woman. The Massachusetts Constitution's guarantee of civil equality thus mandated same-sex marriage. In at least a partial vindication of

Scalia's prediction in his minority opinion less than five months earlier, the Massachusetts justices cited *Lawrence* as a foundation of their ruling.

Supporters of gay marriage, elated and energized by the Massachusetts ruling, began in some cities and counties to take the law into their own hands. A number of clerks and justices of the peace announced they would open their doors to same-sex marriage, and they immediately began doing so. Mayor Gavin Newsom of San Francisco, himself a photogenic, recently married heterosexual, began personally granting same-sex marriage licenses in violation of a California statute passed by a 62 percent majority in a statewide referendum in November 2000. The number of such extralegal gay marriages may have been relatively few in number, and state-level rulings eventually brought them to a halt, but adulatory press coverage made it appear for some months after *Goodridge* that the country was being swept forward on an unstoppable tidal wave of same-sex marriage.

Social-conservative activism concerning the definition of marriage proceeded to take a quantum jump at the state level. Within less than a year, voters in 12 states passed referenda adding a two-sex definition of marriage to their state constitutions, preventing the possibility of a Massachusetts-type ruling in these states. The voters' preference for traditional marriage was overwhelming, ranging from 57 percent for traditional marriage in socially liberal Oregon to 86 percent in Mississippi, where the nation's largest black electorate proved no less vehemently conservative in its definition of marriage than the white majority had. There was polling evidence that popular opposition to same-sex marriage had risen significantly in the wake of *Goodridge* and its euphoric aftermath.

Despite the overwhelming popular opposition, few Democratic elected officials joined in attempts to lock in the traditional definition of marriage. Many expressed support for that definition but in the next breath condemned attempts to codify it at the state or national level as thinly disguised forms of bigotry. This meant that in nearly half the states—states in which state legislatures had to sign off on taking constitutional amendments to the ballot—it would be difficult for voters ever to get a chance to put the institution of marriage out of the reach of state-level judicial or legislative redefinition.

Democratic opposition also doomed any near-term chance for a federal constitutional amendment reaffirming the traditional meaning of marriage. Republicans had slim majorities in both houses of Congress, but near monolithic Democratic opposition would leave them far short of the two-thirds majority needed to send such an amendment to the states.

Prior to *Goodridge*, Republican elites had also shown little urgency about moving forward on a constitutional amendment. They argued that the Defense of Marriage Act (DOMA), passed overwhelmingly by a newly elected Republican Congress and signed into law by President Clinton in 1996, would be sufficient to prevent the imposition of same-sex marriage on states that didn't favor it. Moreover, social-conservative groups had difficulty agreeing on the wording of the proposed amendment.

But the U.S. Supreme Court's ruling in *Lawrence* cast serious doubt on the future of DOMA. If sodomy was now a constitutional right, one state's enactment of same-sex marriage would have far greater standing in other states. DOMA's attempt to override the Constitution's Full Faith and Credit provision, under which one state's legal arrangements traditionally are respected by other states, would likely be thrown out as a violation of the new civil rights defined by *Lawrence*.

When the Massachusetts high court followed less than five months later with *Goodridge*, social-conservative concern turned into alarm. With federal and state courts now moving forward in tandem, Scalia's warning of court-imposed same-sex marriage seemed not only plausible but also imminent. There were six pro-*Lawrence* votes on the Supreme Court, so the cooperation of only a few liberal states could lead to the invalidation of DOMA and invocation of the Full Faith and Credit clause, geared toward one result: compulsory recognition of same-sex marriage in all 50 states. And it could in theory happen exclusively through court decisions rather than by decisions of voters or legislators in any of those states.

Bush's Ambivalence

The leaders of social-conservative groups became more and more focused on President Bush; he had never endorsed the Federal Marriage Amendment (FMA) and continued to resist doing so for more than three months after the historic court decision in Massachusetts. At one gathering held in the White House's intimate Roosevelt Room in early 2004 for a small, predominantly Catholic group of social conservatives, the president departed from normal practice at such sessions by talking nonstop for nearly 40 minutes without ever taking questions.

When he finally endorsed the constitutional amendment on February 24, 2004, Bush described marriage as "the union of a man and a woman" and as "the most enduring human institution, honored and encouraged in all cultures and by every religious faith." He said marriage "cannot be severed from its cultural, religious, and natural roots without weakening the good influence of society."

At the same time, Bush made clear his endorsement of the FMA had been triggered by the actions of the Massachusetts high court and of local officials, in particular San Francisco's Mayor Newsom: "After more than two centuries of American jurisprudence and millennia of human experience, a few judges and local authorities are presuming to change the most fundamental institution of civilization."

Echoing Scalia's minority opinion in *Lawrence* eight months earlier, the president argued that laws banning same-sex marriage in most states and the Defense of Marriage Act "express an overwhelming consensus in our country for protecting the institution of marriage." He added cautionary words, however: We have "no assurance that the Defense of Marriage Act will not itself be struck down by activist courts," he said. "In that event, every state would be forced to recognize any relationship that judges in Boston or officials in San Francisco choose to call a marriage."

Further underlining his own reluctance to engage the issue, the president called for a civil debate: "We should also conduct this debate in a manner worthy of our country, without bitterness or anger. In all that lies ahead, let us match strong convictions with kindness and good will and decency."

Social liberals promptly made clear that kindness and civil debate were very far from their thoughts. Cheryl Jacques, president of the Human Rights Campaign, accused the president of gay-bashing. Stephanie Cutter, a spokesperson for Democratic front-runner John Kerry, said the president's announcement made clear that his reelection strategy was to "use wedge issues and the politics of fear to divide the nation." And the chairman of the Democratic National Committee, Terry McAuliffe, proclaimed, "It is wrong to write discrimination into the U.S. Constitution, and it is shameful to use attacks against gay and lesbian families as an election strategy."

Social conservatives, in the Bush administration and out, could not help but see such rhetoric as disingenuous, misinformed, or both. They vehemently denied that reaffirming the age-old meaning of marriage could be equated with bigotry. Every social conservative who worked for Bush or had been in a meeting with him knew the president deeply disliked the idea of using marriage as a wedge issue, indeed as any kind of issue, and that he had endorsed the FMA only under intense pressure from his social-conservative base. As to "attacks against gay and lesbian families," they knew that a significant part of the president's ambivalence was that he was deathly afraid of being seen as attacking one lesbian couple in particular: the one composed of Vice President Cheney's younger daughter, Mary, and her lesbian partner.

Bush's endorsement, measured though it was, was enough to put the FMA on the agenda of Congress in 2004. The amendment had no chance to achieve the two-thirds majority of each house necessary to refer it to the states (where it would need 38 ratifications, three-fourths of the 50 states). But the votes of approval—almost all Republicans for, almost all Democrats against—left no doubt that unlike the idea of gay marriage or even the DOMA vote eight years earlier, the measure designed to stop the redefinition of marriage had polarized along unmistakable Republican-Democrat lines.

This still didn't have to matter very much in the presidential election unless it emerged as a widely perceived disagreement between Bush and Kerry, and for a few months after Bush's February endorsement of the Federal Marriage Amendment, the president's reluctance to speak out on the topic made it appear that the definition of marriage would remain a nonissue. Democratic strategists certainly hoped so, and they found numerous ways to threaten dire consequences, for the nation and for Republicans, should the president try to elevate the issue to his advantage.

Toward the end of his acceptance speech at the Democratic convention in Boston, as one example, Kerry suddenly assumed a tone of high drama, hauling the issue into the limelight: "I want to address these next words directly to President George W. Bush: In the weeks ahead, let's be optimists, not just opponents. Let's build unity in the American people, not angry division. Let's honor this nation's diversity; let's respect one another; and let's never misuse for political purposes the most precious document in American history, the Constitution of the United States."

It proved to be the biggest applause line of the speech, and in its way quite adroit. Everyone in the hall knew that, in the guise of calling for a civil debate, Kerry had accused President Bush of prostituting the Constitution by endorsing an amendment that would define marriage as between a man and a woman—and Kerry never had to actually mention either the amendment or the controversy that lay behind it.

Kerry was also demanding that conservative leaders cease opposing, or even debating, federal and state judges' increasingly visible drive to redefine marriage. In a town hall meeting in Wisconsin the week after his nomination, the senator declared: "We've got leadership that tends to try to drive a wedge between people. It picks one of the hot-button, cultural issues and drives that at you, whether or not that's the most important thing on America's mind."

U.S. Polarization vs. European Capitulation

This clash over what to do about the judicial elevation of same-sex marriage is in many ways a microcosm of the rise of social issues and of social conservatism in America. The process works like this: The left proposes a major change in society—e.g., unilateral divorce, removal of references to God in public places, abortion on demand, suppressing the words "husband" and "wife" as components of the meaning of marriage. Social conservatives mount resistance—at first perhaps only polemical, then legislative. If social conservatives have a measure of success at the legislative stage, social liberals bring to bear their dominance of the American legal profession. Their lawyers win judicial rulings proclaiming newly discovered legal and constitutional rights, eventually taking the social issue in question out of the realm of legislation and of democratic decision-making. Any attempt by social conservatives to battle this process, particularly in its later stages, is attacked as divisive, as a form of bigotry or political extremism, as demagoguery—above all as a cause of political polarization.

In an important sense, one reflected in the title of this book, the charge of polarization is not only true but inarguable. The existence of an American political movement called social conservatism is the main factor that triggers political polarization. If the movement did not exist—or, in the case of the "no fault divorce" debate of the 1970s, was in a rudimentary form and only beginning to take shape—no political polarization would exist.

What would happen instead—what has happened in Western Europe—is a peaceful social revolution, utterly changing the face of society in ways that would have been both recognizable and pleasing to Rousseau and his heirs, history's first leftist politicians in the French National Assembly of the 1790s. The political resistance of social conservatives is what causes political polarization in the United States, and the absence of comparable movements is why political polarization is negligible in Western Europe, if indeed it can be said to exist at all.

Also increasingly in question is the extent to which European or Western civilization, widely understood as the world's most influential force of the last five hundred years or so, can be said to exist in Europe. The long-lived cultural critic Jacques Barzun, born in Paris in 1907 but for many decades a naturalized American and Columbia professor, believes he has lived to see "the end of the high creative energies at work since the Renaissance":

"The forms of art as of life seem exhausted."[*] The existence of American political polarization, decried by multicultural European and American elites, is the most tangible evidence that the battle over Western civilization is not quite over—or conceivably that the ideas of the American founding have a chance of creating some new hybrid to replace the European ascendancy of the half-millennium just passed.

Whatever the larger roots and implications, Western Europe is rapidly and with little fuss accepting a transformation of marriage; John Kerry's implied demand in his 2004 Boston acceptance speech that heterosexual America do the same did not meet with the reception he hoped for.

Social Issues and Voter Movement

Only weeks after Kerry's acceptance speech, in early August, the state of Missouri held its primary election and at the same time voted on a referendum to add a prohibition of same-sex marriage to the state constitution. This border state had narrowly chosen Bush over Gore in 2000 (50.4 percent to 47.1 percent), had voted for every electoral college winner since 1960, and was seen at the time as critical to Kerry's hopes of ousting Bush in 2004. According to the daily political newsletter *Hotline*, two of the three most recent public polls gave Kerry-Edwards a small lead over Bush-Cheney in the state, while the third registered a tie.

Missouri's vote in favor of the constitutional amendment locking in traditional marriage was not close: 71 percent for, 29 percent against. This took place despite an estimated 40-to-1 advantage in campaign spending by opponents of the amendment, and in the

---

[*] Quoted in the *New Yorker*, "Age of Reason: In his hundred years, Jacques Barzun has learned a thing or two," by Arthur Krystal, October 22, 2007.

context of a disproportionately Democratic turnout in the election (due to a fierce primary challenge that ousted the incumbent Democratic governor). This meant that not only Republicans but also a solid majority of active Democratic voters wanted Missouri to stick with the old-fashioned, heterosexual version of marriage.

As it happened, Senator Kerry was campaigning in St. Louis the day after the vote. The Democratic nominee said he had no problem with the outcome. He said he would have voted the same way as the 71 percent did. He, after all, unlike President Bush, said each state should be able to make up its own mind on the future of marriage. (Kerry didn't add that in 1996 he was one of 14 senators, all of them liberal Democrats, who voted to *prohibit* individual states from defining marriage as they wished. This would have meant that all states would be required, under Full Faith and Credit, to recognize same-sex marriages that had been performed in any state permitting such marriages. At the time of this 1996 debate, Kerry said he cast his no vote because he believed the Defense of Marriage Act to be unconstitutional.)

The day after the Missouri primary, the same day Kerry was answering questions in St. Louis, a judge in Washington State ruled that the 19th-century authors of that state's constitution had made the institution of exclusively heterosexual marriage unconstitutional. The nationwide gulf between judges and voters concerning marriage did not seem to be going away.

For the Democrats, the presidential dead heat in Missouri soon did go away. The only state in 2004 to vote on same-sex marriage earlier than November saw the Bush-Cheney ticket take a solid lead in the weeks following the vote. The Kerry-Edwards ticket soon pulled its television ads, a sign that Democratic strategists no longer believed Missouri to be within reach. (Bush carried Missouri in November by 53.3 percent to 46.1 percent.)

If a midsummer referendum in a closely contested battleground state such as Missouri could contribute to a decisive swing toward Bush-Cheney, what about the 11 additional states that would be voting on similar referenda in November? Could national polling even measure the issue's impact on the race? On the one hand, the *Goodridge* decision in Massachusetts, the wave of announced redefinitions of marriage by the mayor of San Francisco and other officials, Bush's endorsement of the FMA, the party-line floor votes on FMA in the House and Senate, and Kerry's high-profile shot across Bush's bow in Boston had all made national news. But long periods went by without either Bush or Kerry attempting to elevate the issue and without prominent press coverage, and neither side ran any television commercials on the subject.

In recent presidential election years, media firms have taken and made public dozens of surveys. The 2004 campaign was no exception. But these public polls seldom seemed to test or analyze same-sex marriage, or social issues in general, as a factor in voters' presidential preferences.

An important exception was *Time* magazine, which retained the New York firm of Schulman, Ronca, and Bucuvalas to take a series of national polls. In five polls taken between July and September, 15 percent to 18 percent of voters said they were basing their vote on "moral values issues like gay marriage and abortion."

This was higher than anyone might have expected in a wartime election. But even more striking was that Bush led among these voters, 70 percent to 18 percent (the figures for the *Time* poll taken September 21–23). The poll found Kerry well ahead of Bush among voters motivated by all other issues combined. If the voters choosing "moral values issues" in the *Time* poll were taken out of play, a late-September 4-point Bush-Cheney lead in the national popular vote would turn into a 5-point lead for Kerry-Edwards.

Moreover, the *Time* poll found that a significant portion of the *undecided* voters were those planning to vote on "moral values issues like gay marriage and abortion." Interestingly, the larger number of voters planning to vote on their view of war-related issues seemed much more locked in to either Bush or Kerry. This suggested that further upside gains on "moral issues like gay marriage and abortion" were available to Bush-Cheney.

But these were only national numbers. With 2004 shaping up in most projections as a tight popular vote not very different from 2000, even more salient would be the effect of social issues on the handful of states expected to be close. Conceivably Bush's advantage on social issues was concentrated in Southern and other conservative states where the GOP ticket had an unbreakable hammerlock in almost any electoral scenario. The story might be very different in battleground states, which in 2004 seemed to be predominantly outside the South.

In mid-September the cable TV network MSNBC partnered with the Knight-Ridder news conglomerate to survey 10 battleground states. They made the selection based on a compilation by a panel of political experts of which states were likely to determine the outcome of the electoral college. None of the states selected were in the South. A few, such as New Hampshire and Oregon, were classified by most analysts as socially liberal but were no doubt selected because they had been close in 2000 and appeared to be close once again in 2004.

Mason Dixon Polling & Research, the firm retained by MSNBC and Knight-Ridder to take the state polls, offered in its questionnaire "moral issues and family values" as one of the options on the question, "Which one of the following issues will be most important in determining your vote for President this year?"

Anywhere from 12 percent to 16 percent of the 10 state electorates chose "moral issues and family values" as their "most important" issue. Consistent with *Time*'s national poll, an overwhelming majority of these voters planned to vote for Bush.

The ratios ranged from 8–1 in Oregon to 10–1 in Ohio to 12–1 in Missouri. As with *Time's* national findings, in states where Bush had the lead, his advantage on these issues more than outweighed a Kerry advantage on all other issues combined. On only one other issue offered to the voters by Mason Dixon—"terrorism and homeland security"—did Bush have a clear lead over Kerry.

Of particular interest to strategists on both sides was Ohio. In mid-October 2000, the Gore campaign had made what was subsequently seen as a miscalculation by pulling its ads in a state whose 21 electoral votes were much more in play than analysts had thought. (The 2000 Bush-Cheney campaign, running unopposed TV commercials in Ohio's closing weeks, won by 50.0 percent to 46.5 percent over Gore-Lieberman.) The same factors the Democrats faced in 2000—an economy weaker than the national average, presided over by a tax-increasing Republican governor and legislature—had accelerated and become an undiluted Bush-Cheney vulnerability in 2004.

In 2000 Florida had been the dead-even state that drove the national outcome, but its economy by 2004 was enjoying a boom, and Governor Jeb Bush, the younger brother of the president, was far more popular than he had been in 2000. (Although it remained the closest state in the South, Florida was carried by Bush-Cheney in November by a margin of 5 percent.) As the 2004 campaign headed for the homestretch, strategists for both Bush and Kerry locked onto Ohio as the irreplaceable building block of an electoral college majority. Both sides devoted huge amounts of money and manpower to voter turnout in the state.

The Bush-Cheney campaign had one significant advantage. Over the opposition of the Ohio Republican establishment, social conservatives had managed to place a proposed constitutional amendment banning same-sex marriage on the November ballot. It came under widespread attack among Ohio's journalistic and legal elites, including many Republicans, because it was seen as effectively banning not only same-sex marriages but also the "moderate" compromise proposal of same-sex civil unions. Nevertheless, the amendment cruised to a 63 percent victory in the state, which made it easier for the Bush campaign to motivate social conservatives in a year when the Ohio economy was weak, the Iraq war was increasingly unpopular, and Democrats had invested heavily in their own superb turnout operation.

In a state with weakening demographics—Ohio was reduced from 21 to 20 electoral votes by the 2000 Census—Democrats increased their presidential vote from 2,183,628 (Gore 2000) to 2,741,165 (Kerry 2004), an extraordinary jump that would normally have guaranteed victory. They lost the state, and the electoral college, when the Bush campaign simultaneously pushed the president's vote from 2,350,363 to 2,859,764.

The Final Debate

High-profile events in October further ensured the salience of social issues, including marriage, not only in Ohio but all over the country. Eight days before the election, it was announced that Chief Justice William Rehnquist had been stricken with thyroid cancer and had undergone an emergency tracheotomy and begun chemotherapy. The day before the election, Rehnquist's spokesman announced that he had not been physically able to return to his office at the court, as he had earlier planned. On a court whose membership had remained unchanged for more than 10 years, Rehnquist's illness was potentially a major development for both sides of the debate on social issues.

In John Kerry's final debate with President Bush on October 13, the issue of same-sex marriage occasioned what most observers saw as his only serious misstep of the three debates—a misstep that arguably deflected momentum Kerry had achieved by his otherwise adroit performance in the debates. The circumstances of the exchange are worth recounting in some detail.

Moderator Bob Schieffer of CBS began by asking Bush a question whose premise could not have been more consistent with the Kerry-Edwards strategy of playing down differences on the marriage issue: "Mr. President, . . . let's shift to some other questions here. Both of you are opposed to gay marriage. But to understand how you came to that conclusion, I want to ask you a more basic question. Do you believe homosexuality is a choice?"

Bush replied that he didn't know, but that respect was due to people and their life choices. Given his diffidence on this issue, it would have been easy for the president to stop there, but instead he implicitly challenged the premise of Schieffer's question and went on to explain how much more active his opposition to same-sex marriage was than Kerry's:

> But as we respect someone's rights, and as we profess tolerance, we shouldn't change—or have to change—our basic views on the sanctity of marriage. I believe in the sanctity of marriage. I think it's very important that we protect marriage as an institution, between a man and a woman.
>
> I proposed a constitutional amendment. The reason I did so was because I was worried that activist judges are actually defining the definition of marriage, and the surest way to protect marriage between a man and woman is to amend the Constitution.
>
> It has also the benefit of allowing citizens to participate in the process. After all, when you amend the Constitution, state legislatures must participate in the ratification of the Constitution.
>
> I'm deeply concerned that judges are making those decisions and not the citizenry of the United States. You

know, Congress passed a law called DOMA, the Defense of Marriage Act.

My opponent was against it. It basically protected states from the action of one state to another. It also defined marriage as between a man and a woman.

But I'm concerned that will get overturned. And if it gets overturned, then we'll end up with marriage being defined by the courts, and I don't think that's in our nation's interest.

It was in response to this foray that an annoyed-looking Kerry began his own answer to Schieffer: "We're all God's children, Bob. And I think if you were to talk to Dick Cheney's daughter, who is a lesbian, she would tell you that she's being who she was, she's being who she was born as."

This answer by Kerry was to become the most widely remembered moment of the three presidential debates. It came across as a cold, gratuitous use of Mary Cheney as a debating point. Unlike his running mate John Edwards in a similar exchange with Cheney in an earlier vice presidential debate, Kerry neglected to soften his attack by praising the vice president and his wife for being supportive of their daughter, or even by referring to Mary Cheney by name. In context, it's hard to see Kerry's answer as anything other than an attempt—consistent with his acceptance speech, but far cruder—to demonize Bush for daring to open ideological space between himself and Kerry on their approach to dealing with judicially decreed same-sex marriage.

On Election Day, the National Election Pool exit poll asked voters what issue influenced them the most. Of the choices provided, the surprise winner was "moral values," running ahead of economy and jobs, terrorism, and Iraq. Among these voters—22 percent of the national vote—Bush bested Kerry 80 percent to 18 percent. Broken down to percentage points, 18 percent of all voters were in the "Bush Moral Values" category, 4 percent in the "Kerry Moral Values" category. In an election he won by just under 2.5 percent of the popular vote, in other words, Bush won self-described moral values voters by 14 percentage points, while losing all other voters combined by 11.5 percentage points.

Persistence of Red and Blue

Bush defeated Kerry in the electoral college, 286 to 252, receiving 50.7 percent of the popular vote to 48.3 percent for Kerry. Only three states voted differently for President than they had in 2000: Iowa and New Mexico flipped narrowly to Bush, New Hampshire to Kerry. This was how minimal a net change the electoral college saw between the 2000 election, which had little or no foreign-policy component, and 2004, a wartime election. However fervent the 2004 debates over Iraq and the war on terrorism were, most Americans found themselves voting not very differently than they had during the Red vs. Blue near stalemate of 2000. Despite the heart-stopping swings in President Bush's first-term job-approval rating, and even greater swings in his rating as a wartime president, the defection of New Hampshire meant that not a single socially liberal state cast its electoral votes for the Bush-Cheney ticket.

The pattern of Republican gains in the House and Senate confirmed the continued prevalence of Red vs. Blue polarization. Republicans netted four seats in the U.S. House; but if House Majority Leader Tom DeLay had not pulled off a second and (this time) GOP-controlled redistricting in his home state of Texas, Republicans would have suffered a net loss of two House seats nationally. This slight underlying GOP erosion was confirmed by the fact that while Republicans nationally won the House popular vote 51 percent to 46 percent in 2002, their margin slipped to 50–47 in 2004.

Republicans went from 51 to 55 seats in the U.S. Senate, gaining six seats while yielding two. Five of the six pickups came in the South, all five in the wake of Democratic retirements. In the 13 states of the greater South—the Old Confederacy plus Kentucky and Oklahoma—Republican senators now predominated 22 to 4. Following the election of 1960, Democrats controlled the senators from these Southern states, 24 to 2. None of the five southern Democratic senators who retired would have been clear underdogs had they sought reelection in 2004. The GOP Senate gains, not unlike those in the House, were more about the unfinished business of Southern realignment than about a Bush-Cheney or Republican tide.

The 2004 returns in elections for the state legislatures, the best indicator in determining the underlying national strength of the two parties, further confirmed that there was no significant Republican trend. 2002 had seen modest but historically unusual Republican gains in state legislators, leaving a 73-seat (1 percent) Republican majority. 2004 saw an even smaller trend back toward the Democrats, leaving that party with a microscopic 10-seat lead in a universe of 7,382 state legislators. At the grass roots, then, the familiar picture of a 50-50 nation could not have been clearer.

Unquestionably, the patriotic rallying to the Bush administration in the immediate aftermath of 9/11, together with the president's decisive, widely supported response in Afghanistan and Iraq, offered Bush and his party at least a shot at breaking out of Red vs. Blue polarization. There was a hint of this in the 2002 elections, and through the end of 2003, even renewed polarization at home and the appearance of a powerful insurgency in Iraq could not prevent the president from maintaining nearly 60 percent approval, mostly a function of his conduct of the war.

The turning point for Bush as a war president was chief U.S. weapons inspector David Kay's announcement in early 2004 that, much to his surprise, no weapons of mass destruction were in Iraq at the time of the American invasion. From then on, Bush stopped being seen as a highly competent war president and became, from that time to the end of his incumbency, at best a highly controversial war president.

Moreover, as a presidential candidate, John Kerry proved adept at maximizing Bush's growing vulnerability on the war. Unlike Howard Dean, who blundered in December 2003 by saying the recent capture of Saddam Hussein would not make Americans any safer, Kerry welcomed progress on the Iraqi battlefield and the administration's push toward holding Iraqi elections. Throughout 2004, Kerry continued to defend his 2002 vote authorizing the invasion, and he picked a running mate, John Edwards, who not only had voted the same way in 2002 but had been an even more consistent and outspoken advocate of toppling the Baathist regime. In terms of forward-looking policy regarding Iraq—elections, maintaining an American presence until the Iraqi people could achieve self-government—there was surprisingly little difference between Bush and Kerry through Election Day.

Instead, Kerry's strategy centered on converting the intelligence failure concerning WMDs into a competence issue, with the aim of undermining Bush's character. Kerry stopped short of accusing Bush of outright fabrication but dripped disdain on such issues as mistreatment of prisoners at Abu Ghraib and alleged mishandling of European allies. Military embarrassments, such as on-again, off-again campaigns to retaliate for anti-American atrocities in the insurgent stronghold of Fallujah, only increased popular qualms about Bush's ability to handle the war.

If the war on terrorism had continued to dominate the stage in 2004 to the extent it did in 2002, the sharp decline in Bush's approval rating as a war president would almost certainly have put him on a trajectory to defeat. And right up to Election Day, as

Bush again and again fell short of 50 percent approval, numerous Democratic strategists and media analysts believed Bush would lose.

The reemergence of high-profile social issues for the first time in a presidential election since 1988 changed the equation and enabled Republicans to keep their Red coalition stitched together. A number of Democratic strategists dreaded the elevation of same-sex marriage as a national issue (particularly after *Goodridge*), but the president's palpable discomfort in talking about it caused many of them to believe the danger would pass them by. But the social-conservative mobilization at the state level, most dramatically in Missouri and Ohio, together with Kerry's sometimes clumsy attempts to put the issue off-limits, caused Bush to rise to the occasion and help make the partisan divide on the marriage issue unmistakable.

More crucial than either Bush or Kerry in resurrecting social issues was the increasingly impatient eagerness of liberal judges, state and federal, to force same-sex marriage into the heart of American law and culture. When William Rehnquist was stricken just days before the election, the nexus between the liberal view of constitutional law and same-sex marriage became even harder for voters to overlook. Anyone who cared to think about it knew that the kind of judges likely to be appointed by President Kerry would settle the issue once and for all, probably even if Kerry had only one term. In November 2004, from the point of view of John Kerry, not enough American voters were ready to have judges make that decision for them.

6

THE ENDING OF POLARIZATION?

As soon as he was reelected, President Bush undertook a series of conciliatory moves—some of them on social issues, but by no means limited to them—that could be analyzed individually as logical outcomes of unrelated conditions and motives. Added together, they look more like a determined, systematic attempt to end Red-Blue polarization by moving from the right to the center of the political spectrum, and by offering compromise and conciliation to his adversaries on a number of issues.

One might argue that Bush did this because he is not really a conservative, and that in 2000 and 2004 he used conservative ideas to win the nomination and election, fully intending to jettison or de-emphasize them once he knew he would never again face the electorate.

This seems implausible. To judge from his speeches and press conferences, President Bush remained a Reagan-style conservative on foreign policy, economics, and social issues. What does seem plausible is that he came to see ending polarization as a more important goal and a more promising framework than continuing the stark right-left battles that characterized much of his first term.

By most accounts, Bush never believed polarization was an inevitable feature of contemporary politics. He arrived in Washington vowing to lessen raw partisanship and with a credible track record of having done so as governor of Texas. All six of his years as governor coincided with a Democratic-led legislature; even when Republicans gained a slim majority in the Texas House, Democrat Pete Laney was reelected Speaker. Yet Bush succeeded in passing major state legislation on such subjects as tort reform and property tax relief by reaching out to powerful Democrats such as Laney and Lieutenant Governor Bob Bullock, who in Texas's unique political configuration served as uncrowned king of the State Senate.

Bush was well aware that Washington's atmosphere was very different from Austin's, and not only because Republicans controlled Congress in the late 1990s. As I argued in Chapter 3, the impeachment, trial, and acquittal of Bill Clinton in 1998–1999 had sharply accelerated the trend toward polarization that had been building since the 1960s, and by the time that Bush declared his candidacy in 1999, Washington's mood had risen to a toxic level. At one point early in his campaign, Bush singled out a fellow Texan, House Majority Whip Tom DeLay, for divisiveness and lack of compassion for the poor.

The 40-day legal battle over Bush's razor-thin Florida victory over Al Gore, concluded by a bitter 5–4 decision of the U.S. Supreme Court and viewed in the light of Gore's half-million-vote plurality in the national popular vote, left most congressional Democrats feeling cheated; they were in no mood to compromise with the incoming Bush team. The president used his slim GOP majorities to pass a larger-than-expected tax cut (which under budget rules he could do with a bare majority). At the same time, he reached out to liberal Democrats like Senator Edward Kennedy to craft his education-reform bill, No Child Left Behind, which traded provisions for rigorous testing of public school performance in return for increased federal aid. Conservatives, many of whom (including for a time Ronald Reagan) favored abolition of the Department of Education, were unhappy. So were politically powerful teachers' unions such as the National Education Association, to whom extensive student testing was anathema. But passage of No Child Left Behind came with overwhelming bipartisan support in Congress, and no one cited the debate or the new law as products of polarization.

The Faith-Based Initiative

The first-term legislative battle over Bush's faith-based initiative, by contrast, did at times take on the hallmarks of polarization. But, to the surprise of players on both sides of the debate, its outcome was an unambiguous victory for the left and defeat for the administration and the social conservatives who supported Bush's position. The defeat came when the president abandoned his efforts to pass a compromise faith-based bill in the Senate that had met with virtually no public opposition. In earlier chapters, I argued that Bush's advocacy of the faith-based initiative as a distinctive campaign theme was an effective strategy in 2000. It allowed Bush to sound both fresh and different from his opponents, Republican as well as Democratic, while it avoided programmatically challenging any specific Clinton-Gore policies associated with widely applauded declines in unemployment, violent crime, and welfare dependency during the 1990s. The 2000 campaign's faith-based theme generated considerable enthusiasm among socially conservative voters who had felt somewhat disengaged from the presidential politics of 1992 and 1996, yet it was consistent with the Bush campaign's desire to avoid detailed debate on social issues such as abortion and gay rights. Moreover, as Democrats were well aware, Bush's emphasis on the role of faith at both the personal and policy levels set up a contrast with Clinton's second-term scandals.

Yet it is also true that Bush gave many indications of a strong commitment to the faith-based issue. In April 2001 in a speech at Notre Dame University, the president argued that bringing faith-based approaches to bear on intractable social pathologies could represent a "third wave" of modern welfare policy—the earlier waves being the creation of the welfare state and the drive toward local and personal accountability embodied in the 1996 welfare reform.

At first quite a few Democrats—including Vice President Gore in the 2000 campaign—echoed Bush's desire for a greater policy role for faith-based activism. Bush tried to build on this convergence by appointing a socially conservative Democratic professor, John DiIulio of the University of Pennsylvania, to a newly created position as assistant to the president in charge of the faith-based initiative. But in the debate on House Resolution 7, the ambitious faith-based legislation put together by the White House and Republican House leaders in the first half of 2001, secularist qualms returned to the fore among congressional Democrats. Final House passage in June included several dozen Democrats, but most of these were from socially conservative districts. A degree of ideological polarization had now emerged, and the issue as it stood in midyear could no longer be seen as bipartisan.

By the time the debate shifted to the Senate, Democrats had persuaded a just-reelected liberal Republican from Vermont, James Jeffords, to leave the Republican Party and caucus with the Democrats. As a result, liberal Democrat Tom Daschle had replaced conservative Republican Trent Lott as majority leader, and Democrats gained control of the Senate calendar for the first time in seven years.

Even had Jeffords not defected, however, only a much less sweeping version of the faith-based legislation would have stood a good chance of passage in the Senate, where social liberals had greater strength than they did in the House and in any case needed only 41 votes to kill any bill they thought deserving of filibuster.

Administration officials and Senate Republicans showed the appropriate flexibility and came to agreement on a less sweeping bill, the CARE Act. Majority leader Daschle endorsed the legislation and committed in writing to bringing it to the Senate floor for an up-or-down vote.

The legislation, which had a number of innovative tax incentives to increase charitable giving to local faith-based ministries, cleared the Senate Finance Committee in 2002 with only one dissenting vote. But it didn't come to a vote that year. Time after time, it failed to receive the unanimous consent needed to send it to the floor in the course of normal business, and Daschle, although still a nominal supporter of the bill, effectively broke his written commitment to overcome the procedural barriers and hold a vote.

Why? Quite late in the process, Senate Democrats with close ties to the gay-rights movement demanded repeal of the Ministerial Exemption as a condition for allowing the CARE Act to come to a vote. The Ministerial Exemption is a narrow exception written into the Civil Rights Act of 1964 that protects churches and other faith-based organizations from being forced to hire opponents of their beliefs under the rubric of nondiscrimination. One of its effects is to allow traditional-minded faith-centered groups to refrain from hiring workers living an openly homosexual lifestyle.

Until the rise of the gay-rights movement in recent years, the Ministerial Exemption was never terribly controversial. It had survived a number of challenges in the courts, and the landmark welfare reform signed into law by President Clinton in 1996 had reaffirmed it with little or no opposition. Repealing such a widely backed religious-freedom provision in the name of nondiscrimination against gays was a complete nonstarter in the Senate of 2002, much less the House, as both Daschle and the recalcitrant Democrats with whom he was dealing undoubtedly knew. So the legislative embodiment of Bush's faith-based initiative, even though passed by the House and virtually without open opposition in its Senate version, died in the first Congress of the Bush years without ever coming to a Senate vote.

President Bush publicly excoriated Daschle for breaking his commitment to permit a floor vote, but he never said a word about the gay-rights forces' assault on the Ministerial Exemption, which was the unspoken reason that Daschle reneged. Rather than defend a role for locally based urban ministries (almost all of which, most definitely including inner-city black ministries, espouse traditional morals), and rather than forthrightly respond to inevitable accusations of gay-bashing, the administration all but decided to stop fighting for its legislation. When Republican senators attempted to revive the CARE Act in subsequent Congresses, the same senators for the same reasons blocked all efforts to allow a vote, and the administration remained inactive on the issue.

This episode runs directly counter to the widespread belief that Bush and Rove instigated and welcomed partisan polarization in the first term. At each stage—e.g., the appointment of a Democrat to run the initiative and the move to craft a milder Senate version that could attract liberal Democratic support—the administration gave ground and attempted to reach out to Democrats rather than fire up a polarized congressional debate that could have had elective consequences. In the end, Bush gave up on the legislative version of his most distinctive domestic policy goal rather than ignite a polarizing clash with liberal advocates of gay rights.

Even the wartime issue that triggered polarization in the 2002 election—creation of a Department of Homeland Security—was one in which (as we saw in Chapter 5) Bush eventually adopted the Democrats' position, only to see polarization on the issue anyway, on the seemingly peripheral controversy over unionizing airport security workers. Similarly, in the 2003 debate on instituting a prescription drug benefit within Medicare, Bush moved toward what appeared on the surface to be a Democratic-leaning, pro-entitlement position, only to win final passage with virtually no Democratic votes in either house of Congress.

On these issues in the first Bush term, polarization happened despite Bush's best efforts to avoid it. And as we saw earlier, the 2003–2004 debates on the invasion of Iraq and same-sex marriage already were or (in the case of Iraq) later became highly polarized. But the thesis that Bush, with Rove whispering in his ear, did his best to polarize each and every issue that came along seems on closer inspection to hold little water. The intensifying polarization around hot-button issues was more a derivative of the toxic political climate than a preconceived strategy of the Bush team.

Bush's political strategists, led by Rove and 2004 campaign manager Ken Mehlman, most certainly accepted polarization as a governing fact of today's politics and designed a reelection strategy that went against conventional wisdom: They focused on turning out pro-Bush voters rather than wooing the undecided (of whom there appeared to be very few). Democrats followed a mirror approach, but the return of polarizing social issues such as same-sex marriage gave Republican turnout efforts a saving edge (as was especially evident in states like Ohio).

The Second Bush Term

Yet one of the first things Bush did following his reelection was announce that he would no longer pursue passage of the Federal Marriage Amendment. He argued that until and unless the courts overturned the Defense of Marriage Act, there was no chance of getting the two-thirds majority of each house required to pass the amendment along to the states.

This left a sour taste in the mouths of social conservatives. Bush's reelection had for the moment brought a pause in the headlong federal and state judicial drive toward same-sex marriage, but his decision to largely drop the issue in his second term was close to an engraved invitation to social liberals to keep the pressure on at the state and local level, which they proceeded to do. Although in political terms Bush clearly won the 2004 marriage debate against Kerry, his willingness to retire the issue meant there were no lasting consequences for the losing side. In fact, Bush's announcement was of a piece with his decision not to revive the fight for his faith-based legislation: It had the effect of avoiding opposition to a vocal gay-rights movement that enjoyed wide support among American elites.

Several other things happened right after Bush's reelection that also suggested a desire to tamp down polarization. Bush quietly asked three first-term cabinet members for their resignation: Attorney General John Ashcroft, Energy Secretary Spencer Abraham, and Education Secretary Rod Paige. The first two were senators who had been defeated for reelection in 2000, and Paige was a longtime Bush ally who had held some top school-administration posts in Texas. The one thing they had in common was that they were known to be among the most ideologically conservative members of the Bush cabinet. Their three successors were all known as much less conservative. Two of them—Attorney General Alberto Gonzales and Education Secretary Margaret Spellings—had served as influential staffers in the first-term Bush White House.

Not surprisingly, Bush's 2004 campaign manager Ken Mehlman, a socially conservative Rove ally, was named as chairman of the Republican National Committee. But as if to balance the appointment of this sophisticated practitioner of polarized politics,* Bush also named a longtime pro-choice activist from Ohio, Jo Ann Davidson, as co-chairman.

Miers and Alito

The one act in the second Bush term that no social conservative was likely to disapprove was the elevation of John Roberts and Samuel Alito to the Supreme Court to replace Chief Justice Rehnquist, who died in office in 2005, and Justice Sandra Day O'Connor, who announced her retirement earlier that year. This moved the Supreme Court measurably toward greater judicial restraint on social issues—something Presidents Nixon, Reagan, and George H. W. Bush all tried and failed to do.

Yet even this social-conservative gain was, in the eyes of many, for a time put in doubt by the President's attempt to elevate White House counsel Harriet Miers to the second vacancy, which occurred when Chief Justice Rehnquist died and John Roberts, already headed for confirmation as associate justice to succeed O'Connor, was nominated instead to succeed Rehnquist as chief justice. Nominating Miers for associate justice meant that one Republican woman would succeed another, leaving women still occupying two of the nine seats on the Court.

To President Bush, always keen to elevate women and minorities to visible roles in his administration, the Miers choice thus

---

* This is, I believe, an accurate description of Mehlman in 2004–2005. In August 2010, however, Mehlman announced he was gay and a supporter of same-sex marriage.

had the attraction of avoiding a step backward in women's share of the nine justices. It also conformed to the early second-term tendency, so evident in the new look of the Bush cabinet, of elevating close White House associates whose primary loyalty was to him, in preference to ideologically committed conservatives or policy activists with a base at least somewhat independent of Bush.

But in its first wave of leaks on the genesis of the Miers nomination, the White House also cited the fact that Senate Minority Leader Harry Reid, a harsh Bush critic on Iraq and most other subjects, had praised Miers in informal pre-nomination vetting as someone whose confirmation he could support. In approvingly citing this quasi-endorsement from Reid, the White House was tacitly acknowledging that reduced polarization was prominent among the motives for the Miers nomination.

But a politics that is polarized for deep-seated reasons is not easily set aside. The same qualities in Miers that sparked Reid's favorable reaction generated suspicion among social conservatives and adherents of judicial restraint as advocated for many years by the Federalist Society, an influential association of elite conservative lawyers. These disquieting qualities included Miers's pragmatism and her seeming lack of engagement on social issues as well as on the constitutional issues that conservatives had been grappling with since the emergence of the Warren Court in the 1950s. Bush and his political aides privately assured social conservatives that they could count on Miers's vote to help overturn *Roe*; she had, they noted, been "born again" a few years earlier in Texas. A number of conservatives with direct knowledge of Miers were nonetheless far from persuaded.

Then, in private meetings with Republican senators, Miers seemed baffled and unprepared for the kinds of questions that Roberts had deftly handled in his own confirmation hearings only a few weeks earlier. When the conservatives' skepticism was joined by mounting Republican fears that her hearings would be disastrous, Miers asked that the administration withdraw her nomination. The Bush team quickly sent up the name of Samuel Alito, an experienced, respected conservative judge of the circuit court of appeals well versed in constitutional law. As the prospective justice whose confirmation to replace O'Connor would change the ideological balance of the court, Alito was predictably opposed by most Senate Democrats, particularly after a decades-old Reagan administration memo made clear that the young Alito believed no right to abortion exists in the Constitution. But liberal attempts at a filibuster fizzled, and Alito was confirmed 58 to 42. Little more than a year later, in April 2007, Alito's was the swing vote in upholding the Bush-signed Federal ban on partial-birth abortion by a 5–4 margin, a reversal from the Court's 2000 decision in *Stenberg v. Nebraska* to disallow state partial-birth abortion bans.

Alito was confirmed not because he successfully reached out to liberals but because his letter-perfect legal credentials and sure-footed testimony in the Senate hearings made it impossible for Republicans (and a handful of Democrats from conservative states) to vote against him. A leading liberal opponent of Alito, New York's Charles Schumer, cheerfully acknowledged that the Ivy League–trained Alito had all the right credentials but should not be allowed to serve on the Court because of how he was likely to vote on future cases.

A similar mix of world-class qualifications and conservative beliefs had not been enough to save President Reagan's nomination of Judge Robert Bork 18 years earlier. Bork was defeated on the Senate floor 58–42, the same margin by which Alito was confirmed in 2005. The bulk of the difference lay in the simple fact that Republicans had only 45 votes in the Senate of 1987, compared with 55 in the Senate of 2005. But some other things had also changed.

In previous confirmation battles, Republican nominees to the Supreme Court had gone through a prescribed ritual of claiming to be undecided on overturning *Roe* and on other controversial cases. Republican strategists generally assumed that if a nominee became known as an enemy of *Roe*, he or she was likely to go down. A number of well-qualified judges were taken off Supreme Court lists under Reagan and the two Bushes because their past opposition to *Roe* was too transparent.

When Alito's Reagan-era memo implying opposition to *Roe* surfaced unexpectedly amid a voluminous release of documents by the executive branch, social-liberal master lobbyist Ralph Neas, a key figure in the rejection of Bork, proclaimed the Alito nomination to be in grave trouble. But nothing much happened. The division in the Senate changed little, and a public poll showed a slight strengthening of popular support for Alito's confirmation in the wake of the "revelation."

This meant little to the final floor vote, given that liberal Democrats, under almost any scenario, were set to vote against a clearly conservative nominee replacing a social liberal such as O'Connor. But the lack of public or Senate reaction to indications of Alito's anti-*Roe* stance certainly helped eliminate any chance for a successful filibuster. This aspect of the nomination fight confirmed that Democratic strategists could no longer use a GOP anti-*Roe* stance as a "smoking gun" to ensure Democratic gains. Indeed, in 2002 and 2004, liberal stonewalling of conservative judicial appointees was among Republican Senate candidates' most effective talking points.

The change in the balance of forces in judicial politics was also evident in the appearance of a sophisticated, well-financed pro-confirmation lobbying effort that proved surprisingly independent of the Republican administration. The lobbying campaign both highlighted and cemented an alliance between social conservatives and Federalist Society–style legal conservatives interested in ending judicial elitism—for which *Roe v. Wade* had long served as Exhibit A. When Bush named Miers, major elements of this alliance between social and legal conservatives rose up in rebellion against her, a huge factor in scuttling her nomination. Many on the Bush political team concluded that any gain the president might make in moving toward the center would more than likely be offset by disillusionment in Bush's conservative base if a "moderate," nonpolarizing nominee were confirmed.

So, in effect, Bush's single biggest second-term success with social and legal conservatives—and truth be told, virtually all conservatives—in changing the composition of the Supreme Court came in spite of his own initial instincts. In the early part of his second term, those instincts clearly seemed to be telling him again and again to split the difference with Democrats in the interest of trying to lessen polarization.

Economic Issues

When it came to economic issues, Bush in 2005 devoted a big measure of his political capital to a far-reaching proposal to restructure Social Security. This was a goal many conservative activists favored, but it was also one that Bush seemingly could not achieve without at least some Democratic support. In angling for this support, Bush deferred other conservative goals, particularly in tax policy, without in the end finding a formula to win passage of Social Security reform. This was an instance of pursuing a conservative-backed policy goal that seemed to require reducing polarization as a condition of success. Not only was success not achieved, but it was pursued at the expense of what many conservatives saw as Bush's greatest first-term domestic success, the 2001 and 2003 tax cut–tax reform packages.

This earlier success grew out of thoroughly Reaganite assumptions, in two dimensions. One was the supply-side nature of the tax cuts; the other was that Bush aggressively and unapologetically pursued them in time of war.

In the 2000 campaign and in his first term, Bush bypassed the advice of many supply-siders who were arguing for a consumption-based flat tax. He pressed instead for moderate cuts in tax rates, generous expansion of the pro-family child tax credit, and (in such cases as the death tax and double taxation of corporate dividends) outright abolition of some federal taxes. As noted earlier, in the first half of 2001, he fought hard for a much larger tax-cut package than was expected of a president who had recently lost the popular vote, and he got much of it—but at the price of an overly long "phasing in" of the rate reductions, a delay that supply-siders believe postpones a good deal of the economic advance the tax cuts are designed to achieve.

When the issue was reopened in 2003, following the unexpected GOP gains in the 2002 congressional elections, Bush demanded and won immediate effective dates for the income tax reductions and passage of a reform provision that reduced the personal side of the double taxation of dividends by nearly two-thirds, from a top rate of 39.6 percent in the Clinton years to 15 percent under Bush. The stock market went into a bull mode, and the economy began to accelerate from its sluggish 2001–2003 recovery. However, the 2003 tax package made none of the first- or third-year Bush tax cuts permanent, leaving some of the key ones with statutory expiration dates before the end of Bush's second term.

Bush's other Reaganesque action on the economic front concerns the relationship between tax policy, domestic spending, and military expansion. Reagan, after his 1980 election, and Bush after 9/11 both faced the same challenging context: With a sizable tax cut as a given, each president was pledged to increase defense spending and restrain domestic spending at the same time. After Reagan's 1981 honeymoon year, when he got a measure of each, tensions between these two policy goals became acute. Reagan's forward global strategy dictated giving precedence to the military buildup, which eventually would shake the will of the Soviet Union to continue the arms race and thus help end the Cold War. Facing a Democratic House throughout his tenure, Reagan needed Democratic swing votes to sustain his military spending surge. As a result, he and his team had to give way more than they liked to Democratic spending demands on the domestic side.

Reagan broke from all previous hawks and war leaders— Lincoln, Wilson, and FDR in this country and virtually every democratic war leader abroad—in refusing to finance his sharply increased military spending with stiff tax increases. Taking over the presidency from the hapless Jimmy Carter, Reagan faced an economic as well as a foreign-policy crisis, and he decided he had no choice but to address both at once. He allowed the Federal Reserve under Carter appointee Paul Volcker to sharply raise interest rates to break the back of inflation, while he cut the top rate on personal income taxes from 70 to 28 percent, rescuing the economy from the stagflation of the 1970s and successfully sustaining his defense buildup.

Bush after 9/11 gained great credit from supply-siders and other economic conservatives for emulating Reagan's double achievement rather than reverting to earlier, high-tax wartime models. Bush had the advantage of a tax-cutting Republican-controlled House for his first six years. But that same House had been badly burned by Bill Clinton in the spending showdown of 1995–1996, and it had developed its own domestic-spending habits as a kind of compensatory adjustment.

Unlike Reagan, though, Bush had to deal with the most damaging military attack on the American mainland since the War of 1812 and the abrupt economic contraction that accompanied it. His 2001 tax cut, though designed in peacetime, proved a well-timed stimulant that helped keep that year's recession brief. The bolder 2003 tax cut, with its immediate effective dates and the stunning breakthrough on ending most of the double taxation of dividends, left Reaganite supply-siders powerfully impressed. At the same time, many conservatives who applauded the tax cuts were critical of Bush for failing to control domestic spending.

Because it was wartime, the politics of all this tended to follow Bush's ups and downs as a war leader. In 2002, with the economy sluggish and the global war on terror going well, Bush's economic rating in the polls was high. In 2004, when Bush was looking less impressive as a war leader while the economy had become strong, his economic rating was actually lower.

But to supply-siders, the policy substance on taxes was superb. In the 2004 campaign, Bush argued that his tax cuts needed to become permanent, while John Kerry made clear he would let a large portion of them expire, partly in pursuit of "fairness" but also to gain new revenue for his domestic-spending proposals.

Reforming Social Security

Coming out of his reelection, Bush had a clear, forward-looking mandate on the economy to make his 2001 and 2003 tax cuts permanent (this was the economic issue where he had most starkly differed from Kerry during the campaign). In 2005, it would have been virtually impossible for a new Congress with 55 Republicans in the Senate and 232 Republicans in the House to deny such a request.

Instead, Bush decided not to make the permanence of his tax cuts a legislative priority. Nominally, he asked Congress to do this. In reality, he put all his domestic emphasis on Social Security reform—an idea he had offered and defended only in the vaguest terms during the 2004 campaign.

Beginning in his 2000 race, Bush campaigned as a backer of partial privatization of Social Security via a diversion of some payroll tax revenue into accounts listed under the names of future retirees. The privatization proposal drew vehement Democratic opposition whenever it came up, most audibly from the Gore-Lieberman campaign in the closing weeks of that race, when Democratic strategists believed it was helping overcome the lead Bush had established by doing well in the fall debates against Vice President Gore. Over the years, relentless demonization of various words used to describe the proposal caused backers to keep changing its name. The word "privatization" itself became taboo, as did "private accounts" and other attempts to describe the destination of the putatively diverted payroll taxes. Eventually Bush and other backers settled on "personal accounts" as the most innocuous description, one that the plan's critics predictably never used.

In his first term, Bush repeatedly (and courageously) insisted on the need to deal with Social Security's long-term fiscal deficit, always to the applause of conservative elites (as well as editorial writers of virtually all stripes). But no amount of elite applause could persuade congressional Republicans to touch this issue in Bush's first term. In particular, Speaker of the House Dennis Hastert, fortified by extensive polling as well as anguished pleas from his members, became known at the White House for his willingness to inform the President on numerous occasions that elevating the Social Security issue would mean a swift end of the House Republicans' majority status. Bush deferred to these fears in his first term and downplayed Social Security reform in his 2004 race, although without backing off in the smallest degree from his advocacy of it. After the election, he decided to make Social Security reform the centerpiece of his second term, de-emphasizing all other issues due to the magnitude of the challenge.

Social Security reform as conceived by Bush tried to tackle two main questions: How can future retirements be paid for, given the steep post-baby-boom decline in the ratio of workers to retirees? And should Social Security remain a "pay as you go" government-run program, with workers being taxed to pay not for their own future retirement, but for the *present* retirement of their parents' generation?

The first question is one that stirs vast fears in the population and causes voters to be intensely engaged, perhaps even open to significant changes in Social Security if they become convinced their future benefits or those of their loved ones are in doubt. And one might address the first question without dealing in any way with the second question, which is what most Democratic reform advocates prefer to do. To them, it is axiomatic that the way to solve Social Security's fiscal deficit is to raise payroll taxes and reduce the growth of future benefits, preferably with greater emphasis on the tax side.

President Bush and his allies believed it would be irresponsible to address the fiscal deficit without addressing the structural flaw they believed had created the deficit in the first place—a structural weakness that could lead to a repeat crisis if left unchanged.

Up until 2005, one of Bush's greatest strengths among conservatives had been his adamant opposition to tax increases. Even Reagan, the world record holder as a cutter of income tax rates, had in his fiscal deal-making succumbed a number of times to loophole-closing tax increases as well as (in the bipartisan 1983 Social Security reform) a greater burden of payroll taxes. Bush had never gone down that path. In the closely divided politics of polarization in which he found himself operating, it was a refusal that served him well with his Red State base.

But to get what he wanted from Democrats on Social Security—a limited beginning for personal accounts carved out of the payroll tax, plus a downsizing of growth in future benefits via a severe cut in benefits for future retirees among the top half of wage earners—Bush concluded he would have to open the door to higher payroll taxes. Early in his selling efforts in 2005, Bush intimated that he would oppose an increase in payroll tax rates, which (combining the shares of workers and employers) amounted to 12.4 percent for Social Security; but he might in the interest of bipartisanship be willing to consider some increase in the taxable income to which the rate applied (at the time the first $90,000-plus of wages).

It is theoretically possible such a deal could have happened in 2005. But Bush, perhaps in a fit of impatience to make progress toward a difficult goal, had put his conservative credentials at risk much too soon. Alarm bells rang loudly on the right. As anti-tax activist Grover Norquist, a leading advocate of Social Security reform, observed at the time, the conservative House would never back a Social Security fix that included tax increases; but—once Bush had opened the door—the not-so-conservative Senate would never agree to Social Security reform *without* tax increases.

At that moment, in February 2005, Bush's campaign for reform probably died. But the president didn't act as if it had. For a solid six months, the quest for Social Security reform dominated his public appearances, putting not only tax cuts but also active defense of his Iraq strategy on hold. By the end of those six months, a time of visible and heightened terrorist gains in Iraq, the president had lost much of his popularity.

On Social Security, he got nowhere. Despite Bush's flexibility on taxes, congressional Democrats took not a single step toward negotiations. His plan never even came to a vote in so much as a subcommittee of either house of Congress. After a first term in which a less Republican Congress repeatedly gave him much of what he asked for, it was a failure so complete that it invited comparison to Hillary Clinton's health-care reform fiasco of 1994.

Even worse, the decline in Bush's performance rating meant that the window for asking Congress to make the first-term tax cuts permanent had slammed shut as thoroughly as the chances for Social Security reform had. Bush and congressional Republicans had to settle for extending those tax cuts scheduled to expire in his second term to the most distant expiration date possible: December 31, 2010. That may have seemed far away in 2005, but when Democrats took control of Congress in November 2006, making the most innovative of the tax cuts permanent took on the contours of a long shot, if not quite a lost cause.

Bush evidently thought the issue of Iraq could use a rhetorical rest following the successful parliamentary elections in Iraq in January 2005. This proved to be a serious error in judgment. In almost any circumstance, it is a mistake for a war leader in a democracy to act as if his war is on autopilot. It was especially damaging in the first half of 2005, a time when the enemy in Iraq was showing new strength.

Momentum Shifts to the Left

For Bush, leaving the war rhetorically undefended only served to underline the failure to find weapons of mass destruction, as well as the ongoing debacle of the Valerie Plame investigation. Combined with a loss of momentum or loss of will on other war-related issues (Iran, North Korea, Lebanon, Afghanistan, and the drive for democracy in the Arab world), Bush now seemed completely on the defensive on what had once been his strong suit, his leadership against global terrorism.

A mere six months after his second inaugural, the American electorate saw Bush as an unsuccessful war president, without any significant compensating successes in domestic policy. It was a complete reversal from their view of him in the first two years after 9/11 and a remarkable political shrinkage even from the image of an embattled but determined president who fought through to reelection in November 2004.

His one big success later in 2005 and early in 2006, the confirmation of Roberts and Alito to the Supreme Court, did not improve his overall standing. In purely political terms, it combined with the post-election decisions to suspend his campaign for the Federal Marriage Amendment and drop his effort to pass faith-based legislation to take social issues pretty much off the table in the November 2006 congressional elections. Once these social issues were not part of the debate, the values voters of 2004 drifted away to vote on other issues, issues on which Bush now had relatively weak talking points.

From the beginning of 2006, Democratic campaign themes centered on the failure of the Bush presidency and the need for change. Their gain of 30 House seats and 6 Senate seats, enough to oust Republicans from their majority in both wings of the Capitol, shifted the momentum of national politics to the left.

The left's momentum did not flag in the remaining two years of the Bush presidency. Even Bush's most significant and successful move of his entire second term, the appointment of Army General David Petraeus as Iraq commander in early 2007 and the success of the shift toward a hands-on counterinsurgency strategy that became known as the Surge, brought no improvement in Bush's approval ratings, which remained through Election Day 2006 no higher than the mid-30s.

The surge did increase credibility for one of its congressional architects, Arizona's Senator John McCain, and helped him gain the upper hand in his campaign for the Republican nomination in early 2008. By election day, thanks to Petraeus, America's Iraq involvement, while still unpopular, had become far less of a negative for Republicans than it had been in 2006. But in the interim, the U.S. economy (which had appeared reasonably strong in 2006) had badly weakened, and starting around September 15, the day Lehman Brothers announced its bankruptcy, the economy entered a period of financial meltdown that made it the kind of political liability that no incumbent party in the White House would be likely to survive. A slight lead by the McCain-Palin ticket shortly after Labor Day turned into a solid Democratic victory. The Democratic ticket of Barack Obama and Joe Biden carried 28 states and received 52.9 percent of the popular vote, the Democrats' second-best showing since FDR. The gain of 21 House seats and 7 Senate seats—bringing net Democratic gains to 13 senators and 54 representatives since November 2006—confirmed that the change in momentum toward the left that took hold early in Bush's second term was still the framework of national politics.

Surprisingly, what showed no sign of changing was the polarized nature of that framework. Voters motivated by social issues in 2008 were almost as likely to vote Republican as they had been in 2004. If their total number had declined, it was mainly because, as in 2006, social issues were a far less significant part of the general-election debate than they had been in 2004. But the millions who told the national exit pollsters that social issues shaped their presidential choice were far more likely to vote for John McCain than for Barack Obama. And even though its share of the popular vote was 5.1 percentage points below that of Bush-Cheney in 2004, the McCain-Palin ticket prevailed or came close only in socially conservative states.

Nothing that happened in the 2008 campaign better underlined the persistence of social-issue polarization than the reaction to McCain's August 29 announcement that he had selected Palin as his running mate. From the first instant, the American left went into a kind of collective mass seizure, in which dozens of left bloggers became indistinguishable from both supermarket tabloids and the mainstream media in their willingness to find and use anything to demonize and humiliate Palin and her family. Yet at the time this firestorm broke, all that was widely known about the governor of Alaska was that she was married with five children, the last one of which she had knowingly carried to term with Down syndrome, and that she was a pro-life social conservative. Palin also had a thriving political career, which flagrantly disproved the adversarial feminists' zero-sum notion that women had to choose between traditional marriage and a fulfilling career (but could never have both). These biographical details were enough to propel Palin instantly to the top of the left's enemies list. Naturally, the spectacle of this elite rage, alongside Palin's own qualities, made her an instant heroine to millions of socially conservative Republicans. In fact, it was in the wake of her selection that McCain unexpectedly scored a net gain around the time of the two party conventions and took (right before eruption of the financial crisis in mid-September) the only polling lead over Barack Obama he ever enjoyed.

Why does such a high level of polarization persist? Many believe it was the essence of the Bush presidency. Yet, particularly in 2005, Bush made more of an effort to end polarization than any prominent Democrat ever had before. It would be a caricature to blame all of Bush's second-term political decline on his failure to end polarization, or even on congressional Democrats' near complete lack of interest in bipartisan harmony. But no one could argue that his second-term effort at conciliation worked out well, either for Bush, his party, or the policies he cared about. It failed because it went against political reality.

The argument of this book is that the United States has polarization, while Western Europe does not, because the United States has a social-conservative movement and Western Europe does not. We have a social-conservative movement because many Americans still believe that the words of the Declaration—that all men are created equal—are literally true. That is the defining battle of our politics, domestic and foreign. It follows that to the left, Bush's chief sin was not that he was a polarizer, or even that he was a warmonger, but that he believes the Declaration is true, that its values are universal, and that therefore America's role is to promote those values in the world.

Because that view is anathema to an elite opinion dominated by the left, not only in America but in the world, a politician who espouses it will be fought bitterly by the left as long as the left exists.

II

SOCIAL CONSERVATISM: ORIGIN AND FUTURE

7

WHERE DOES IT COME FROM?
American Social Conservatism and the Conservative Enlightenment

In the Introduction, I argued that both the existence and uniqueness of American social conservatism are driven by the central assertion in the Declaration of Independence: "We hold these truths to be self-evident, that all men are created equal, that they are endowed by their Creator with certain unalienable Rights, that among these are Life, Liberty, and the pursuit of Happiness." That many Americans take these words literally not only says something important about Americans; it's also the most plausible explanation for the rise and continued power of social conservatism in American politics.

Our belief in the literal truth of these words also defines the link between America's social-conservative movement, a comparatively new force in politics, and a much older struggle between two rival political interpretations of the Enlightenment. If there is one word in the above sentence from the Declaration that illuminates this link, it is the word "self-evident." Social conservatives believe there are things that are self-evident. Many if not most opponents of social conservatism question the existence or possibility of the self-evident, either in general or specifically as applied to politics.

The American Revolution was the culmination of what at first seemed to be the line of political advance most likely to emerge from the European Enlightenment of the 17th and 18th centuries: the path inspired by what is sometimes (not inaccurately) called the Anglo-Saxon enlightenment but what I believe is better described as the conservative enlightenment.

The founders of the United States all saw themselves as men of the Enlightenment. They saw the political implications of the Enlightenment as enormous and contentious, but they were conservative in swearing allegiance to the notion of a universe that rests on self-evident truths, which most of them saw as flowing from a God-centered universe—from "Nature and Nature's God." Moreover, they envisioned God not as an archaic holdover deity from unenlightened times, but as the only conceivable authority capable of demolishing humanity's immemorial rule by blood elites. That is, the only way to justify ending millennia of domination by kings and nobles was by facing the implications of what they saw as a simple, self-evident fact: Humans are innately equal because God created us that way. This view of equality as equal human dignity, they believed, was what mandated republican self-rule, in North America and (eventually) everywhere else.

This set up a paradox. The American founders' version of enlightenment was undeniably conservative in its retention of Europe's age-old monotheistic framework, and it's true that the institutional and social changes generated by the colonists' defeat of Great Britain took the shape of a conservative revolution, especially compared with the chaotic and destructive French Revolution that followed a few years later. But our founders' version of equality is far more radical than that of the left enlightenment, and it demanded far more respect for human rights than the kind of equality—elite management *toward* equality—favored by the secular-leaning left enlightenment. The more God-centered one's view of equality's origin, the more respect people's rights must receive *in the present*.

The left enlightenment, shaped by Rousseau and put into practice for the first time by the Jacobins and their radical allies in the France of the 1790s, was also committed to the overthrow of blood elites, holding as it did the belief in human equality that united most strands of the Enlightenment. But the left was not at all sure in what sense human equality could be said to exist in the present, and it was therefore much less inclined to believe in the currently existing equal rights of each and every human being. From its beginning, the left attempted to raise up, train, and empower revolutionary vanguards and elites to guide society to its ultimate destination, often at the expense of benighted social groups and individuals tied to the old order. It should come as no surprise that the first political program instituted by the left once it came to power, the Terror, involved the mass arrest, imprisonment, and (often) execution of aristocrats, believers, and others committed to institutions of the old regime.

These institutions proved more durable than the left perhaps expected. Even in France, the ever-boiling cauldron of the left enlightenment, the left experienced a restoration of the Bourbon dynasty and the revival of the Catholic Church within a few years of having decreed the extinction of both. But the left proved at least equally resilient and developed an ability to set more and more of the agenda of global politics, even while (as outlined in Chapter 3) assuming many different shapes and pursuing many different political, cultural, and economic projects.

How the 1960s Changed the Left

During the more than one hundred years when socialism was the left's highest-profile project, many assumed that the left's central goal was equality of economic result. Adherents of the conservative enlightenment argued that this goal of equal results took the enlightenment's central idea of equality too far or (more accurately) attempted to apply it in the realm of economics, where it did not belong, rather than to politics, where it does. And despite huge losses of prestige as well as intermittent persecution, a number of pre-enlightenment institutions and opinion streams survived and helped contain the socialist left as well.

But the upheavals of the 1960s opened the possibility that socialism would prove for adherents of the global left not the final destination but only one more in its long list of means to an end, easily de-emphasized or discarded when socialism's political and economic credibility drained away. Though nothing was very clear during the 1960s or even its immediate aftermath, the ultimate result of that decade was to bring the left overtly back to its roots in the liberationist vision first set forth by Rousseau.

For it gradually became clear that the left's own two-century-old image of itself as a force for comprehensive human liberation was far more authentic and persistent than conservative critics (or disillusioned leftists such as George Orwell) had been willing to admit—that the left's ultimate aim is perfect, autonomous human freedom rather than some mathematically exact equality of economic or social standing. If socialism or equality of result became attractive to the masses, achieving it could be instrumental in breaking down the human institutions that the left sees as the greatest barriers to human liberation and fulfillment. Many on the left, both before and after the heyday of socialism, believed that universal equality of condition is a necessary precursor to true liberation. But if doctrinaire socialism lost its popular appeal, the left would be happy to shift its emphasis toward other means of deconstructing human institutions.

In fact, the 1960s were about a radical, worldwide assault on social institutions. The decade's fallout left people all over the world with greatly diminished trust in institutions that they had previously obeyed or at least respected. Some of these institutions, particularly but by no means exclusively in the Communist world, had themselves been fathered by the socialist left. But the institutions that came under the fiercest attack were pre-Enlightenment ones that, often in alliance with adherents of the conservative enlightenment, had kept the left in check for almost two hundred years.

If it is correct that Rousseau was the true founder of the left and that the ultimate aim of the left is to deliver humanity to the "state of nature" liberated from corrupt institutions and free of laws and binding obligations, then the seeming collapse in the 1960s of institutions and moral codes all over the world would surely have heartened Rousseau had he been alive to see it. It also would have opened up a vista of definitive, society-wide victory for the left as had no other event or series of events since the modern left was named and took shape in the 1790s.

Its scope in the end was worldwide, but the assault on institutions began in the United States as a somewhat surprising outgrowth of a landmark institutional success: the victory of the black civil rights movement in the early 1960s, culminating in the civil rights acts of 1964 and 1965.

An institution that should have gained enormous self-confidence from these civil rights gains was the Democratic Party, particularly its predominant liberal wing, which had held a reluctant Congress's feet to the fire and insisted that the government grant and safeguard the equal social and political status of Southern blacks. With passage of the Voting Rights Act of 1965, which brought millions of Southern blacks into the electorate, the paramount project of political equality (one person, one vote) had in a tangible sense reached completion in the world's first and most influential mass democracy.

But instead of heightened self-confidence, American liberalism soon found itself questioning its core premises and enmeshed in racial and generational conflict. Between 1963 and 1968, most American cities experienced rioting in their black ghettos, rioting that was more widespread and violent after enactment of the civil rights bills than before. Between 1964 and 1970, a wave of student unrest, at times violent, swept through America's college campuses, which had been peaceful in their entire previous history. With the dispatch of American combat troops to South Vietnam in 1965, debate about a limited war in Asia unexpectedly took on the contours of a national moral crisis that seemed to pit entire generations and social classes against each other in a way that bore no resemblance to debate over a comparable limited war in Korea 15 years earlier. And as nearly everyone knows, the decade was pockmarked with three stunning assassinations: President John F. Kennedy in November 1963, civil rights leader Martin Luther King in April 1968, and New York's Senator Robert F. Kennedy, mortally wounded just minutes after his victory speech in Los Angeles on the night of the California Democratic presidential primary, June 4, 1968.

1968

In that year, 1968, the revolt against institutions, a revolt first felt in the United States, not only peaked but also became global. In reach it far exceeded the year 1848, when monarchies across Europe tottered. Civil unrest attained crisis proportions in countries as varied as Mexico, France, West Germany, Japan, China, and Czechoslovakia, among others. Vehement dissent jolted even the most stable institution in human history, the Roman Catholic Church, after its July publication of Pope Paul VI's encyclical reaffirming a ban on artificial contraception.

In the short run, as with events following 1848, most of the political elites that came under attack in 1968 remained in power or regained it after a brief period of chaos. In China, the Great Proletarian Cultural Revolution ignited by Communist Party chairman Mao Zedong in 1965 concluded its violent phase, while in Czechoslovakia the Soviet Army restored the status quo. Despite President Charles de Gaulle's resignation in 1969, following his defeat in a referendum, the Gaullists under Georges Pompidou won the subsequent national election and stayed in power in France, as did the Institutional Revolutionary party in Mexico, along with most other long-ruling elites.

But in every instance, the challenge was radical in nature and directed primarily at "the system" and only secondarily at specific local grievances. The eruptions of 1968, coming at the end a decade that had seen the broadest economic growth in history, represented a worldwide explosion of the values politics that had begun with the early-1960s civil rights revolution in the U.S.

The assault on institutions emanated mainly from the left, but regimes where the left already held sway did not escape the storm. In the Marxist-Leninist sphere, which at the time made up about a third of humanity, the challenge came from two very different directions.

In China, party chairman Mao orchestrated a campaign of intimidation and terror against the increasingly bureaucratic party he nominally led. Mao identified the major sin of Communist elites as elite status itself. How could such status be consistent with the Marxist ideal of equal results? Mao and his allies tried to resolve this tension at the heart of Marxism by such measures as abolishing military ranks and herding professors and scientists to the fields during harvest season to purge them of their attachment to elite status.

Czechoslovakia's entrenched pro-Soviet elites, by contrast, came under attack not for ideological lassitude but for rigidity. The anti-institutional assault here was comparatively nonviolent, at least until Soviet Army units occupied the country and ended the new reformist government of Alexander Dubcek in June. Yet Dubcek's efforts to put incentives into economic life and openness into political life proved far more prophetic of future reform efforts in the Communist world than did China's Cultural Revolution.

In the context of 1968, this outcome would have come as a major surprise. The Dubcek experiment was snuffed out with minimal resistance and appeared to have few imitators, in Eastern Europe or anywhere else. Though the violent phase of the Cultural Revolution peaked in 1968 and ended shortly afterward, Mao and his radical allies remained firmly in power in China and won many admirers among intellectual elites of the Western and Third Worlds.

This was important because in the non-Communist world, intellectual elites—particularly professors and their students—were instrumental in driving the rebellion almost everywhere. And the intensely anti-institutional nature of the New Left meant that much of its fury was directed at institutions the Old Left had brought into being or had taken over, such as university administrations and the national bureaucracies attempting to run Europe's welfare states. Moreover, many analysts were surprised that stalwart adherents of Old Left politics, such as the Communist politicians who then dominated the Paris suburbs, failed to support the student revolt that paralyzed that city.

As for the New Left's Maoist sentiments, despite its heavily intellectual demographics, the movement seemed more inspired by the Cultural Revolution's anti-intellectualism than by Mao's stated goal of economic equality. In fact, according to James Billington in his seminal study of revolution, *Fire in the Minds of*

Men, the New Left's ideology bore a striking resemblance to the populist, anti-Marxist socialism preached in the first half of the 19th century by Pierre-Joseph Proudhon: "There was, first of all, the intense moralism and quasi-anarchic rejection of almost all established authority. There was the accompanying Proudhonian desire to put power directly in the hands of 'the people,' primarily by the nonviolent strengthening of local communal structures. At the same time there was a deep antagonism to dogma and 'idea-mania' as well as an indifference to history, and suspicion of science. They followed Proudhon in protesting against remote central power, and arguing for immediate concrete benefits against the distant, symbolic goals promoted by governments."[*] The gulf between the "scientific socialism" of the Old Left and a movement that thrived on such slogans as "Power to the People," and "Don't Trust Anyone Over 30" could hardly have been wider.

But in the light of the New Left's short-term failure to destroy the political institutions it targeted, the more influential wing of the 1960s rebellion went by a revealing name: the "counterculture." This strain of thought advocated the rejection not only of conventional politics, but of conventional society itself. The rise of the counterculture, with its disdain for middle-class Western society and its norms, was on the surface nonpolitical, but on a deeper level it was the ultimate manifestation of the left's values politics. Its withdrawal of allegiance from previously respected institutions and moral norms had a profound impact on its predominantly youthful mass base and on the older generation as well. In the United States, the special strength of both the New Left and the counterculture on elite campuses ensured that the 1960s ushered in not only generational revolt but also a crisis of confidence within the world of elite opinion as a whole.

---

[*] James H. Billington, *Fire in the Minds of Men* (New York, N.Y.: Basic Books, 1980), 304–305.

Around 1967, the powerful, predominantly liberal elites who set the terms of much of the political debate in the two decades after World War II began visibly to tip toward society's harshest critics, toward the darker view of America these critics held. One milestone was the appointment of the Kerner Commission on urban rioting, which in its 1968 report assigned the blame for the riots to "white racism"—in effect, to American society as a whole. Another milestone was an announcement that same year by *Time* magazine that it opposed the American war effort in Vietnam. In those days the most influential mass-circulation magazine among American elites of both parties, *Time* was especially known for its hawkishness on Far Eastern affairs and for proclaiming the 20th century as the "American Century." Its defection to the dovish side echoed like a thunderclap and was quickly followed by the defection of CBS's Walter Cronkite, America's most authoritative face and voice at a time when TV network news was in its historic prime.

In late 1967, Secretary of Defense Robert McNamara, the chief architect of Vietnam war strategy in the Kennedy and Johnson administrations, privately concluded that the doves were right, and he resigned his office, effective early the following year. President Lyndon Johnson, still determined to bring the war to a successful conclusion, chose as McNamara's successor Clark Clifford, a widely revered pillar of the Washington establishment who, as a young White House aide in the 1940s, had been a pivotal advocate of President Truman's turn to a hard anti-Soviet stance in the Cold War's early days.

But Clifford quickly turned against the war as well and began maneuvering to steer Johnson toward a speech (eventually delivered on March 31) in which he announced a partial halt in the bombing campaign against North Vietnam, as well as (it turned out) his own withdrawal from his race for a second full term. Clifford's initiative was facilitated by an informal advisory group of senior statesmen, a group created several years earlier by Johnson himself and led by former Secretaty of State Dean Acheson. In the wake of the Vietnamese Communists' spectacular Tet offensive in February 1968, this group of senior advisers, a virtual Who's Who of the post–World War II moderate-to-liberal foreign policy elite, shifted en masse from hawkish to dovish. Elite support for the Vietnam war had disintegrated in a matter of months. Officials who had been lifelong hawks suddenly became agonized, articulate doves. Those who did not change found themselves marginalized.

This phenomenon of swift, unexpected elite realignment happened in one form or another in other countries deeply affected by the upheavals of the 1960s. During the 1968 unrest in Mexico, the justice minister, Luis Echeverria, responded to Mexico City riots by carrying out a bloody suppression that led to the deaths of hundreds of student protesters. In 1970, he was elevated by the then one-party Mexican state to the presidency, at least in part as a reward for preserving the status quo. After taking office, he stunned most of his backers by shifting government policy sharply to the left at home and abroad. In West Germany, Willy Brandt, known as a Social Democratic hard-liner concerning the Cold War in his years as mayor of West Berlin, became a near pacifist after he won election as Chancellor in 1969. Similarly, French premier Valery Giscard d'Estaing had been regarded as on the right wing of the ruling Gaullist-conservative coalition; but after winning the presidency in 1974, and without much warning, he became a socially liberal crusader for abortion rights. Giscard's metamorphosis was by no means universally welcomed in France, but the disapproval never took on a political form. France repealed its pro-life laws virtually without debate, and the country moved on to other subjects.

When it came to social issues, similar top-down transforma-
tions happened all over Western Europe in the aftermath of the
1960s.

Double Realignment in the U.S.

The United States did not differ from Western Europe and
other affluent democracies in the scope and magnitude of its elite
realignment. What was strikingly different was that the United
States experienced, beginning in the fateful year 1968, a simultaneous realignment in popular opinion that went in precisely
the opposite direction—toward conservatism. This realignment
ended 36 years of mainly Democratic presidencies and ushered in
four decades of presidential politics during which a more conservative yet more populist Republican Party gained the upper hand.

Initial signs of this double realignment—elite opinion moving well to the left, popular opinion realigning in a conservative
direction—appeared before the 1960s had ended. The change
was both completely unpredicted and, in retrospect, fairly easy
to measure, given that the Republicans nominated the same man,
Richard Nixon, both in their narrow defeat of 1960 and their narrow victory of 1968.

In 1960, student polls taken on the eight Ivy League campuses—a reasonably good barometer of America's elite opinion—
found majorities for Nixon on six of the eight (the exceptions
were Columbia and Harvard, Kennedy's alma mater). In 1968,
Democratic nominee Hubert Humphrey won overwhelmingly
on all eight Ivy League campuses. On some campuses, Nixon
received fewer votes than did minor-party candidates such as
black comedian Dick Gregory.

In 1960, the hyper-affluent "Silk Stocking" congressional
district that includes the East Side of Manhattan, a bastion of
elite opinion, went solidly for Nixon. In 1968, with the nation

narrowly favoring Nixon and the Republicans, the Silk Stocking district voted overwhelmingly for Humphrey.

This disconnect in American politics between popular and elite opinion, nearly nonexistent in the debates of the 1950s, has persisted ever since. The tension between the two opinion streams has manifested itself most starkly on social issues, but it's also proved important in pivotal economic and foreign-policy debates.

In the late 1970s and 1980s, for example, most elites opposed Ronald Reagan's emphasis on sharp cuts in personal income tax rates, and they showed nearly unanimous disdain for the supply-side theory of economists Arthur Laffer and Robert Mundell that lay behind it. Prestigious conservative economists and business leaders for the most part shared their disdain.

This was not simply a matter of elite skepticism about tax cuts. The economy of that era was so listless that almost everyone in national politics or elite journalism favored some kind of tax cut. But elite opinion's view of the kind of tax cut Reagan favored is well captured by a *Washington Post* editorial of April 15, 1983: "[M]anipulation of the tax code isn't a terribly effective way of changing most people's habits in managing their personal money. It works beautifully in the business sector, where funds are handled by professionals using the tax system's incentives to increase returns. But people very frequently have other values to follow in disposing of their own incomes."

By the same token, Reagan's strategy of attempting to win the Cold War by a combination of a forward military posture and renewed ideological confrontation with the Soviet bloc had far more popular than elite support. Most of elite opinion was certain that the Cold War could be ended only by nuclear arms-control agreements between the United States and the Soviet Union, accompanied by U.S. acceptance of permanent Soviet control over Eastern Europe. Elite approval of Reagan's 1982

London speech consigning Communism to the "ash heap of history" was close to nonexistent. Probably only two of Reagan's own top aides—CIA Director William Casey and William Clark, one of six different men who served as Reagan's national-security adviser—agreed with Reagan's emphatic premise in private meetings that we had a realistic hope of pushing the Soviet empire into early extinction.

In the eyes of most voters and even a small slice of elite opinion, Reagan won a measure of vindication in these debates by visible successes at home and abroad, especially when the Berlin Wall fell and the Soviet Union disintegrated in the immediate aftermath of his presidency. Reagan had a rare combination of adamantine will and serene temperament that enabled him to pursue his goals relentlessly and cheerfully in a landscape of virtually unbroken elite disapproval.

But we should underline the word "rare." Talented political leaders have great motivation and discipline, but their preference is to maximize approval at all times from as many quarters as possible. In principle, the goal of a career politician in a democracy is election victory, leading to confident actions in the government arena. In practice, politicians fear disapproval from their highest-status day-to-day "audience" (the term of sociologist Tamotsu Shibutani). This makes election victory, the supposed holy grail of politics, seem remote and even hard to envision, given a prospect of elite criticism that is both instantaneous and articulate.

The Left and Feminism

Reagan's stunning successes in economics and foreign policy were predominantly at the expense of the Old Left—the socialist, big-government left that lauded top-down economic "planning" as a superior growth strategy. In the years following World War

II, this statist stance became an embarrassment to the left, and many found it increasingly hard to defend.

As indicated in Chapter 3, the left had prepared for the possible demise of Marxism and democratic socialism in two ways. An intellectual vanguard within Marxism itself, led by the Frankfurt School in Germany and Antonio Gramsci in Italy, was dismayed by the resilience of conventional society and morality. In response, they developed the concept of a "march through the institutions." To them, according to Hudson Institute scholar John Fonte, this meant the capture of elite opinion within the key institutions of European society. They set aside the old dream of armed revolution and opted instead for a tactic of "change from within." Through a rolling takeover of the institutions, they could more effectively call traditional morality into question and alter the power structure, once they'd raised the consciousness of key leaders. According to Fonte, many new movements of the left that have arisen in the 1960s and subsequently—black power, radical feminism, even homosexual rights—were uncannily forecast by this neo-Marxist school, particularly in the work of Gramsci. Interestingly, some of the key figures of the Frankfurt School, most prominently Herbert Marcuse, who had emigrated from Germany to the United States, emerged as mentors of the American New Left in the 1960s.[*]

The left had prepared for the decline and fall of socialism in another way as well, through self-critique. Left theoreticians, during the 1970s and well in advance of the Reagan presidency, painstakingly internalized the left's failures and successes of the 1960s, especially the climactic experiences of 1968.

---

[*] John Fonte, "Liberal Democracy vs. Transnational Progressivism: The Future of the Ideological Civil War Within the West" (Hudson.org/files...transnational_progressivism.pdf).

By the end of the 1970s, the left's biggest failure was clear: The social and cultural upheavals of the 1960s had not translated into significant leftward movement in economic policy, either in the affluent democracies or in the Marxist-Leninist sphere. Even the one seeming exception of Maoist China, with its drive toward radical economic egalitarianism in the years of the Cultural Revolution, abruptly reversed course after the death of Mao and the arrest of his would-be ideological heirs, the Gang of Four, in 1976. From around 1978, with Deng Xiaoping's rise to power, the trajectory of the economic reform in China was in the direction of capitalism, though never under that name.

The left's biggest success was also clear: Institutions and groups that had stoutly resisted the left prior to the 1960s had suffered a sharp decline in status and self-confidence and were no longer widely trusted, much less obeyed. Morality was said to be not absolute, but subject to variation depending on one's cultural identity. In many institutions but particularly those of higher education, "political correctness" had become a tool for stifling debate. A mind-set was understood to be correct if it recognized claims of those who had suffered at the hands of antiquated power structures. Out groups such as women and racial minorities were owed not simply recognition and justice before the law, but transfers of power from the "haves" to the "have-nots." If an existing institution acquired the correct consciousness, it would voluntarily yield power, achieving change from within, rather than by violent revolution or by an explicit electoral debate followed by a decision of the voting public.

For the post-1960s, post-socialist left, the single most important development has been the alliance between modern feminism and the sexual revolution. This was far from inevitable. Up until around 1960, most educated women resisted attempts at sexual liberation. In the wake of the success of *Playboy* and other mass-circulation pornographic magazines in the 1950s, men appeared as the initiators and main beneficiaries of sexual liberation, women as intolerant of promiscuity and as potential victims of predatory "liberated" men.

In Europe, women formed a big majority of active churchgoers. Men were expected to learn sexual technique prior to marriage, often with legally sanctioned prostitutes, but seek marriage to a girl from a good family with decent standards. In the United States, where a higher level of male-female social equality had been the norm for many years, young men might "sow their wild oats" without disapprobation but were urged to move on to a field of "nice girls" when getting serious about marriage. In mainstream American culture, female virginity was not only a mark of respectability; it carried an aura of magnetic attractiveness for young men wanting to "settle down."

With the introduction of the Pill around 1960, things abruptly began to change, rapidly accelerating in the latter part of the1960s and throughout the 1970s. Fears of overpopulation legitimated a contraceptive ethic throughout middle-class society in North America, Europe, Japan, and the Soviet bloc. China, which discouraged contraception and welcomed population gains under Mao, flipped to the extreme of the One Child policy in 1979, shortly after pro-capitalist reformers took charge and fixed on strict population control as an integral and unquestioned part of Western-style development.

The fact that women, not men, took the Pill gave many women a greater feeling of control over their sexual activity and eroded their social and psychological resistance to premarital sex. "No fault" divorce, a term borrowed from the auto-insurance industry, in reality amounted to unilateral divorce and began to undermine the idea of marriage as a binding mutual contract oriented toward procreation and child-rearing. Contrary to nearly every prediction, the ubiquity of far more reliable methods of contraception coincided with a huge increase in the incidence of surgical abortions. Another surprise: The growing ideological separation of sex from pregnancy, far from reducing the rate of unwed pregnancies, instead saw it explode.

Earlier versions of Western feminism had tended to embrace children and elevate motherhood. Beginning in the 1970s, though, a more adversarial feminism preached that children and childbearing itself were the central means by which men subjugated women. This view gained traction in virtually every affluent democracy, and more than anything else on the menu of the post-socialist left, it helped forge a cultural consensus that the institution of the family was inherently oppressive. Rousseau was right: Family anchored by monogamous marriage was the single greatest threat to the "natural" freedom that in Rousseau's vision is our birthright, freedom from all laws and bonds of mutual obligation.

In the 1960s and 1970s, the rising tide of moral and cultural revolution (or, harking back to a key term of the 1960s, the rise of the "counterculture") seemed to fulfill the Frankfurt School's vision of a march through the institutions. With the surge of contraception, divorce, promiscuity, abortion, and nonmarital pregnancy, no institution in Europe showed much ability or inclination to halt or slow down this march. The old institutions, including the churches, had seen their authority drained away or relativized by the emerging post-1960s cultural mainstream.

Things were not appreciably different in those European countries where powerful political parties carried a Christian brand. Ruling Christian Democratic parties in Germany and Italy had successfully triggered post-war economic growth, won elections, and kept the socialist and Communist left largely out of power. But in the face of the sexual revolution, these parties and the churches that helped found them seemed as helpless as the long-enfeebled state Lutheran churches of Scandinavia.

The key to these triumphs of the social left, it would seem, is that the dynamic unleashed in the 1960s largely achieved what no previous revolutionary wave in Europe ever had accomplished: the destruction of the authority of the surviving pre-Enlightenment institutions and moral codes. It helped that the left no longer carried the albatross of Communism and rigid socialism. But the victory of a liberationist counterculture meant that surviving pre-Enlightenment institutions such as the church and the family no longer had the popular allegiance or political clout to prevent the marginalization of traditional faith, family, and "self-evident" morality.

Earlier in this chapter, I argued that a largely center-right alliance between the forces of the conservative enlightenment and surviving pre-enlightenment institutions and values had headed off a decisive leftist victory for nearly two centuries. Indeed, the willingness of elements of this alliance to regroup behind Ronald Reagan, Margaret Thatcher, and a handful of other aggressive, optimistic leaders in the 1980s revitalized capitalism and won the Cold War, dealing what at first appeared to be a devastating setback to the global left. But the weakening, obliteration, and (in a few older realms such as higher education and the legal profession) the conquest by the left of pre-enlightenment institutions meant that in most of the affluent democracies, the forces of the conservative enlightenment were, by themselves, not enough to prevent the emergence of a Rousseau-like revolutionary wave in the direction of autonomous, amoral human freedom—that is, a historic breakthrough for the core vision of the left enlightenment.

Religion and the Two Enlightenments

This breakthrough, in turn, might've prompted political pushback and might even still be in doubt in some parts of Western

Europe and Japan, were it not for the marginalization there of key ideas of the conservative enlightenment. By contrast, in the U.S., this would suggest that belief systems opposed to the counterculture retained enough of a foothold to (so far) prevent a comparably definitive victory by the left enlightenment here.

Many analysts believe the main difference lies in an anomaly: The United States has seen greater levels of religious observance in an era in which broad-based acquisition of wealth and a declining allegiance to religion have widely been assumed to be two sides of the same coin. In this view, the decline of American religious practice—and by many measures it is declining—will eventually bring the United States into line with the irreligious, tolerant, unpolarized societies of Western Europe and Japan.

But historically, periods of economic innovation and growth have not always been accompanied by widespread loss of faith. In the first half of the 19th century, America's second Great Awakening was also a time of economic boom. In the second half of that century, Victorian England in the age of Gladstone saw a simultaneous explosion of wealth and of religious observance, accompanied by a trend toward fertile and monogamous family life.

If in our own era we look beyond the First World of North America, Western Europe, and Japan, the last two or three decades also paint a decidedly mixed picture. In the boom years between 1983 and 2007, globalization brought billions of people into a measure of urbanized economic affluence with little if any sign of religious collapse in countries such as India, Indonesia, and South Korea. And in China, where an antireligious one-party state presides over a capitalist boom, one of the government's most visible and vehement activities is a campaign to repress a trend toward mass-based Christianity and the neo-Buddhist meditative practices of Falun Gong.

The truth is that of the three main political paths of the Enlightenment—the left enlightenment originating in France, the British or parliamentary version of the conservative enlightenment, and the American version of the conservative enlightenment as embodied in the Declaration and the Constitution—it was the American political founding of 1776–1789 that most *limited* the political role of religion.

This, as Alexis de Tocqueville later noticed, proved to be the healthiest alignment for both religion and politics. It is a settlement whose rough outline continues today, and it's reflected in the rise of American social conservatism as the clearest ideological heir of the conservative enlightenment. Reversing the conventional apportionment of cause and effect, one might argue that the higher levels of religious observance in the United States should be understood as a *result* of our conservative founding, rather than as the sole cause of America's persistent values war. It is one aspect of why social conservatism is more accurately seen as the application of natural law to politics—the self-evident truths of the Declaration—rather than as a political manifestation of religious revelation.

The Glorious Revolution of 1688–1689 correctly came to be seen as a political landmark of the modern era, but at the time it had the feel of a squabble among three forms of religion: Roman Catholicism (the faith of King James II), the Church of England, and Calvinism. The Anglican victory of William and Mary—ironically, William of Orange was himself a Calvinist— left Britain with both legislative supremacy and a state church completely dependent on Parliament. The ability in 1690 of non-Anglican Protestants, of Catholics, and of Jews and unbelievers to participate in political life was either nonexistent or very much in doubt; Britain did not fully resolve this quandary for another two hundred years.

In the France of the early 1790s, where the left came into being as a revolutionary movement, the Rousseau-influenced Jacobins and their radical allies gained the upper hand over advocates of the conservative enlightenment who had influenced the revolution's first stages. The liberationist, anti-institutional belief system of the left led the new regime to execute the King and Queen of France, outlaw the nobility, and abolish the Catholic Church.

If anything, the left saw the anti-Catholic element as the most essential of the three prohibitions. Robespierre and his associates, fearing the people's desire for some form of moral and religious authority, adopted an idea advocated by Rousseau and attempted to erect a substitute neo-pagan religion honoring the Goddess of Reason. The revolutionary government's bloodiest, most ruthless war was waged against the peasants of the Vendée in western France, almost exclusively because the people of that region refused to abandon Catholicism, while Napoleon's rise revealed the left's opposition to ruling monarchy as considerably less than categorical. In France no less than the Britain of a century earlier, the question of religion's role was deeply and obsessively intertwined with the political struggle.

One might presume that what became the United States had too much religious diversity for fights over religion to become a major factor, or even a significant sideshow, in the political struggle between the Crown and the colonists. Anglicans and Calvinists (who were called Congregationalists in New England and Presbyterians elsewhere) made up the bulk of the population, but one could hardly ignore the role of (to list a few) Quakers, Baptists, Lutherans, Deists, Catholics, and Jews. Portions of all these, but especially Anglicans and Quakers, chose the side of King George III. Unlike the Glorious Revolution, the political struggle did not neatly divide along sectarian lines. Unlike the

French revolutionaries, our republican revolutionaries saw no need to suppress or restrict traditional religion.

In fact, the kind of religion prevalent in America was on balance a major influence in favor of independence, as well as for the independence of religion from government.

In this, as conservative theoretician M. Stanton Evans documents persuasively in his 1994 book, *The Theme Is Freedom,*[*] the American Revolution was conservative not simply in its allegiance to Western civilization's theistic origin, but in its tendency toward separate spheres for religion and politics, a tendency rooted in medieval Europe as well as in biblical texts familiar to all Christians.

Jesus's admonition to "Render unto Caesar the things that are Caesar's, and to God the things that are God's" is depicted in the Gospels as a conversation stopper, and with good reason. The idea of separate realms, each with its own independent sphere and appropriate functions, does not seem to derive from earlier pagan or eastern belief systems; nor can we find an analogy for it in the later faith of Islam. Jesus's words proved no simple teaching for either prince or prelate, even when men made good-faith efforts to carry it out.

Much in medieval European history that is puzzling or opaque to the modern reader can be seen as part of an ongoing attempt to work through this issue. The centuries-long struggle between the pope and the Holy Roman Emperor, as well as the prolonged investiture controversy over the right of monarchs to name church officials, are aspects of the attempt to sort out functions between religion and politics. It was this cauldron of violent disagreement that fostered legal and political theories encom-

---

[*] M. Stanton Evans, *The Theme Is Freedom: Religion, Politics, and the American Tradition* (Washington, D.C.: Regnery Publishing, 1994).

passing not only apportionment of powers between church and state, but covenants such as the Magna Carta that encouraged diversity of rule in the purely secular realm as well.

Unitary Rule and Marginalized Religion

Evans argues that the Renaissance, whose biggest political idea was the Divine Right of Kings, represented Europe's reversion back toward the unitary rule (unity of political command) that had characterized the earlier paganism of Greece and Rome and, for that matter, virtually all previous known history other than medieval Europe and (to a lesser but still notable extent) the arrangements of the Davidic monarchy with its distinct religious elite of temple priests.

The Protestant Reformation at first did nothing to change Europe's trend toward unitary rule. In his tract "The Freedom of the Christian Man," Martin Luther downgraded the importance of institutions in favor of the individual conscience, but he did not extend this new freedom to the political realm, as evident in his support for monarchical repression of German peasant revolts. Luther was all in favor of his allies, the Lutheran princes, making religion into a subordinate department of government. The break of Henry VIII from Rome implied no freedom of conscience for believers who wanted to dissent in either a Catholic or Protestant direction. The Tudor monarch was the head of the new Church of England, and questioning his view of doctrine or ritual could bring grave legal consequences.

The drive of kings to take control of religion in the Renaissance and its aftermath was not limited to countries where the Catholic Church was displaced as the dominant faith. Louis XIV pressed forward with attempts to limit Rome's sway over French Catholics at the exact same time that his Revocation of the Edict of Nantes (1685) triggered a new wave of persecution of the French Calvinists known as Huguenots. The movement to domesticate Catholicism in France was called Gallicanism, but it had its counterparts elsewhere, very much including the Holy Roman Empire to the east, where the Habsburg ruling family at times became notably less Roman and more imperial in its treatment of the Church.

The Thirty Years' War (1618–1648) pretty much completed the sorting out of central and western Europe between Catholic and Protestant. The Treaty of Westphalia ratified what was already happening in the war and even earlier: With an odd exception here and there, a Protestant monarch would now have mainly Protestant subjects, and a Catholic monarch would have mainly Catholic subjects. The real winner at Westphalia was the increasingly dominant new arena of war and politics, the modern nation-state.

The clearest loser was religion as an independent force in society. The term "established church," which today connotes an image of a single sect with a leg up on its competition, was at the time of its invention a clear subordination of the church to a newly dominant monarchical state. In the transition from ruling monarchy to democracy, established Protestant churches remained established in most northern European countries but continued to decline as a social force, becoming little more than an empty shell by the early and middle 20th century. Several Calvinist churches were established state churches in New England at the time of the American Revolution, and they remained so for the first several decades after independence. But not only did they not prosper; they actually drifted into Unitarianism by the time their state legislators cut them loose during the first three or four decades of the 19th century.

The domestication of religion that accompanied "establishment" in central and western Europe, beginning in the Renaissance, was a reprise of the loss of vitality that had happened a thousand years earlier for religion in the East. The phenomenon of Erastianism—subordination of church to state—was despite its surface advantages never a dynamic force when it came to Christianity, the religion whose founder wanted to give to Caesar what rightly belongs to Caesar and to God the things that are God's. When Muslims and (much later) Communists displaced Christian dynasties in the East, the Orthodox Church found it difficult to carve out an independent sphere it had long since forsaken.

In the post-Enlightenment politics of the West, predominantly Catholic Mediterranean countries such as France, Italy, Spain, and Portugal were much more likely to see their churches disestablished by secularists of the kind that came to the fore after the French Revolution. Catholics understandably saw the takeover of the state by opponents of traditional religion as a disaster. But compared with the established Protestant churches in the North, southern European Catholics probably gained more from independence than they lost by estrangement from the left-secularist governments periodically in power throughout the 19th and 20th centuries, even when that estrangement turned into hostility and active persecution. In Spain, the status of Catholicism veered wildly through the years: The left prohibited it outright in half of Spain during the civil war of 1936–1939; it played a collaborative cultural and moral role in the three-plus decades of the Franco dictatorship; after Franco's death in 1975, the non-ruling monarchy shaped by King Juan Carlos marginalized Catholicism, both culturally and morally.

In the United States, meanwhile, despite the tenuous foothold of the few state churches of the republic's first decades, the First Amendment ensured that religion operated vigorously and in full independence from the national government. With the exception of many Anglicans and some Calvinists, the churches wanted separation. Many American believers, after all, had come to North America in the first place to escape persecution by European governments and *their* state churches.

The United States, the first country of modernity to consist mainly of people from somewhere else, has always had a multiplicity of religious denominations, even when almost all voters were white Protestant males. Because the country's culture was overwhelmingly Christian and its churches were so used to operating in a sphere independent of the state, for most of our history it occurred to no one to start a party based on adherence to a single religious faith or revealed moral code. Even when a left-influenced form of secularism arrived in the United States a century or so ago and began a long-term campaign to strip religious content and symbols from public life, a party such as the Catholic Church–founded Christian Democrats of Italy was unthinkable.

This was in part because dozens of denominations are scattered geographically throughout the United States. Furthermore, secularism's inroads in the 20th century's first few decades were predominantly in the private sector—e.g., removal of religious affiliation from the high-status Ivy League colleges in the Northeast—and these were correctly seen as voluntary changes rather than due to religious repression by a hostile federal or state government.

Religious instruction had largely been removed from primary and secondary education in the 19th century, not by an upsurge of secularism but by anti-Catholicism. The widely used McGuffey's Readers were drained of biblical content because of Protestant fears that the pope and Mariology would find their way into textbooks in the growing numbers of school districts that had become heavily Catholic.

In the second half of the 20th century, aggressive secularism achieved a political breakthrough, at first most visibly in the federal courts and in the American bar in general. For the first time, believers faced the prospect of a systematic campaign against public religion—or, as their legal adversaries preferred to define it, a wall of separation between public life and religious symbols and language. Legal secularists now openly argued that the First Amendment demands strict neutrality not simply among different faiths, but in the argument between believers and nonbelievers.

For a nation that from its beginning appropriated public funds for congressional and military chaplains, that puts "In God We Trust" on its money, that as recently as the 1950s added (by a near unanimous act of Congress) the words "under God" to the Pledge of Allegiance, this was a huge and unexpected shift in elite opinion. But it was hardly more startling than other matters subjected to comprehensive change in the left's "march through the institutions" that accelerated and became far more visible in the 1960s and afterward.

The "Mystery Passage"

Given the nature of the world's first successful pluralist nation as the stronghold of the conservative enlightenment, there was still zero chance that American conservatives' resistance to the secularists would take the form of European-style confessional politics. Such a response, even if possible, would have been comically inadequate, if only because the left's new, post-socialist offensive had in its way become far more threatening than earlier attempts to restrict or outlaw traditional religion in places such as Russia, France, Spain, and Mexico. True to its deepest roots, the countercultural left was now engaged in an attempt to deny that there are such things as "self-evident truths" at all.

Nowhere was the comprehensiveness of the challenge more clearly stated than in *Planned Parenthood v. Casey*, the Supreme Court's 5–4 decision in June 1992 upholding the universal right to abortion established 19 years earlier in *Roe v. Wade*: "At the heart of liberty is the right to define one's own concept of existence, of the universe, and of the mystery of human life. Beliefs about these matters could not define the attribute of personhood were they found under the compulsion of the state." From the founders' belief in "created equal" resulting in "unalienable rights," this language travels to the furthest opposite pole of individual self-definition, verging on self-creation.

Legal and social conservatives soon came to refer to these words as the "Mystery Passage." The opinion was particularly galling because it was signed by three Republican justices—Sandra Day O'Connor, Anthony Kennedy, and David Souter—who had been appointed by Presidents Reagan and George H. W. Bush over the previous 11 years as three of their five choices to bring a conservative majority to the high court. Instead, these three justices had now provided the decisive swing votes to uphold *Roe*.

"The Mystery Passage," composed and signed by these three Republicans who clearly saw themselves as reasonable centrists, underlines the transformation of the global left after the 1960s from a mainly economic to a mainly social movement. It also makes clear that moral relativism and the age-old vision of autonomous, open-ended human freedom are closely connected. If the "heart of liberty" extends to one's individual right to define "the attribute of personhood," the "concept of existence," and "the mystery of human life," then autonomous, unregulated, individual freedom (Rousseau's return to lawless nature) *must* become far and away the highest political good. And under this premise, society must accept as reality that no standards other than the desirability of autonomous freedom can be objective. Individual opinions are to be respected and protected, but there can be no *common* standards of moral right and moral wrong—other than universal tolerance, accompanied by the maximum conceivable liberation of individuals from moral laws and social institutions.

155

The *Casey* plurality also stated: "Where, in the performance of its judicial duties, the Court decides a case in such a way as to resolve the sort of intensely divisive controversy reflected in *Roe* and those rare, comparable cases, its decision has a dimension that the resolution of the normal case does not carry. It is the dimension present whenever the Court's interpretation of the Constitution calls the contending sides of a national controversy to end their national division by accepting a common mandate rooted in the Constitution."

With these words, it became clear that, in the view of these three self-perceived moderate justices, the biggest error in the first two decades after *Roe* was the decision by the anti-abortion side of the national debate to continue speaking out and fighting as if the court's earlier ruling had not definitively resolved the issue. Given that *Casey* was decided by a high court of which eight of nine members had been appointed by Republican presidents, each of whom with his power of appointment was at least nominally trying to curb judicial activism, many commentators believed the defeat that had not been accepted in 1973 would surely be seen by the most bull-headed of social conservatives as unalterable in 1992. But despite social conservatives' intense disappointment, once again they somehow missed their chance to politely remove themselves from the national debate on abortion and other social issues. Why?

The Unresolved Enlightenment

It is hypothetically possible that social conservatism is an opportunistic concoction that serves the mutual ambition of entrepreneurs from the worlds of faith and politics. In this hypothesis, the very term "social conservative" is misleading, a mild-sounding label that obscures an effort to import primitive religion into politics, bordering on theocracy. This hypothesis sees it as a gradually weakening movement hanging on as long as it provides a net electoral benefit to right-of-center politicians. Inevitably it will cease providing such net benefits at some future tipping point when a mix of improved education and generational change will leave the United States with few remaining "judgmental" voters, even among the religiously observant. Then our political culture, while perhaps still a bit freewheeling, will be much closer to Western Europe's, and the politics of polarization will be over.

It seems to me far more likely that social conservatism's ability to survive so many demoralizing defeats, as well as dismissals by elite opinion, denotes an underlying strength that has something to do with the unresolved political consequences of the Enlightenment.

Most historians agree that the Glorious Revolution, the American Revolution, and the French Revolution represent at least two models of revolution: the two Anglophone revolutions as comparatively conservative and the French as a decidedly more radical model. What they had in common, in pure institutional terms, was the abolition or curbing of ruling monarchy.

The Glorious Revolution was Britain's second attempt during the 17th century to downgrade monarchy. The Civil War of the 1630s and 1640s erupted as a struggle for control of the public purse between Parliament and Crown, but it quickly took on a religious dimension. The war culminated in the execution of Charles I in 1649 and the designation by Parliament of Oliver Cromwell, its Calvinist military commander, as Lord Protector of the British Commonwealth. In practice Cromwell was an elective monarch who soon turned against the Parliament that elevated him. Cromwell's estrangement from Parliament left a constitutionally ambiguous power vacuum at his death in 1658, and a consensus formed in the Commonwealth army to restore the Stuart monarchy in the person of Charles II in 1660.

Viewed as a power player, Parliament had learned its lesson by the time of its next battle with the Crown. With the military defeat and flight to France of the Catholic King James II, Parliament in effect imported its very own monarch, William of Orange, from the Netherlands. Parliament, centered mainly in the House of Commons, became the source of power in Britain and has remained so to this day.

On the surface, the Glorious Revolution seemed not simply conservative but incremental. Parliament, the Crown, and the established Church of England existed both before and after the revolution. What had changed was the locus of ultimate power. Parliament was in the saddle, well on its way to achieving a degree of unitary power that had eluded even the powerful 16th-century Tudor monarchs. But its experience with regicide and subsequent eclipse by Cromwell may well have influenced Parliament's decision to leave the revolution relatively undefined, which is why Britain is often said to have an "unwritten constitution." In other words, Parliament may have been motivated not so much by humility as by a desire to avoid attracting attention to the completeness of its victory. In practice, of course, having an unwritten constitution also means that a nation's governing arrangements can be completely altered at any time by any bill passed by a simple majority of its legislators.

Many historians believe Parliament's discretion misled Montesquieu, an 18th-century advocate of the conservative enlightenment who praised the British constitution as a model of separation of political branches. It is true that in 1600, England (Scotland was a separate kingdom until 1603) was the one European country that still had a degree of political separation between the executive (the monarch) and the legislative (Parliament). Every other European country had by then more or less succumbed to the new wave of centralizing Divine Right monarchical takeovers that marked the politics of the Renaissance. England was the one holdout in favor of the separation of powers and subjection to a higher law that had marked Europe's medieval political order.

The American Divergence

As we have seen, the idea of a check on power was overwhelmed in Britain during the 17th century as Parliament struggled nominally for its ancient rights, but in reality for the undivided power it achieved in the Glorious Revolution. Yet, as Evans documents in *The Theme Is Freedom*, many of the English emigrants to what became the United States retained their commitment to a higher law that requires a check on ultimate political power, an idea that translated intact to the New World and survived to influence the Declaration and the Constitution. So not only was the American Revolution conservative in believing its rights came not from the state but from God; it was conservative in its devotion to a related *medieval* tradition of biblical origin that put a premium on denying unitary power to government or any one branch of government.

At the beginning of this chapter, I noted a paradox: Even though the American Revolution is the most conservative of the three earliest revolutions of the modern age, most indisputably in comparison with the French Revolution that immediately followed, its centering of America's self-evident human rights in the Creator—"Nature and Nature's God"—makes its vision of equality far more consequential *in the present* than that of the left, which prefers management *toward* equality by a semi-permanent vanguard or elite. In the United States, it is this radical view of equality that undergirds the prime characteristics of the conservative enlightenment's translation into modern, post-monarchical politics.

The Declaration of Independence is known to have been drafted by Thomas Jefferson and modified by other members of the Second Continental Congress prior to its adoption in early July of 1776. These particularities have led many to assume that the Declaration's central assertions, while interesting and important, might have been very different had someone other than Jefferson drafted the document.

In her 1997 book *American Scripture*, MIT historian Pauline Maier documents that the Declaration was the culmination of perhaps 90 declarations issued by colonial legislatures, municipal councils, and less official groups of American colonists, and that the similarities of these earlier documents to the Declaration are far more striking than the differences.[*] Maier's title, dripping with irony, encapsulates her thesis that there was nothing unique or sacred about Jefferson's draft or the ratified version. But to anyone who sees the American founding as the central event of a broad ideological movement that can with reasonable accuracy be described as the conservative enlightenment, her research provides striking confirmation that many Americans were broadly conscious of the content and importance of what they were fighting for. It's therefore useful to attempt a brief analysis of the first two sentences of the Declaration not for their level of acceptance by Americans or other peoples of that time, but with an eye for what belief in them implies for political action in concrete, practical terms.

"When in the Course of human events it becomes necessary for one people to dissolve the political bands which have connected them with another and to assume among the powers of the earth, the separate and equal station to which the Laws of Nature and of Nature's God entitle them, a decent respect to the opinions of mankind requires that they should declare the causes which impel them to the separation.

---

[*] Pauline Maier, *American Scripture: Making the Declaration of Independence* (New York, N.Y.: Alfred A. Knopf, 1997).

"We hold these truths to be self-evident, that all men are created equal, that they are endowed by their Creator with certain unalienable Rights, that among these are Life, Liberty and the pursuit of Happiness."

1. Only one authority is cited for the colonists' right to break away from Great Britain and found a republic: "the Laws of Nature and of Nature's God."

2. "Truths" that are "self-evident" could only follow from a belief in universal natural law.

3. Human rights are given by the Creator, together with human existence. This means that they predate or at least take priority over the founding of any state, whether monarchical or republican. This is also why it is immoral for the state, or anyone else, to try to take them away: They are "unalienable."

4. The first self-evident truth the document mentions is that we are "created equal." It comes first because the idea of innate equality, if true, is the irreplaceable principle, the starting point of politics.

It is preeminently a Christian belief, but it has important antecedents in Hebrew and Stoic thought. Innate equality does not imply equal abilities by all people in all fields. It is not uniformity and does not imply that people are copies of each other. It means that by virtue of being human, everyone has an equal dignity and therefore an equal stake in decisions concerning the whole community—that is, in political decisions. People's human rights—to life, liberty, the pursuit of happiness, and all other rights—must be exercised in a framework in which equal respect is paid to the rights of all others. If innate equality is a fact, no one can be born a king or made a slave. Equality also means political leadership may legitimately operate only with the consent of those led. (The very next sentence of the Declaration—the document's third sentence, stating its third self-evident truth—underlines the importance of consent: "That to secure these rights, Governments are instituted among Men, deriving their just powers from the consent of the governed.")

Because the conservative enlightenment believes equality is so compelling and so central to politics that it must be honored in the present, the imperative that it be so honored must take precedence over any one goal of politics. The conservative enlightenment, centered in natural law, believes certain things are always wrong—for example, the taking of innocent life is wrong in the present and at all times—but in general it is by necessity relativistic in terms of goals that properly belong to politics. This is because each generation comes of age in a different political landscape containing a different mix of public goods and public evils, and by virtue of the new situation, it will see different goals as urgent. Even if political goals are broadly shared at a given moment, people who value equality may disagree vehemently about how to get there.

Moreover, the fact that each new generation is entitled to its freedom—its rights being unalienable—means that no political decisions can claim to be permanent. The idea that all of political life should be channeled (presumably by some elite) toward repeating exactly some decision or decisions of the past violates equality because it violates consent. A further implication is that there is no such thing as a perfect destination in politics. There can be no Utopia on the horizon of the conservative enlightenment. Perfect outcomes, if any, are for a higher realm.

The left enlightenment is by no means sure there is a higher realm—or, in the event there is, none that should moderate the possibilities of political fulfillment in this one. The Declaration of the Rights of Man of 1789, by no means a pure left document, makes its proclamation "in the presence and under the auspices of the Supreme Being" but says nothing about God as the originator of the rights it proclaims. (In this it is similar to the constitutional preamble of the Federal Republic of Germany and most other

European founding documents that mention God.) In the words of Evans, God's role appears more in the nature of a legal witness or notary public. Later French constitutions (and there have been many) usually describe themselves as "secular" and do not mention God at all.

Because the left enlightenment is fundamentally utopian, the *goal* of political action is its center of gravity, and its adherents are far less likely to agonize about the means of achieving it. Humanity in the midst of confining social institutions, in the analysis of Rousseau, Marx, and the counterculture, is fundamentally unfree and in no sense in possession of operational equality, or even of sufficient discernment to make rational political choices in the present. Humanity will fulfill its true nature, attaining everything worth having, only with full future liberation. The human condition is so defective prior to liberation that proactive elite guidance and (in the vision of the nondemocratic left) active coercion are often necessary. As mentioned earlier, the centrality of the goal of liberation and the drive to inculcate moral relativism throughout society fit seamlessly together, given the urgent need for draining legitimacy from, taking over, or (if necessary) dismantling the unjust "structures" of an oppressive society.

In an era that has seen the decline and fall of Marxism, the transfer of the left's center of gravity from economic to social issues has meant a renewed focus on liberation, especially the multitude of liberations involved in the sexual revolution. This has left equality a bit of an orphan.

Some years ago Professor Charles Kesler, of Claremont University, a leading conservative theoretician, remarked that for American conservatives, the main thing worth conserving is equality. Although he clearly meant equal human dignity in the sense of the God-created equality of the Declaration, it still was a shocking thing to say to conservatives. For most conservatives, "equality" is a word the left has misused to justify never-ending redistribution up to and including full-fledged socialism. In the many past debates when left vs. right seemed synonymous with socialism vs. capitalism, the idea of conservatives as the defenders of equality seemed unthinkable.

Today that may be changing. The old arguments have by no means disappeared, but for the heirs or would-be heirs of the conservative enlightenment, God-given equality and the resultant right to life, liberty, and the pursuit of happiness are at the core of what is still defensible, of what is still seen as properly *American* to the rest of the world. Even though most of American elite opinion has come to side with Europe's victorious social left on the centrality of relativism and personal liberation, social conservatism still has a pulse because the conservative vision of equality retains its place at the root of American identity.

8

COUNTERATTACK
ON EQUALITY

After the British Army and native Loyalists had been overcome in the Revolutionary War, the idea of political equality was virtually unchallenged in American politics. The 13 colonies (soon to be states) had no native monarchy and no blood-defined aristocracy after the handful of titled British noblemen withdrew along with the Union Jack. Primogeniture (inheritance of land exclusively by the eldest son) existed but was repealed in the states with little resistance. Unlike nearly all of Europe, the central government had no established church and (with passage of the First Amendment) no realistic possibility of getting one. Yet there was no serious effort to marginalize religion in general or prohibit a single denomination in the national or state capitals.

This is not to say that American politics was tame in the early years of independence. The chaos of competing, economically predatory state governments under the Articles of Confederation generated an existential crisis, perhaps the only sort of crisis sufficient to compel adoption of the U.S. Constitution.

In Philadelphia beginning in 1787, two pillars distinctive of the American version of the conservative enlightenment were debated: decentralization (to be modified, relative to the Articles) and separation of branches (to be enhanced). To come to agreement on a workable constitution, states gave ground to centralizers on issues relating to the powers of the federal government; and populist advocates of legislative supremacy, which under the Articles had characterized politics at both the national and state levels, had to allow for an independently chosen (and therefore more robust) executive branch.

To most republican theorists of the 18th century, a time of no vigorous ongoing examples of popular rule in anything larger than a city-state, a more robust executive meant a return, or the danger of a return, to some version of ruling monarchy. (That is essentially what had happened when, in the aftermath of its regicide, the British Parliament in 1649 elected Cromwell as Lord Protector.) Advocates of innate equality could not and did not anticipate the rise of an elected presidency that, in instances from Andrew Jackson to Ronald Reagan, led populist or egalitarian reform against a more elitist and more cautious Congress. Many of those who accepted the institution of an independently chosen president did so out of the need to end the chronic disorder under the Articles of Confederation. Also key was the fact that George Washington, the principled, widely trusted military hero of the republican revolution, made himself available to serve. Even these weighty factors were not enough to induce egalitarian populists such as Patrick Henry to endorse the Constitution

The fact remains that when the first constitutional Congress was called to order in 1789, the United States had achieved a far more rooted and egalitarian version of the conservative enlightenment than Great Britain had in its Glorious Revolution exactly one century earlier. There was no king or nobility. There was no established national church and no religious test for voting or holding office. The branch of the federal government designed to wield the power of the purse, the House of Representatives, was chosen by direct popular vote. There were significant elective power centers in the states, cemented by a U.S. Senate that awarded each state two votes, no matter how large or small it was. The states retained control over moral and cultural issues. And (completely unlike Britain) there was a written constitution, amendable only by two-thirds majorities in the U.S. House and Senate, followed by ratification by three-quarters of the states. The continued power of the states was further underlined by the framers' choice of a backup system for adopting constitutional changes, in the event of a possible deadlock between Congress and the states. In that circumstance, states could initiate and enact constitutional changes without any support or participation of Congress; for its part, Congress could do nothing to amend the Constitution without winning the support of three-quarters of the states.

Yet given the fact that equality is what all political applications of the Enlightenment have in common, it is undeniable that Britain was precocious in having achieved its understated version of political equality a full century earlier. The Glorious Revolution elevated Britain's most egalitarian institution, the House of Commons, into a position of dominance. The institutions of monarchy and aristocracy, while still wielding some influence as late as the first years of the 20th century, were on a path to ultimate extinction as holders of political power.

The Continental Difference

On the European continent, by contrast, blood elites were not so easily abolished (as in the U.S.) or marginalized (as in Britain).

The survival of monarchy and aristocracy as important political structures, in some cases until the aftermath of World War I, significantly slowed the advance of equality. By the time old-fashioned blood elites did pass from the European power mix, political equality found itself gravely threatened by the rise of nonaristocratic versions of blood elitism: among others, "scientific" racism and fascism, post-Enlightenment movements that vehemently denied all claims on behalf of equal human dignity.

How did Europe, the one part of the world whose very identity was formed by Christianity, become the breeding ground of antiegalitarian movements that were deeply anti-Christian as well as anti-Enlightenment?

The simplest answer is that Europe's decline in religious faith created a vacuum, first noticeable among some elites of the 16th and 17th centuries, but extending to a more popular base by the second half of the 18th century. The political and cultural following gained by the left enlightenment of course played the role of an accelerator, beginning with the left's appearance as a named movement in 1790s France; but it is also true that earlier declines in Christian observance created some of the essential preconditions for the left's rise. It's unclear which over time predominated as cause, which as effect.

Moreover, the well-chronicled conflict between Christian churches and the secular left, or for that matter the struggle between the conservative and left enlightenments over the political meaning of equality, does little to explain the vulnerability of Europe to racism and fascism, which in their radical rejection of human equality seem contrary to Europe's main path of political development over many centuries prior to around 1850.

There are any number of ways to analyze this recent and violent phase of European history, a history that culminates (post-1945) in a marked decline in Europe's weight in global politics.

For the purpose of this book, a look at the tension between unity and diversity in European history may be helpful.

The fall of the western Roman Empire in 476 brought a thousand years of second-class status to Europe, in comparison with what proved to be its main rivals for global preeminence, Confucian China and the successive Islamic caliphates. These two civilizations had systems of elite idea-driven control that leant themselves to territorial expansion and the economic power and cultural prestige this brought. Compared with its main rivals, Europe was split into countless political jurisdictions that constantly waged war with each other.

But centralized political consolidation sometimes proved a mixed blessing. When the Ming emperor decided to outlaw China's extensive sea commerce in 1430 to increase defenses against raiders from the steppes, the efficient Confucian bureaucracy was able to enforce the order with considerable success. This was a disastrous setback for China on the eve of the Age of Exploration.

Beginning in the early 15th century, under the leadership of tiny Portugal in the era of Prince Henry the Navigator (1394–1460), western Europe's advances in navigation and shipbuilding enabled it to fill the vacuum left by China at the precise time when the world's strategic center of gravity was beginning to shift from the Mediterranean and the Eurasian land mass to the Atlantic and Pacific oceans with their global reach.

According to William H. McNeill, the retired University of Chicago professor whose prize-winning 1963 book *The Rise of the West* established him as perhaps the preeminent modern historian of comparative civilization, Europe by 1500 had two qualities that set it apart from the rest of the world and fitted it for the global dominance it assumed in subsequent centuries.

First, Europe had an exceptional ability to learn from its encounter with other civilizations. Just as in the classical period

Rome had benefited from its ability to absorb the older and more sophisticated Hellenistic culture, medieval and Renaissance western Europe, which was predominantly Catholic, had taken aboard elements of classical, Byzantine, and Islamic high culture and combined them into an overpowering presence in every dimension, from the military to the artistic and scientific.

Second, according to McNeill, "[P]opular participation in economic, cultural, and political life was far greater in western Europe than in the other civilizations of the world. . . . Despite the dominance of aristocracy in the European countryside and of oligarchy in the towns, a larger proportion of the total population participated in the war and politics of medieval Europe than was true of any of the civilized Asian countries, with the possible exception of contemporary Japan. Thus, for example, pikemen recruited from the towns of northern Italy and later from the villages of Switzerland challenged the military supremacy of aristocratic knights from the twelfth century onward, while in the fourteenth century, the cream of French chivalry could not prevail against English bowmen, recruited originally from the poverty-stricken Welsh marchlands. As for politics, such representative institutions as the English Parliament, the French Estates-General, and the Ecumenical Councils of the Church all brought varied social groups into the highest arenas of the political process.

"The result," concludes McNeill, "was to mobilize greater human resources within European society than was possible within the more rigidly hierarchical societies of the other civilized lands."[*]

And Europe's persistent political divisions, however costly in terms of blood and unrest, were clearly a force for dynamism at a time when centralized elite rule had the power and self-confidence

---

[*] William H. McNeill, *The Rise of the West: A History of the Human Community* (Chicago, Ill.: University of Chicago Press, 1963), 558–559.

to perform dubious feats such as stifling China's long-range naval and maritime capacity.

Europe's Roman Obsession

But recognition that Europe benefited from diversity does not mean it lacked common aspirations. The same Europe that in 1500 was on the verge of unparalleled modernization and global reach still devoted much of its warfare and politics to efforts to reconstruct Europe's ancient empire with Rome as its capital.

In its final two centuries beginning around 250 AD, the Roman Empire was in decline politically and militarily, but not as an ideal of political and social order. The idea of a predictable, written rule of law, regnant in a vast domain whose many cities were connected to each other by the finest roads the world had ever seen, a domain where the best and brightest (and most useful) among the people it had conquered could even obtain citizenship—this was a powerful vision that increasingly captured the imagination of the same barbarians from the east who were trying to overrun Rome. Just as in the earlier case of Greek art and culture, Rome was to a surprising degree willing and able to absorb them and their vitality. Many joined the legions and some rose to the imperial seat.

When the Edict of Milan made Christianity the empire's favored religion in 313, the idea of the empire became even more attractive to the warrior peoples from the east, many of which had already encountered the Christian message. The vision of a Christian empire with the emperor as political leader and the pope as spiritual leader, first articulated by Pope Gelasius I around 450, gradually took hold in the West.

In the Greek-influenced eastern Roman Empire, separated administratively from the west in the will of the emperor Constantine, and which survived the western empire for nearly a thousand years, the emperor and the state were paramount. They limited if not eclipsed the church—an arrangement that recalls the all-encompassing role of the polis in the Greek city-states of classical times as well as the persistent Asian pattern of autocratic rule. For the first thousand years after Constantine renamed it, the eastern empire's capital of Constantinople usually surpassed Rome as a cultural and financial center. Yet even in the east, the vision of a reunited Roman Empire held considerable sway, and in the sixth century the emperor Justinian mounted an impressive though unsuccessful military campaign to make this happen.

The fall of the last Latin emperor of the west in 476 did not end western Europe's fascination with Rome and its empire. Emergence of the Frankish monarchy as the dominant military power in western Europe went hand in hand with its emergence as the leading champion of the Roman Catholic Church. In 800 AD, Charlemagne journeyed to Rome to be crowned by the pope as head of the Holy Roman Empire.

As mentioned in Chapter 7, the pope and emperor were not always in such accord. The struggle between these two primary institutions of the West defined much of medieval politics. After the 13th century, the roles of pope and emperor became better defined; they were often on different sides of wars and political alignments, but the two seldom posed a mortal threat to each other.

The Holy Roman Empire under the Carolingians had been centered in eastern France; later, under the Hohenstaufens, its power base was to the northeast, along the borderlands with Germany. In the late medieval period, when the Habsburg family gained dominance in the electoral college that chose each new emperor, the empire anchored itself in Vienna. There, it became Europe's champion against the expansive Islam of the Ottoman

Turks, especially after the fall of Constantinople and the definitive end of the eastern empire in 1453.

The 16th century saw the closest approach to European political unity since the Roman Empire itself. Due to both military prowess and advantageous marriages, the Habsburg family in the person of the Holy Roman Emperor Charles V assumed control of Spain together with its vast overseas empire from the Americas to the Philippines; some of what is now northern France, important parts of Italy, and a majority of what is now Germany and Austria; Hungary and huge chunks of Slavic eastern Europe; and the economically advanced Low Countries corresponding to today's Netherlands and Belgium. Charles V, triumphant over Protestant forces at the battle of Muhlberg in 1546, sat atop much of Europe as well as history's first overseas empire of truly global reach.

But given powerful opposition from the tenacious Protestant princes of the north, the ambitious French monarchy to the east, and continued pressure in the south from the aggressive Ottoman caliphate based in Constantinople, uniting Europe proved a task even beyond Europe's greatest dynasty at its peak. In abdicating in 1556, Charles V split his vast empire: He left the Spanish throne to his son Philip and his central European holdings to his younger brother, Ferdinand, who subsequently won election to succeed Charles as Holy Roman Emperor. Charles hoped his eldest son, now Philip II of Spain, would inherit the family's eastern, Austria-based lands and win election as Holy Roman Emperor on the death of his brother, Ferdinand I; but this was not to be. Charles died in a Spanish monastery in 1558, the two branches of the Habsburgs never reunited, and the family lost the Spanish throne to the France-based Bourbons in 1702. A century later, struggling to survive in the Napoleonic wars, the

Habsburgs agreed to drop the title of Holy Roman Emperor and became mere emperors of Austria.

The Left as Unifier

By that time, it was the newly birthed French-led left, in uneasy alliance with the emperor Napoleon, that had taken over as the main driver of European unity. As noted in Chapter 7, in the Treaty of Westphalia in 1648, European religion had surrendered the last vestige of its independence from the rising nation-states. By 1800, long marginalized in the politics of the Protestant north and fighting for survival against left secularizers in the Catholic south, the forces of institutional Christianity all over Europe found themselves by stark necessity on the side of the conservative enlightenment, whose stronghold was the Protestant, parliament-centered government of Great Britain.

Napoleon Bonaparte, a Corsican whose first language was Italian, emerged from the ranks of the French revolutionary army because his military genius was indispensable to the left. When the revolutionary republic first elevated him above all others, the title agreed on was First Consul, reaffirming Europe's Roman aspirations even with the Christian content freshly removed. Elsewhere in Europe, such monarchical titles as "Czar" and "Kaiser," both variants of "Caesar," joined "Emperor" in underlining Europe's continued Roman obsession. Even in the eastern periphery of Europe, where few Catholics lived, Russian nationalists had long defined that country's destiny as establishing Moscow as a "third Rome," succeeding Rome itself as well as Constantinople.

Napoleon was a man of the left who departed from important precepts of left orthodoxy when he found doing so attractive or convenient. The most obvious instance was his maneuvering to resurrect ruling monarchy, for his personal dynastic benefit. Nearly as great a deviation was his willingness to sign a Concordat to make peace with the Catholic Church of France. He had a stormy relationship with the papacy: He held the pope prisoner for years at a time and struggled to reestablish for himself the Bourbon monarchy's grip on the appointment of French bishops. But Napoleon was focused on conquest, so he prized the domestic stability gained by recognizing the church (and having it recognize him). Further, a show of good will toward the church neutralized still formidable papal opposition to his effort to control the rest of Europe. The left sullenly acquiesced, hoping to curb the church more radically after Napoleon had conquered and transformed Europe.

Even in its compromised Napoleonic form, the left enlightenment had a universal vision that sought specific local outcomes. Every country that saw the victory of French arms also experienced egalitarian social change. In many if not most countries, such changes had broad popular support. For example, in the many continental countries where Roman legal tradition already predominated over English-style common law, the Napoleonic Code was widely welcomed and largely survived the fall of Napoleon himself.

But in the entire 20-year-plus duration of the French revolutionary and Napoleonic wars (1792–1815), it was never clear to the rest of Europe if the main story was one of transnational liberation or French colonization. In a sense, Europe's age-old tension between unity and diversity was now focused on a single nation, at times even on a single man. When the pendulum swung toward fear of a French-run Europe, a fear always encouraged by Britain and its monarchical allies on the continent, Napoleon's position became more doubtful.

In the closing years of this epic struggle, an increasingly strong European nationalism, buoyed by older institutions and belief systems, managed to swing the balance against France and the left. The role of both the traditional and modern wings of this anti-French impetus was famously evident in Orthodox Russia's patient but thorough annihilation of Napoleon's *Grande Armée* in 1812–1813. In the less bloody but perhaps equally important Peninsular War, a British expeditionary force commanded by Sir Arthur Wellesley (later successively Viscount, Earl, Marquess, and Duke of Wellington) combined with nationalist guerrillas in Spain and Portugal to defeat a proud succession of previously invincible French field marshals between 1808 and 1814.

When Napoleon escaped from his Elba exile in 1815 to propel France through the Hundred Days, the newly created Duke of Wellington, now serving as Britain's chief envoy to the Congress of Vienna, faced a choice between completing the work of Vienna and commanding a multinational allied force in Belgium. Wellington calmly accepted command and rode across much of Europe in time to confront and defeat Napoleon's massive French army at Waterloo, the battle that definitively ended the Napoleonic Wars.

While it is true that the absence of the left enlightenment enabled the statesmen at Vienna to restore Europe's pre-Enlightenment ruling monarchies, it was the small island nation run by its Parliament that continued to get its way in the politics of the 19th century. In that century, Britain dominated the oceans and with a comparative handful of officials administered a growing global empire that, at its height, well exceeded that of Charles V, becoming the most populous and far-flung in human history.

But in contrast to the Habsburgs at their peak three centuries earlier, Britain and its Parliament-centered elites seldom saw themselves as architects of a unified Europe, Roman or otherwise. British and continental blood elites could sense that the main potential of playing this role had passed to the left enlightenment. The Jacobins and Napoleon had been contained, but their imprint was everywhere in the form of a pan-European left ideology.

This happened at a time when technical advances and overseas conquests were making European civilization the first ever to become truly worldwide. By virtue of becoming the likeliest unifying force of 19th-century Europe, the left had become a threat to sweep over the world.

No one understood this better than the man the Habsburg emperor Francis I designated to represent Austria at the Congress of Vienna: Prince Klemenz von Metternich. It was Metternich who fashioned the Holy Alliance, still remembered in the Americas as the overseas threat that gave birth to the Monroe Doctrine. Despite its name, so suggestive of a return to the ideal of a Holy Roman Empire, the Holy Alliance was mainly about the struggle between republicanism and pre-Enlightenment ruling monarchy. This was underlined by the fact that the Alliance's three founding powers—Austria, Prussia, and Russia—were products of mutually antagonistic religious traditions—Catholic, Lutheran, and Orthodox. This reflected a new division, unseen in Europe previously: traditional Christian believers of all stripes vs. predominantly secularist revolutionaries active all over Europe. To Americans of the 1960s and afterward, of course, this isn't at all surprising: It is a species of realignment that invariably kicks in when the left enlightenment achieves critical mass. Disparate religions temporarily unite not from a desire for conquest but merely to survive secularist onslaught.

In Austria's domestic scene, Metternich's various efforts to modernize were thwarted by the emperor Francis—according to at least some interpreters, the reforms might have become a continental version of the conservative enlightenment. But Metternich's failure only deepens the image of early post-Enlightenment European politics as a polarized clash of old vs. new, ruling monarchy vs. human equality. What in fact emerged in the 1780s was a comparatively peaceful struggle between ruling monarchies and advocates of political enlightenment, who pressed for reforms such as written constitutions and modification of the unitary rule of the powerful Renaissance monarchies; the reformers also pressed for some movement toward expanded voting rights and recognition of innate human equality. This is also an apt description of the debate over reform even in France as late as 1788 and 1789, and of many reform efforts in 19th-century monarchical Europe.

Following the eruption of the left as the dominant revolutionary force on the continent, however, much of the debate polarized in a manner that never happened in Britain, and never could have happened in the United States. Appalled by the chaos and destructiveness of the French Revolution, continental conservatives (a word first used in post-Napoleonic France) came to favor either outright restoration of the pre-Enlightenment order or a restructuring that emphasized economic reform and development, without ending monarchical or aristocratic rule. As the idea of equality spread and became more and more compelling in popular opinion, continental conservatives increasingly found themselves an unpopular minority allied with wealth and social privilege. Concluding that the anti-Christian nature of the left enlightenment left it no choice, traditional religion was similarly driven toward an alliance with society's upper crust in a way that had never occurred in the medieval or early modern eras, when royalty and nobility were usually the chief predators of church property and independence.

For all its economic innovation and global military reach, Great Britain saw itself in the 19th century as a small country in comparison with populous continental powers such as France, Russia, the Austro-Hungarian empire, and (after 1870) the German Second Reich. Having effectively ended its ruling monarchy more than a century earlier and having gained in economic and political power ever since, Britain was firmly committed to its parliamentary version of the conservative enlightenment, which was both admired and resented in Europe. All else being equal, British foreign policy tended to side with republican reform and nationalistic revolts against autocracy, such as Greece's successful drive to free itself from Ottoman rule in the 1820s. A similar tension was at play in Britain's prolonged debate over the morality of human slavery, the important first phase of which was won by Tory Evangelical parliamentarian William Wilberforce with enactment of a ban in 1807 on British participation in the global slave trade.

But all else was often not equal. British foreign policy alternated between support for democratic reform and national liberation, on one side, and maintaining a comparatively peaceful balance of power on the continent, on the other. In the initial post-Napoleonic period, the leading antagonists in this debate were the Tory reformer George Canning, a moralist, and the Tory architect of the pro-monarchical Congress of Vienna, Lord Castlereagh, who was what today we would call a realist. The 19th-century British version of realism often advocated that country's intervention on the side of the weakest continental nation or coalition—even when (as was frequently the case) the weak power was the most antithetical to the forces of enlightenment. This was certainly true of Britain's intervention in defense of the beleaguered Ottoman Empire in the Crimean War of the 1850s, the only European land war Britain fought in the 99 years between Waterloo and World War I.

The rise of nationalism, so greatly accelerated by the charisma conferred on the institution of the nation-state by the Westphalian system after 1648, brought a volatile new dimension to the byplay between the left and conservative enlightenments, on the one hand, and ruling monarchy on the other. Competitive and often predatory nationalism fostered overseas empire-building and (as earlier noted) was a force both for and against the left during the French revolutionary and Napoleonic wars.

As to Europe's monarchical land empires after 1815, nationalism enhanced the rising powers of Russia and Prussia and was a constant drain on the declining multiethnic empires based in Vienna and Constantinople.

Conflict Theory

On balance, a surging nationalism, which had helped rapidly marginalize religion's independence from the state at Westphalia in 1648 and succeeding decades, was a powerful challenge to the idea of a united Europe. This was true whether the unifying vision was of the Christian empire of the Carolingians and Habsburgs or, after the 1790s, the secular, liberated utopia sought by the left enlightenment. But beginning in the 16th century with Machiavelli, an approach to political analysis rooted in the centrality of conflict in human affairs made nationalism a far greater threat to Europe's common identity than almost anyone could have anticipated. An understanding of how this happened may be aided by a look at the way competing modern worldviews regard conflict.

It goes without saying that no serious analysis of politics excludes the existence or importance of conflict. The disagreement is over the extent to which conflict is the animating force of political change.

In modern times, there are at least three influential views. They differ strikingly in the relationship each sees between the idea of equality and the nature and prevalence of conflict, up to and including war.

One line of thought can be summed up by the French revolutionary slogan, "Liberty, Equality, Fraternity." These three values are seen as intimately related to each other, and growth of belief in one tends to enhance growth of belief in the other two. Growth in all three affects all areas of human society, but for a believer in the conservative enlightenment, it helps to see equality—in the sense of universal human dignity in the present—as a central and necessary foundation of politics, as outlined in Chapter 7. Belief in this equal dignity implies freedom for broad popular participation as a superior means of political decision-making, and fraternity or concord as a reasonable and attainable outcome of politics, consistent with actual human nature. Given this optimistic view of human potential in the present, those with this worldview tend to value cooperation (rather than conflict and competition) as both a desirable and effective means of attaining political and economic goals. An example of this mode of thought is the inclination to support free trade among nations in preference to mercantilism (defining mercantilism as protectionism structured to give the comparative advantage to one nation).

A second view shares the Enlightenment allegiance to liberty, equality, and fraternity but believes that acting as if the three can thrive in the present is unrealistic. Instead, it favors elite management toward a future social order maximizing equality of status and human liberation, usually seen as preconditions of fraternity. While a revolutionary vanguard or informed elite can smooth the way if it gains control of the government and other institutions, brass-knuckled political conflict is accepted as invariably necessary to oust elites committed to retrograde institutions that hold humanity back from its future fulfillment.

This second view comprehends the Marxists and most other strains of the left, as well as a range of liberal democratic egalitarians. Immanuel Kant (1724–1804), as one example, disapproved of conflict as a chosen tactic of political reformers, but he acknowledged that, given his view of human nature, conflict and war are concretely the most efficacious ways of advancing toward human rights and "perpetual peace."

The third view is that human equality is neither possible nor desirable. Freedom and fraternity can exist for some, but only as an outgrowth of conquest and mastery. Conflict is not only inevitable, but also ubiquitous and desirable. It is the way nature works its will and is therefore the irreplaceable means of humanity's advance. Nietzsche was the most eloquent among the growing number of post-Enlightenment European thinkers who held this view, which opened up politics to theories of natural aristocracy, scientific racism, eugenics, and predatory nationalism up to and including Fascism and National Socialism. In the politics of the 19th and 20th century, these movements were nearly always anti-Christian as well as an explicit rejection of the Enlightenment.

Of course, rejection of equality and fraternity was hardly new. For most of civilization's history, political equality in the modern sense of equal human dignity was never even entertained as a possibility. The great Athenian historian Thucydides had a typical pagan's fatalistic view of the inevitability of human conflict. Like most other Greeks whose writings have come down to us, he had little good to say about democracy as a political system or framework for justice. Aristotle believed slaves were fated to stay that way "by nature."

The Hebraic vision of a single personal God as ruler of all peoples implied the possibility of salvation and dignity for all peoples, an idea several of the prophets made explicit in the first millennium BC. Christianity's teaching about the trinity—three interactive persons within the single godhead—first introduced the concept of personhood to humanity, which in turn led to the rise of belief in universal human dignity and human rights.

By analogy, the trinitarian framework may also have helped foster the medieval idea of separate realms for church and state. Coupled with Jesus's dictum about giving to Caesar the things that are Caesar's and to God the things that are God's, the notion of the trinity was consistent with plurality of rule and separation of powers (sometimes known as "checks and balances"). No single institution of society, or even of government, should possess unchecked, unchallengeable dominance of society as a whole. In medieval Europe, every monarch, including the Holy Roman Emperor at the peak of that institution's grandeur, was believed subject to a higher law.

Regression to Unitary Rule

Marsilius of Padua (1275–1342), writing a century or so after the Magna Carta, was the most influential European Christian to begin to push back toward the belief in unitary rule that has been the political norm for most of humanity's recorded history. An antagonist of the papacy, Marsilius rejected the autonomy of the church as well as the existence of natural law (meaning that neither the church nor natural law could provide a check on the political authorities). In a foreshadowing of conflict analysis, Marsilius believed that the improved order he saw as a consequence of unitary political rule trumped all other values likely to be overridden in the process.

As outlined in Chapter 7, the Renaissance doctrine known as the Divine Right of Kings swept through Europe and had eliminated parliamentary independence nearly everywhere on the continent by 1600. It took two civil wars and most of the 17th century to bring unitary rule to Britain, this time in the form of rule by Parliament. The rise of the idea of established churches, Catholic as well as Protestant and Orthodox, had nearly everywhere relegated religion to the status of a department of government.

Among influential European Protestants, only the Calvinists tended to reject the subordination of the church to the state. Their vision, implemented by Calvin himself in the city-state of Geneva, was not theocracy but a complex collaboration between lay councilmen and moral advisers drawn from the clergy. Calvinists who attained political power did not believe in toleration of religious minorities (in the 16th and 17th centuries, such intolerance was the norm), but a series of military and political setbacks to Calvinists almost everywhere on the continent led them to develop a doctrine of "free churches"—free, that is, of control or regulation by Europe's mostly non-Calvinist states. It was the emigration of so many English Calvinists to North America in the early 1600s that kept the ideas of autonomy for religion and separation of powers—ideological bulwarks of a medieval Europe no longer prized in Europe itself—alive in a kind of suspended animation, awaiting the founding of the United States to reemerge on the world stage in a completely post-monarchical form.

Particularly on the continent, the triumph of unitary rule was a critical precursor to the rise of competitive nationalism and, not much later, the dominance of conflict theory. Unitary rule and conflict theory, both representing a sharp break from medieval Europe, logically reinforce each other. If unitary rule is assumed to be the only viable way to achieve a measure of political order, it follows that politics will be analyzed as a perpetual struggle for this unappetizing but necessary supremacy. Looked at from the other end, belief in politics as an unending competition for raw power leads logically not to a morally based, comparatively stable, diversified, shared power, but to eventual triumph by a single force, in the form of either autocracy or some milder version of top-down, hierarchical government.

In 19th-century European social thought, a theory of race-determined human differentiation gained standing as a "scientific" refutation of equality and emerged with new credibility when egalitarian thought split into the competing schools of innate equality and the managed, conflict-driven equality championed by the left. Not surprisingly, many of Europe's blood elites in the later 19th century welcomed as a godsend this intellectual challenge to equality.

As was often the case during many centuries of Europe's history, Germany displayed in exaggerated form the trends affecting the continent as a whole. Germans had been the Europeans most captivated by the vision of a multinational Catholic empire in the medieval period, only to become the most influential defectors to Protestantism in the 16th century. Led by chancellor Otto von Bismarck in pivotal European wars and diplomacy of the 1860s and 1870s, the kingdom of Prussia succeeded in forging an extensive and dynamic German-speaking empire, known as the Second Reich. On the instant of its formation in 1871, it became Europe's preeminent land power. It was monarchical, aristocratic, and economically a formidable challenger to Great Britain. The new Germany permitted elections, but its rulers showed little interest in political equality.

What they did show interest in was aggressive, competitive nationalism. In an effort to catch up to Britain and France, a German overseas empire was launched in Africa. A formidable navy was assembled at warp speed. Victorious in every major land battle since forces led by the ancient cavalryman Gebhard Blucher had marched to the aid of Wellington as evening fell on Waterloo, Prussian-led Germany by the late 19th century boasted the best-trained and most feared army in the world.

Now forgotten racial theorists such as French Count Arthur de Gobineau (1816–1882) and the English historian Houston Stewart Chamberlain (1855–1927) elevated Aryans as a master race and the key to future human progress. Rather strikingly given their wide separation in age, Gobineau and Chamberlain both paid court to the German composer Richard Wagner in his home in Bayreuth, which was emerging as the center of a neo-pagan, anti-Semitic circle of German literary and artistic elites. Eventually Chamberlain married the deceased composer's daughter and, though the son of a British admiral, became a radio propagandist for Germany during World War I.

Berlin, capital of the Prussian monarchy and later of the German Empire, became an intellectual center of nationalistic conflict theory. In the wake of Prussia's crushing defeat by Napoleon at the battle of Jena in 1806, Johann Gottlieb Fichte, who held the chair of philosophy at the University of Berlin, began an electrifying series of "Addresses to the German People." Fichte praised the German language as the purest and most original in the world and excoriated Jews and Latins (including the French) as decadent races. Only a united Germany led by a small elite free of "private" moral restraints, he argued, was capable of leading the world to a new and higher stage of history.

Interestingly, Heinrich von Treitschke, the dominant figure at the University of Berlin in the closing decades of the 19th century, a time when Berlin had become the capital of the mighty Second Reich, was if anything even more committed than Fichte to the need for German preeminence in a world of conflict and hierarchical power politics. He extolled the Prussian martial spirit as "a jewel as precious as the masterpieces of our poets and thinkers," although he was not himself Prussian. His priority was clear: "War is not only a practical necessity, it is also a theoretical necessity, an exigency of logic. . . . That war should ever be banished from the world is a hope not only absurd, but profoundly immoral. It would involve the atrophy of many of the essential and sublime forces of the human soul." As for the idea of human equality, "It does not matter what you think, so long as you obey." Treitschke's history lectures were praised by Kaiser Wilhelm II and attended by the cream of the German General Staff and the powerful civilian bureaucracy.

Germany was unique not in its commitment to raw nationalism and power politics, but in its seeming ability to defeat any and all competing versions of the same. Even France, which was still the stronghold of the left in the Third Republic of the later 19th century and in the process of excising any role for religion in public life, including schools, seemed at least equally obsessed with avenging Bismarck's humiliation of Napoleon III at the Battle of

Sedan in 1870 (which led to the annexation of Alsace and Lorraine). Britain, particularly following elections won by William Gladstone and the Liberal Party, remained a lonely voice for a cooperative, peaceful Europe centered on political reform and economic development, but it found itself spending the bulk of its foreign-policy time constructing shaky alliances with France and Russia to keep Germany in check. By 1900 the age-old European balance between unity and diversity was tilting lopsidedly toward predatory, conflict-driven nationalism. Any potential European unity seemed destined to become subject to a chauvinistic blood elite, rather than offered in service to a universal ideal.

Hegel and Bismarck

If the claustrophobic infighting of 16th-century Italian city-state politics was an appropriate venue for the introduction of conflict theory to Europe by Machiavelli, 19th-century Berlin will perhaps in retrospect seem fitting as its apotheosis, thanks above all to the powerful, multifaceted mind of Georg Wilhelm Friedrich Hegel (1770–1831). In contrast to Fichte and Treitschke, the two Germanophiles who dominated the University of Berlin at the beginning and end of that century, Hegel—who held the university's chair of philosophy between 1818 and 1831—elaborated a "systematic" theory of history as a conflict-driven yet progressive process, a vision that captured imaginations all over the world.

Hegel's was so protean a mind that it is harder to specify what he was not than what he was. He laid down the predicate for the theory of Marxist class conflict at the same time he was mounting a serious post-Enlightenment defense of ruling monarchy. Hegel praised the human liberation brought by the Lutheran reformation at the same time that he celebrated secularization in the context of the modern state, which he saw as the inevitable outgrowth of Christianity's triumph.

187

At the heart of Hegel's analysis of politics is his belief that every historical breakthrough carries within itself its own contradiction, up to and including self-destruction. His vision of the pre-political centers not on Rousseau's "natural man" of lawless freedom but on the relationship between master and slave. The master prevails, commands the work of the slave, and spends his resultant leisure dreaming of glory and preparing for war (which Hegel not surprisingly believed to be humanity's most creative medium). The slave, whose primal motive is fear of violent death, develops the material and cultural side of civilization. The state emerges out of the unresolved tension between the two, forcing them to recognize each other.

Hegel believed the French Revolution was an epochal breakthrough for human freedom, but that the totality of its success in erasing the past made inevitable the Reign of Terror, which came from elements within the revolution's own nature rather than from outside. As a young academic in 1806, Hegel observed Napoleon's arrival in Jena prior to the battle of that name as the appearance of a "world-historical" figure. He praised the revolutionary ideals of Liberty, Equality, and Fraternity but defined equality as juridical equality—equality before the law, most definitely not at the ballot box. He attacked England's proposed Reform Bill, eventually adopted by Parliament in 1832 to greatly expand the electorate. He opposed demands for political reform that led to riots in Berlin in 1830, and the following year, the last of his life, King Frederick William III decorated him for his service to the Prussian state.

Despite all these seeming paradoxes, when the influence of Hegel had worked its way through modern thought, people all over the world came to understand history as a violent progression or dialectic, driven by self-contradiction and universal in scope. Tacitly or explicitly, political truth therefore inhered not in moral reasoning but in whatever institutions had proven strong and resilient enough to emerge from a creative process motored by recurring human conflict.

If there were ever a perfect Hegelian example of a historical breakthrough containing within itself its own destruction, it was the rise of the Second Reich fashioned by Bismarck, the Prussian aristocrat who became the political grand master of Europe. Bismarck remained in power in Berlin for 28 years—19 of them after he brought forth the new German Empire in 1871. These latter years proved for him a time of frustration and gridlock, in a sense because the iron chancellor had achieved too much in his wars and maneuvers of the 1860s and 1870s. He knew exactly how to maximize German power in the cockpit of predatory nationalisms, but in doing so, he had made Germany the predominant threat to everyone else.

Determined to preserve the huge gains in territory and population he had won for his monarch, Bismarck's main goal after 1871 was to avoid another European land war. But he possessed only a conflict model, more often than not involving duplicity, and distrust of Germany steadily mounted. There seemed no chance of returning to earlier European visions of multiethnic fraternity— certainly not under Bismarck, who in 1866 had maneuvered a reluctant king of Prussia into a war to eject the internationalist Habsburgs from most of their German possessions.

Other elements of Bismarck's agenda reflected his deep-seated belief in conflict theory, which in his case included hostility to anything that implied a transcending of national self-interest. In the late 1870s, he switched the Second Reich's trade policy toward protectionism so German manufacturing could rival that of previously dominant Britain. And in 1871, as his first order of business after founding the Second Reich, he turned his wrath toward the Catholic Church in what came to be known as the "Kulturkampf." This included a drive to secularize marriage and remove Catholic content from the schools even of heavily Catholic regions of the new Germany. His friend and confidant, the British diplomat Odo Russell, said Bismarck concluded that "the pretensions of the Vatican were fundamentally inconsistent with the supremacy of the state." Bismarck could not, Russell said, "conceive that a faithful child of the church could also be a loyal son of the fatherland." Eventually Bismarck accepted détente with a new and more conciliatory pope, Leo XIII, and enlisted the Catholic-backed Center Party as an ally in his campaign to demonize still another transnational enemy, the parties of the German left.

Apart from Bismarck's precarious, widely mistrusted peacekeeping, the only viable political path for German foreign policy was to use the threat of its military power to become the openly acknowledged arbiter of Europe—first among equals among the great European states. That was the path favored by the newly crowned Kaiser Wilhelm II, and his dismissal of the aging, nearly exhausted Bismarck in 1890 was the first step along a path that decisively emphasized power over peacekeeping, which also proved to be the path to World War I.

It seems ironic that in the decades before 1914, European wealth, technology, and power peaked at the very time when its aspirations toward unity had been almost completely erased. The shift of European politics in the Renaissance toward belief in unitary rule had become universal, surviving transitions from ruling monarchy to republican forms of government. Previously vibrant European churches, Catholic and Protestant as well as Orthodox, had increasingly been absorbed into the state, steadily shrinking the independent role of religion in the 250 years prior to 1900.

The idea of human equality, the political hallmark of the Enlightenment, had been checked by the resilience of Europe's blood elites and—above all—by the near universal belief in conflict as the main engine of political change: Any desire of pro-Enlightenment reformers to permanently divide or decentralize rule by means of a written constitution was inhibited by the growing belief that multiple power centers would prove merely way stations in a conflict-driven progression to unitary rule. Given this mental architecture, any *existing* plurality of power centers was seen as a temporary flaw within the system, rather than as an achievement consistent with a comparatively stable and balanced politics.

Combined with the related and growing influence of scientific racism and predatory theories of human anthropology, conflict theory thus leant credence to authoritarian political models, whether based on primordial blood elites, secular nationalism, or (quite often) some combination of the two. Many of the most charismatic modern writers, epitomized by Nietzsche, argued that this relentless process of conflict inevitably and appropriately led to greater inequality, perhaps to culminate in the appearance of some higher form of humanity.

Gladstone and Lincoln

The two bastions of the conservative enlightenment, Great Britain and the United States, were far from immune to the rise of conflict theory, which came to characterize the analytical side of English-speaking politics nearly as much as on the European continent. But British and American politics in the 19th century had a significant offset: two eloquent practitioners, Gladstone and Lincoln, who were explicit and thoroughgoing opponents of conflict theory.

William Gladstone (1809–1898) was at or near the center of British politics for more than 50 years, beginning with his appointment to the Board of Trade under reformist Conservative prime minister Robert Peel in 1843 until the fall of Gladstone's final Liberal ministry over his determined but unsuccessful effort to achieve Irish home rule in 1894. A supply-sider long before such a term had been invented, Gladstone was a relentless tax,

budget, and tariff cutter as well as an advocate of economic cooperation among nations. He was a skeptic of his era's competitive
empire-building, in Africa and elsewhere—a key issue between
him and his formidable Conservative election opponents, Ben-
jamin Disraeli and the Marquess of Salisbury. On the issue of
political reform, he started as a Tory opposed to expansion of the
franchise but gradually became more and more optimistic about
the wisdom and disinterestedness of British voters. In fighting to
give the vote to allegedly ignorant rural laborers in the Reform
Act of 1884, Gladstone said: "[W]e are firm in the faith that the
people may be trusted—that the voters under the Constitution
are the strength of the Constitution."[*]

In an 1862 speech, Gladstone attacked those who argued that
"the people cannot be trusted—that they are fit for nothing except
to earn daily bread—that you must not call them to the exercise
of higher functions, or look to them for enlightened views." As
a contrary example, Gladstone cited what he believed to be the
conscious sacrifice of North Country voters who accepted unemployment owing to the cotton famine as a painful but necessary
cost of the struggle to end slavery in the American civil war. In
the words of the late American historian Robert Kelley, of the
University of California at Santa Barbara: "He had come to the
view that the ordinary man had both the intellectual capacity to
understand great issues and the moral character to act rightly
upon them. When he spoke to his audiences, he assumed that
they were serious and reflective. His speeches moved freely over
all areas of statecraft, as if they were given on the floor of Commons itself. . . . He gave them the sense that they were being
invited to join him in making moral judgments on public events
of worldwide importance. He appealed confidently to a sense of

---

[*] Robert Kelley, *The Transatlantic Persuasion: The Liberal-Democratic Mind in the Age of
Gladstone* (New York, N.Y.: Alfred A. Knopf, 1969), 228.

compassion he was sure was in them—and which, perhaps, they therefore felt. The ordinary man standing in Gladstone's audiences was made to feel as though he had become a classless man, a disinterested man, a moral agent in the world."[*]

Similarly, the controversy between Lincoln and his fellow Illinoisan Stephen A. Douglas can be seen in part as a debate over conflict theory in a democratic context. In defending his doctrine of popular sovereignty, Douglas argued that the existing white electorate in each state and territory had the right to enslave or not enslave blacks, depending on the comparative advantage of doing so or not doing so. In his 1854 Peoria speech marking the end of a five-year absence from public life, Lincoln countered that acceptance of such a doctrine, by making human freedom a function of power politics, would deprive "our republican example of its just influence in the world" by "insisting that there is no right principle of action beyond *self-interest*" (emphasis in original).[†] Lincoln believed it was no accident that the pre–Civil War Democrats, at the time the nation's long-standing dominant party, had also become advocates of Manifest Destiny, the belief that the U.S. was entitled to any land it cared to take on the North American continent on grounds of racial or cultural superiority.

So Lincoln and Gladstone both rejected conflict theory and predatory, zero-sum-game imperialism; both also adhered to the conservative-enlightenment belief in innate God-given human equality. The virtual disappearance of such beliefs in the political philosophy of their time magnified their influence, but in strikingly different ways.

The superbly educated son of a wealthy Scottish industrialist, Gladstone was all his life a full-fledged member of the political elite. In his 50-plus years at the top rank of British politics, a time

---

[*] Ibid., 209.
[†] Lewis E. Lehrman, *Lincoln at Peoria: The Turning Point* (Mechanicsburg, Pa.: Stackpole Books, 2008), 129.

in which he became more and more of an egalitarian democrat, he was increasingly and deeply resented by most other members of the elite. After 1859, Gladstone "ruled Parliament through the electorate," Kelley writes in *The Transatlantic Persuasion: The Liberal-Democratic Mind in the Age of Gladstone.* "He was imposed upon the oligarchies in Lords and Commons by social forces coming from every direction. 'Gladstone exercises such a sway over the constituencies,' wrote the Duke of Argyll in a private letter in 1881, 'that the members are afraid to call their souls their own.'"[*]

Brought up dirt-poor and lacking formal education, Lincoln was consistently underrated by other politicians until the day he was mortally wounded by an assassin. His career at the summit of politics lasted only about seven years, including an unsuccessful Illinois Senate campaign in 1858 and a victory in the 1860 presidential election in which he received less than 40 percent of the popular vote in a four-way race. He owed his prominence to a single issue, slavery and the existential threat it posed to the Union, an issue that ceased to exist shortly after Lincoln's death with the successful conclusion of the Civil War.

Gladstone's struggle against the British version of conflict theory ended with his failure to achieve a peaceful transition to Irish self-government in 1894. Gladstone was succeeded for 15 months as Liberal prime minister by Archibald Primrose, Earl of Rosebery, and (after a 10-year interlude of Conservative government) by Sir Henry Campbell-Bannerman (1905–1908), Herbert Henry Asquith (1908–1916), and David Lloyd George (1916–1922), the last Liberal Party head of government Britain would ever have. Lloyd George was also, it is fair to say, the first adherent of Britain's left to achieve political power, and his ascendancy was so divisive for the Liberals that by the end of the 1920s, the

---

[*] Kelley, op. cit., 203.

Socialist Labour Party had effectively displaced them as one of the two contenders in Britain's party system.

In reality, Gladstone had no successor, Liberal or otherwise. Successful and dominant as he had been for so many years, no major figure shared Gladstone's God-centered belief in human dignity or his optimism about the British people as mature actors in both politics and economics. No subsequent British politician made a serious attempt to emulate him. As Kelley's analysis makes clear, Gladstone and his achievements were far more revered in subsequent decades in the United States and Canada than they were in Britain itself. Today he is little more than a name, his ideas and achievements scarcely remembered on either side of the Atlantic, or for that matter anywhere else.

Although Lincoln had far fewer years in the limelight and so many fewer evident advantages, he proved to be a far more enduring influence in democratic political life. The belief systems of the two men, both born in 1809, were remarkably compatible, but Gladstone was effectively the last of his kind, whereas Lincoln was the first president of a new party that in 2012 has held the presidency 92 of a possible 156 years. And more books have been written about Lincoln than any other elective politician in history. Why such contrasting long-term outcomes?

It is tempting to believe this is merely a function of Lincoln's violent and dramatic end in comparison with Gladstone's peaceful death in bed, covered in honors. But at least as salient is the nature and outcome of the climactic crisis each man faced at the end of his career: Each accepted and entered a high-profile, defining battle about political equality. On the persistent, recurring issues of black slavery in the United States and self-government for Ireland, Lincoln won and Gladstone lost.

Even more important, Lincoln's victory was a return to, and reaffirmation of, the American founding as a bastion of the conservative enlightenment. Gladstone's defeat on Irish Home Rule happened because long-marginalized English blood elites, no doubt emboldened by conflict theory and the predatory imperialism that swept over Europe in the second half of the 19th century, rose up to deal a punishing setback to the conservative-enlightenment values Britain had to a considerable degree espoused and embodied on the world stage for two centuries. The setback to Irish political rights did not prove permanent, but Gladstone's politics of inclusion passed from British democracy, leaving a gaping hole that British socialists managed to fill with their politics of conflict.

From 1854 on, Lincoln defined his battle against the slaveholding South as an argument over the Declaration of Independence—specifically its doctrine of innate human equality. His adversaries, including Senator Douglas and Chief Justice Roger Taney, in effect accepted the terms of Lincoln's challenge, arguing that because most American blacks were slaves at the time of the revolution, the founders did not regard them as truly human. Thus the literal words of the Declaration, according to Lincoln's adversaries, should either be disregarded as empty rhetoric or treated as meaning "all *white* men are created equal." By winning this argument, first in presidential politics and then on the battlefields of the Civil War, Lincoln restored and deepened innate equality as the central premise of American existence.

This is something Lincoln all along was highly conscious of doing, as shown by what he said in 1861 as president-elect on a visit to Independence Hall in Philadelphia: "I have never had a feeling politically that did not spring from the sentiments embodied in the Declaration of Independence. . . . I have often inquired of myself what great principle or idea it was that kept this confederation so long together. It was not the mere matter of the separation of the colonies from the motherland, but that something in the Declaration giving liberty, not alone to the people of this country, but hope to the world for all future time. It was that which gave promise that in due time the weights should be lifted from the shoulders of all men, and that *all* should have an equal chance."[*] For Lincoln, no less than Jefferson before him and Reagan after him, the attraction of American exceptionalism was its claim to universality.

When in 1801 William Pitt, parliamentary mastermind of Britain's generation-long struggle against revolutionary France, decided Ireland should join England and Scotland as a full-fledged member of the British nation, he proposed an Act of Union that included voting rights for Catholics as a necessary part of winning Ireland's allegiance. Parliament agreed, but with a kicker insisted on by King George III: Irish Catholics could vote to send members of Parliament to London for the first time, but no Irish Catholic could be seated in Commons. Catholics could vote, but only for Protestants, even in counties where Protestants were less than 5 percent of the population. Pitt called this a betrayal and resigned, ending his remarkable 18 years of unbroken service as prime minister. Like Scotland a century earlier, Ireland had given up its own parliament and now had representation in the British Parliament, but its Catholics had to wait until 1829 for the right to occupy a seat in Commons. Needless to say, the protracted and grudging nature of English resistance to these Irish rights did nothing to enhance the Union, once it was achieved. In fact, well before the end of the 19th century, a time of democratic reforms and an expanding electorate in Britain, Irish aspirations turned away from any thought of participation in an English-led whole and decisively toward self-determination and self-government.

In his climactic drive for Irish Home Rule in 1894, Gladstone won approval in the House of Commons, only to have the unelected House of Lords contemptuously kill his bill by a margin of more than 10 to 1. Like Pitt nearly a century earlier, Gladstone had won

---

[*] Lehrman, op. cit., 221.

a battle for Irish rights in that part of the British system where political equality prevailed or was gaining, only to be thwarted and forced to resign by British blood elites, who held residual power and unfailingly found it repugnant to accept fraternal partnership with Ireland and its Catholics. Gladstone's successor as Liberal prime minister, Lord Rosebery, was unlike Gladstone part of the Liberals' pro-imperialist wing, but he lasted little more than a year before the Conservatives regained power under Lord Salisbury in the 1895 election.

When the Liberals returned to power in 1905 and cemented it by a landslide in 1906, the outgoing Conservative prime minister, Arthur Balfour, became leader of a greatly outnumbered opposition in Commons. Like his uncle and predecessor Lord Salisbury, Balfour was a member of the aristocratic Cecil family that rose to legendary prominence during the Tudor monarchy of the 16th century. Rather than accept the idea that the Liberals were fully in charge because of their landslide electoral victory, Balfour allowed the House of Lords, building on the precedent of the Irish controversy a decade earlier, to nullify a series of Liberal victories in the House of Commons, on Ireland and various other measures of political and economic reform.

This infuriated the Liberals and was a major factor in radicalizing the government's economic policy, which was already moving away from the limited-government, pro-people vision of Gladstone. Eventually the Liberals stripped the House of Lords of the last vestige of its power by having a reluctant King George V threaten to create hundreds of new peers. The decisive ideological change came in the form of the left-redistributionist 1909 budget crafted and pushed through by chancellor of the exchequer Lloyd George (who later forced the retirement of the moderate prime minister Asquith over war policy in 1916). As mentioned earlier, Lloyd George proved to be Britain's last Liberal prime minister, at least in part because his quasi-socialist economic views forced the British debate into a left-right, social-ist vs. capitalist pattern that continued well into the late 20th century. The swift emergence of the British left, inadvertently aided by the residual power and misconceived comeback attempted by Britain's conservative blood elite, had combined to deliver a severe blow to the conservative-enlightenment forces, in part by making a leader of Gladstone's type appear irrelevant in a country he had so recently dominated.

Lincoln, by contrast, never seemed irrelevant in the subsequent politics of the United States. This was partly because he won and the party he led to power survived to dominate American politics for the next 70 years. But it was also because the United States, with its ringing Declaration and written Constitution, was more deeply involved in the idea of universal God-given equality than was Britain, with its unwritten constitution and hierarchical sociopolitical order.

As for his opposition to conflict theory, Lincoln continued to be an anomaly in American politics in the 1870s and afterward. But the broadly based, unflagging hunger to study and understand Lincoln's life, and particularly his words and ideas, may be related to this aspect of his thought. He embodies an approach to politics felt to be lacking elsewhere; and many people (not all of them American) still seek it as an alternative to the pervasive zero-sum-game, pro-conflict premises that have so often given democratic politics a bad name.

Conflict Theory and the Rise of the Left in U.S. Politics

Still, in 1900, Britain and the United States were wealthy, effectively governed adherents of the conservative enlightenment, at a moment in time when (as we have seen) no sizable country on the European mainland could be said to meet that description. But the early 20th century was also a time when the left, stymied everywhere in Europe except France, began to break through in the English-speaking world. As noted, the socialist left rose in Britain at least in part because it opposed blood elites more vociferously than did conservative advocates of innate equality.

In the United States, the country most influenced by the ideas of the conservative enlightenment, the left's emergence took a different form. While some of the early American left did bring forward a socialist-leaning critique of capitalism and big-business monopolies or "trusts," the more important challenge came from within the broad national movement that came to be known as Progressivism.

Progressivism had both a populist and a left component. The populist strain was particularly successful in enacting such political reforms as direct election of U.S. senators, state-level initiative and referendum, and the party primary as a new means of nominating political candidates—outcomes by no means out of sync with the pro-democratic conservative enlightenment. The left Progressives, whose most effective publicist was *New Republic* founder Herbert Croly, influenced the administrations of Theodore Roosevelt and Woodrow Wilson in the direction of greater federal intervention in the economy.

At least equally striking was the left Progressives' blunt critique of the American founding. They argued that the decentralization and separation of powers in the Constitution were perhaps adequate for the first decades of national existence, but in the more complex reality of life in their own time, the Constitution had become cumbersome and—the ultimate insult in the eyes of left Progressives—unscientific. Croly and his acolytes were relentless centralizers, advocating what they described as a Hamiltonian approach to national policy. They resonated to such proposals as that of the younger Woodrow Wilson, who as a college professor had favored curbing America's plurality of power centers and replacing them with a form of parliamentary government. In part, of course, this was an American version of the drive toward unitary rule, already conventional wisdom in Europe on both the left and the right, which went hand-in-hand with the conflict theory of political progress. It also was consistent with the left's quasi-utopian impatience with delay, including the kind generated by the checks and balances instituted by America's founders.

In the short run, the left Progressives' overt attack on the founding went nowhere. By the time he entered politics in a successful race for governor of New Jersey in 1910, Wilson had dropped his support for parliamentary government after observing the strong presidencies of Grover Cleveland, William McKinley, and Theodore Roosevelt, although he still favored the increased role of American presidents as programmatic party leaders. As governor, Wilson was far more identified with the Progressives' populist emphasis on political reform, winning legislative approval of party primaries for New Jersey. And as Democratic nominee for president in 1912, Wilson, a lifelong admirer of Gladstone, advocated far less federal intervention in the economy than did his leading opponent, former President Roosevelt, who had been nominated by the newly formed Progressive Party.

Most left Progressives favored Roosevelt over Wilson, but the combination of the left Progressives' growing influence among elites and the demands of World War I pulled the Wilson administration increasingly toward increased federal intervention in the economy. Yet at the Versailles peace conference, the role Wilson carved out in the wake of his country's hugely successful intervention in the war was one with which Thomas Jefferson and Abraham Lincoln—not to mention Gladstone—might well have identified: pushing for democratic self-determination in the dozens of new countries created by the breakup of the Habsburg, Ottoman, and Russian empires.

The End of Ruling Monarchy

World War I was so destructive that many hoped it would be the war to end all wars. It was not that, but it did prove to be the war that decisively brought to a close humanity's age-old fascination with the institution of ruling monarchy. The suppression, between 1911 and 1922, of the dynasties ruling China, Russia, Germany, Austria-Hungary, and the Ottoman Turkish empire left only Japan among the major powers as a ruling monarchy. Suddenly nearly every country in Europe and quite a few elsewhere, including Turkey and China, either declared itself a republic or seemed to be taking on the contours of Britain as a parliament-centered regime with a royal figurehead. It was a stunning, unexpected breakthrough for the idea of political equality, the most consistent theme of the European Enlightenment.

Proponents of political equality were utterly unprepared for this breakthrough. Despite the encouraging start in the wake of Wilson's drive at Versailles for self-determination, democracy broke down or was shoved aside in most of Eurasia in the 1920s and 1930s (Russia's new republican government was extinguished by Lenin and the Bolsheviks after only a few months in 1917, well before the end of the war). The casualties included most of the new democracies of Europe, most importantly Germany and its Weimar Republic. The big winners were the anti-democratic left, in the form of Soviet Communism and the former Czarist possessions it forcibly reabsorbed as socialist "republics," as well as (preeminently) the anti-democratic right, in numerous variations of fascism and military-backed nationalist dictatorship. Rule by royal and aristocratic blood elites remained dead in Europe, but a far more sinister and threatening version of inequality had risen up to take its place.

Fascism and its cousins did not appear out of nowhere. Tempting as it is today to regard Europe between the two world wars as gripped by a kind of mass insanity, it did not feel that way to Europeans at the time. As much to its opponents as its advocates, Fascism had the look of the wave of the future. It was the logical outcome of a theory of politics as pure power that had been on the scene since Machiavelli and that had taken firm control of continental Europe in the second half of the 19th century, with its competitive and predatory empire-building. This Renaissance-born strain of European political theory was now steadily gaining strength against both versions of equality put forward by the Enlightenment—including the left's vision of class conflict leading to equality and liberation.

Hitler and Conflict Theory

The founder of Germany's Third Reich, Adolf Hitler (1889–1945), was a politician immersed in the ideas and battles of his own time. He was remarkable for the strength of his will and his ability to bend others to that will, rather than for any insight or originality in his thought. Although Austrian by birth, Hitler enlisted to fight in World War I for the German Second Reich, whose architect Otto von Bismarck was one of his heroes. He was deeply moved by Richard Wagner, both his music and his neo-pagan elevation of a constellation of prehistoric Aryan gods. Hitler extended the exaltation of the State that is a hallmark of 19th-century German nationalism, arguing that its sole and sacred purpose is "conservation of the racial characteristics of mankind." He brought to completion Europe's trend since the Renaissance toward unitary rule, abolishing Germany's parliament, the *Reichstag*, in all but a ceremonial sense and closing down all of Germany's state governments in favor of completely executive rule from Berlin. He despised modern finance capitalism, which he blamed on the Jews and correctly saw as a force for globalization.

With its roots in the German Romantic movement of the early 19th century, National Socialism included a self-consciously comprehensive rejection of the Enlightenment. The Nazis denigrated both variants of equality, the elite-guided future equality of the Marxists and the innate equality envisioned in the democratic-leaning conservative enlightenment. Another of Hitler's many accusations against the Jews was that they seduced Aryans into believing in equality; instead, they should accept "the truth that the principle underlying all Nature's operations is the aristocratic principle and . . . that this law holds good down to the last individual organism." Long before winning designation as chancellor in 1933, Hitler pledged to close down Weimar's parliamentary democracy, which he blamed for many of Germany's problems. He made good on his pledge within weeks of taking office.

Above all, Hitler's views were the ultimate elevation of conflict theory as an explicit denial of the potential for human concord, whether in the Judeo-Christian or Enlightenment versions: "Man must not fall into the error of thinking that he was ever meant to become lord and master of Nature," Hitler wrote in *Mein Kampf*. "Man must realize that a fundamental law of necessity reigns throughout the realm of Nature and that his existence is subject to the law of eternal struggle and strife. He will then feel that there cannot be a separate law for mankind in a world in which planets and suns follow their orbits, where moons and planets trace their destined paths, where the strong are always masters of the weak and where those subject to such laws must obey them or be destroyed."*

Traces of Europe's obsession with ancient Rome were present in Fascism, particularly (and predictably) in Mussolini's Italian version. The name "fascism" is itself derived from a Roman

---

* Adolf Hitler, *Mein Kampf* (Mumbai: Jaico Publishing House, 1988), 223–224.

symbol of authority, and the Italian Fascists and later the Nazis adopted the straight-armed Roman form of military salute. But there was no trace of the desire of the Holy Roman Empire or (later) of the left to unite Europe behind a shared set of values. A good working definition of fascism is hyper-nationalism, which, taken to its logical extreme, ends in doctrines of racial purity and in practices such as state-administered coercive eugenics, scientific experimentation on human beings, and genocide.

Defeat of the Axis powers in World War II marked the end of continental Europe's violent challenge to the Enlightenment. The forces of the conservative enlightenment and the left enlightenment, so often mutually antagonistic since the late 18th century, united to defeat both the imposing threat of post-monarchical inequality (as represented by Fascism and its variants) and the dying gasp of ethnocentric ruling monarchy represented by imperial Japan.

Beginning in 1945, for the first time in history, all the major political forces in the world were in some sense egalitarian. All paid lip service to democracy, not excluding the Soviet Union with its unanimous elections returning the Communist Party to power again and again. But even before the end of World War II, the Cold War began to take shape as (at least in part) a struggle between the two Enlightenment versions of equality: innate or democratic equality vs. Marxism-Leninism's version of conflict-driven, elite-managed equality of result. Marxism and other, more democratic versions of conflict theory were very much alive, but there was no longer a powerful conflict-driven ideology attempting to elevate a single nation or race as permanent master of all the others. The two versions of equality, strikingly different as they were, were alike in possessing a universal vision, in principle inclusive of all humanity.

After more than four centuries of preeminence, the nation-states of Europe were no longer the world's most powerful.

Between 1945 and 1975, they shed virtually all their overseas possessions. In the Cold War, Europe remained a key field of contention, but the leading contestants were not Britain, France, or Germany, but the United States and the Soviet Union—"new" countries whose foundations flowed from the egalitarian vision of the European Enlightenment, but either were not geographically European (in the case of the United States) or were at most only peripherally European (the Soviet Union).

At least as striking, the field of the Cold War spanned the entire globe. Far more than the two world wars, the conflict between Marxism-Leninism and its opponents was inescapable in places such as sub-Saharan Africa and Latin America. In effect, the period between 1945 and 1991 saw the clash between two interpretations of the European Enlightenment become the central subject of global politics, even as Europe itself, battered by the two world wars, receded as both a military force and a cultural influence.

9

THE END OF EUROPE

The Eurocentric phase of human history was over, but Europe's debate about its own identity was not. Amid the rubble of a second world war of European origin within 30 years, most Europeans seemed ready to leave racism, chauvinism, and dictatorship behind, opting instead to work out on their own the global implications of the Enlightenment.

European leaders were influential shapers of the Universal Declaration of Human Rights, adopted without a dissenting vote by the newly founded United Nations (the Communist countries abstained). Even though it claimed no theistic origin, this Declaration was an unapologetic assertion of absolute morality and natural rights reminiscent of the American Declaration of Independence, rights with their basis in a universal human dignity that rulers may not violate in the present, no matter how attractive their goals or unassailable their motives.

The European Coal and Steel Community, designed to put an end to predatory, zero-sum-game economic policies and later to evolve into the European Union, was shaped by the three leading countries of postwar continental Europe: France, Italy, and the Federal Republic of Germany (the democratic portion of a divided Germany with its capital in Bonn). The political leaders who conceived of and brought the treaty to completion, Robert Schuman of France, Alcide de Gasperi of Italy, and Konrad Adenauer of West Germany, were all devout Roman Catholics who believed revival and adaptation of Europe's age-old common aspirations were the best alternative to the near suicidal destructiveness epitomized by the two world wars. Whether by coincidence or not, the flag adopted by the community bore a strong resemblance to the halo of 12 golden stars depicted in the Book of Revelation as surrounding the vision of the Virgin Mary.

Europe's commitment to democracy proved more determined and successful than it had been in the wake of World War I. By the end of the 1970s, every non-Communist country in Europe had adopted democracy. The final western European country to go democratic was Spain, which did so after one of the continent's last avowed opponents of democracy, longtime dictator Francisco Franco, attempted to institute ruling monarchy by providing for a posthumous revival of the Bourbon dynasty. But following the death of Franco in 1975, the newly crowned King Juan Carlos took command of a successful movement to render himself a figurehead and bring parliamentary democracy to Spain. The post–World War II trend to democracy culminated in June 1979, when voters in the nine countries who were then members of the European Union (at the time called the European Community) simultaneously went to the polls to choose the first popularly elected European Parliament.

Europe's Democratic Paradox

Beneath the surface of democratic unanimity, though, the commitment of European elites to popular self-rule was less than wholehearted. The increasingly integrated European Union was a smashing success in economic terms, and countries (including Britain) that had at first been reluctant to join found themselves humbly petitioning for admission. But the political ground rules of the new Europe left room for a paradox. To qualify for the EU, a country had to have a democratic system of government; but once admitted, that same country could find itself deciding fewer and fewer important issues by a democratic vote of its people.

It was partly that elected national governments had ceded considerable power to the EU. But the key factor was that the elective European Parliament had only a narrowly circumscribed authority, and bureaucrats based in Brussels, the EU capital, were carrying out the bulk of policymaking. These bureaucrats in turn reported to an appointive European Commission. Composed of representatives of the member states, the commission functioned as an increasingly powerful unelected executive branch. There was some stirring of popular sentiment against this emerging pattern, but elected national elites in the member states remained largely quiescent.

Only after the climactic events of the Cold War in 1989 and 1991 did it become fully evident how decisive the 1960s had been to the politics and culture of Europe in comparison with the United States. In Chapter 7, I argued that the single biggest difference was not the impact of the 1960s on elite opinion—in both democratic Western Europe and the United States, institutions deferential to elite opinion realigned sharply in the direction of a revitalized, socially centered left—but the fact that in the U.S., popular opinion not only resisted the elites but moved in the opposite ideological direction. America's double realignment, evident as early as the presidential election of 1968, led to the rise of social conservatism which, by becoming the single biggest factor perpetuating ideological separation between popular and elite opinion, led to the persistent polarization that marks American politics to this day.

Conservative politicians in post-1960s Europe were still more than equal to beating back leaders of the old left, centered as many still were on fading quasi-socialist economic issues such as confiscatory taxation and nationalization of business. But a post–World War II resurgence of the conservative enlightenment in Europe proved to be a transitory reaction to the destructiveness at the heart of conflict theory in general, and to the nightmare of Hitler in particular. Leaders like Adenauer and de Gasperi were deeply respected, perhaps not so much as harbingers of the future as nostalgic throwbacks to a past moment a century or so earlier when Europe had faced a fork in its road, one where it might have turned toward the conservative enlightenment but in fact did not.

Adenauer and de Gaulle

The remarkable career of Konrad Adenauer illustrates the paradox of the conservative enlightenment in continental Europe—how effective it was capable of being, yet how limited its influence as a framework for other politicians. Adenauer first won a seat on the Cologne city council at the age of 30 in 1906 as a candidate of the Catholic-backed Center Party that had been so hated and feared by Bismarck. He went on to become a central player in founding the Christian Democratic Union (CDU), which became Germany's leading political party, in 1946 when he was 70; and he retired in 1966 when he was 90, after 20 years as its chairman.

Adenauer became mayor of Cologne in 1917 and president of the Prussian state council (which in the Weimar Republic was roughly equivalent to the U.S. Senate) in 1922. He held both offices until 1933, when the Nazis took power and removed him. Adenauer refused to shake the hand of a prominent Nazi official and, after being threatened with arrest, sought asylum in a monastery. Hitler's government imprisoned him three times, including in 1944 in the wake of the failed Claus von Stauffenberg coup d'état against Hitler, when Adenauer was sent briefly to a concentration camp and came close to death. He was released for lack of evidence.

In the formative period of the CDU, the party he helped found as an alliance between German Protestants and Catholics, Adenauer rejected Communism in an emphatic manner then unusual for Germans who had risked their lives opposing Nazism. At a time when most CDU theoreticians were attempting to fashion a left-of-center ideological merger between Christianity and socialism, Adenauer argued that politics needed to be centered instead in the God-given dignity of the individual. He delegated economic policy to Ludwig Erhard, an advocate of free markets who suddenly and unexpectedly ended all allied-imposed price controls and paved the way for what became known as the postwar German economic miracle.

Adenauer was elected four times as chancellor of the Federal Republic, serving from 1949 to 1963. Although he had little or no involvement in foreign policy in his prewar career, he became foreign minister as soon as the allies allowed Bonn to have one, in 1951, serving until 1955, and he remained the prime maker of West German foreign policy until his retirement as chancellor. He pursued a close alliance with the United States, enjoying a particular rapport with Eisenhower's secretary of state, John Foster Dulles, who was a believing Calvinist and a Wilsonian. He took Germany into NATO, and (as mentioned earlier) was one of the three prime political architects of the Coal and Steel Community and of the economic integration of Europe. Although he signed a peace treaty with the Soviet Union in 1955, winning recognition and (as a consequence) spurring the Soviet Union to release its German prisoners of war, he refused to recognize the Soviet-occupied German Democratic Republic. He succeeded in keeping the East German regime diplomatically isolated on the world stage during the remainder of his chancellorship. In the face of vehement domestic opposition, he won approval of German rearmament and of reparations for Israel.

Adenauer and the CDU were weakened in the national elections of 1961, and he was forced to reinstate a coalition with the small libertarian, secularist-leaning Free Democratic party, whose leaders disliked him. As their price for joining the government and keeping the Christian Democrats in power, the Free Democrats extracted an agreement from Adenauer to step down after two years of his new term as chancellor, in October 1963, when he would be three months short of his 88th birthday.

With his forced retirement approaching, Adenauer maneuvered to become president of the Federal Republic, a ceremonial job controlled by German party elites, to try to keep his hand in politics. He had little faith in his widely backed successor as chancellor, the economically brilliant but politically clueless Ludwig Erhard, and he wanted to hang on as a visible presence and stabilizer. But by then the leaders of the national parties, including his own CDU, believed that with a new spirit of détente gaining strength in the Kennedy administration and in Western Europe, the time for Adenauer's politics of moral leadership had passed.

Political elites were acutely aware that during his post–World War II career, almost all of which had taken place in his 70s and 80s, Adenauer had been consistently underestimated; but because of his declining poll ratings, they were no longer afraid of him. Rejected for the presidency, Adenauer did hold on to the chairmanship of the CDU for three more years, until 1966. He died a year later at 91. He had carried forward the values of the conservative enlightenment more successfully than any other leader did during its impressive continental revival after World War II. But like Gladstone at the end of the previous century, he was unique in his time, both as an exponent of the conservative enlighten- ment and a principled opponent of the left and of conflict theory. This isolated him in his success, and he had no successors or seri- ous imitators in his own party or country.

Yet as a virtual lame duck in his last two years as chancel- lor, Adenauer outperformed the expectations of European elites one last time. Seemingly marginalized as the West's last undi- luted cold warrior still in power, Adenauer surprisingly reached out to the most defiant European critic of America and its moral leadership in the Cold War, French President Charles de Gaulle. The result was a historic rapprochement between Germany and France, culminating in de Gaulle's becoming, in 1963, the first incumbent French leader to visit Germany since Napoleon last arrived with his armies.

Despite some obvious similarities—the two leaders were both elderly believing Catholics and champions of democracy who had bravely resisted the Nazis—their view of politics could not have been more different. Far from being an Adenauer-style internationalist, de Gaulle was a fierce and prickly nationalist who had negative things to say and do concerning virtually all his country's prominent international associations: NATO, the United Nations, economic integration within the EU, and alli- ances in two world wars with the United States and Great Britain. De Gaulle's nationalism even at times verged on racially tinged chauvinism, as in his 1967 visit to Canada in which he delivered a stunning and electrifying speech in Montreal all but urging the French-speaking province of Quebec to fight for freedom from English-speaking Canada. By mutual consent, de Gaulle's good- will tour of Canada was cut short before he could go through with a planned call on Canadian prime minister Lester Pearson.

De Gaulle did have a vision of a united Europe "from the Atlantic to the Urals," but he tended to define Europe not in terms of its shared values, but mostly in terms of the desirability of raising its power in relation to the other main power blocs of the world, particularly the bloc led by English-speaking peoples. It was widely noted that de Gaulle's designation of "the Urals" as an eastern boundary seemed to leave Europe's door open to the Soviet Union or at least Russia, but that his chosen western boundary of "the Atlantic" put the European eligibility of the British Isles into considerably greater doubt. In 1963, the same year as his historic visit to Germany, de Gaulle vetoed Britain's first application to join Europe's common market. In 1967, after several years of intricate negotiations, he vetoed Britain's second application. In 1966 he withdrew France from the joint military command of the North Atlantic Treaty Organization, whose headquarters had until then been in Paris.

Neither could the French president be counted as an advocate of a Gladstonian or Reaganite "morality in foreign policy" or as a critic of conflict theory. Asked once about France's friends, de Gaulle famously replied that "France has no friends, only interests."

De Gaulle's Critique of European Democracy

But for all his disdain for the values this book has described as the conservative enlightenment, on one surprising issue de Gaulle tried mightily to break away from a near universal feature of modern European democracy. He despised the parliamentary system that had characterized France's Third and Fourth Republics and most other European countries. In 1946, de Gaulle resigned as the first postwar premier of France because voters in the newly erected Fourth Republic adopted a parliamentary system nearly identical to the chaotic, party-elite-centered snake pit of the Third

Republic, which Nazi Germany had steamrollered earlier in that decade. When the French Army and leading politicians of both the left and right recalled him to power after a military uprising in 1958, de Gaulle consented to return on one condition: The new Fifth Republic he envisioned would replace France's parliamentary system with a strong, independently elected presidency. In this one respect, de Gaulle fervently wanted his country to become much more like the United States. Why?

After stating the necessity of our republic's founding—the assault by Britain on the "unalienable rights" the Creator gave us (and that British elites therefore had no right to take away)—the Declaration of Independence goes on to the real-time consequence: "That to secure these Rights, governments are instituted among Men, deriving their just Powers from the Consent of the Governed." The Declaration does not lay out a map or timetable of how this would proceed, nor does it describe what the new government would look like.

That proved to be wise, because the men who signed the Declaration had no blueprint to consult. A democratic republic with boundaries beyond those of a single city had never lasted for very long. The entities that were even remotely comparable—the Dutch Republic founded in 1588 and Britain's own constitutional monarchy ruled after 1688 mainly by its Parliament—had only a fraction of the territory claimed by the 13 colonies. Unlike the unchanging principles that animated the founding, how to erect a brand-new form of government executing these principles was not self-evident. A good amount of trial and error would be needed.

Three lessons learned by the founders and their immediate successors, all at least somewhat counterintuitive, are particularly important in illuminating the divergence between the U.S. and Europe: the unexpected vitality of religion when cut loose from entanglement with government; emergence of a separately elected, independent executive as a stronghold of democratic values; and the desirability of a plurality of power centers, rather than the unitary rule increasingly favored not only in Europe, but also by many of the founders themselves when it came to the state governments they set up under the Articles of Confederation.

The survival of ruling monarchy and aristocracy in continental Europe until World War I meant, among other things, that the latter two lessons were extremely difficult for Europeans to learn. In the 19th century, there was some plurality of power almost everywhere in Europe, but supporters of equality saw plural power as at best transitional, at worst something to fight tooth and nail, as the power centers were divided between democratic and undemocratic institutions within each state.

The near universality of parliamentary systems in Europe was likewise very much a function of the persistence of ruling monarchy. In most of Europe including England, parliament was a venerable institution left over from medieval times or even earlier, which meant that it had always coexisted with monarchy even when kings had rendered it powerless. In principle, it represented the legislative function of government, while the monarch represented the executive.

As the idea of political equality began to take hold in the wake of the Enlightenment, it was natural that election to parliaments became increasingly competitive and democratic. This was true even in the German, Russian, and Japanese empires, where ruling monarchs retained the lion's share of power until each country's defeat in a world war.

In countries where monarchy slowly and peacefully yielded power, republican reformers (who were invariably members of parliament) had no desire to provoke the local royalty by gratuitous insult. The cabinet continued to be referred to as "his majesty's government" or "the king's ministers." But the natural pathway to bringing the executive branch under greater democratic control was not replacing the king with a separately elected president, but gradually bringing the cabinet and executive branch under operational control of parliament.

This process of course enhanced the status of the head of the cabinet, the premier or prime minister, so the ability of a politician to gain favor among legislative elites tracked closely with his or her ability to gain power in the executive. In this way, the success of Europe's Renaissance monarchies in attaining unitary rule led invariably, with the advent of political equality, to unitary rule by a parliament that fully embodied both the legislative and executive functions. We saw in Chapter 7 how this first took place in Great Britain, not at all peacefully, between 1603 and 1688, years that coincide with the beginning and end of rule by the Stuart dynasty in England.

In Europe, only the rare country that had totally abolished monarchy while remaining (at least intermittently) democratic was capable of experimenting with an executive independent of the legislature, and the few such experiments had not proved uniformly satisfying. The election of Louis Bonaparte, nephew of Napoleon, as president of France's Second Republic in December 1848 led in stages to his crowning as Emperor Napoleon III in 1852. This Second Empire lasted until 1870, when, taken captive by the Prussian army during France's crushing defeat in the Battle of Sedan, the emperor abdicated and fled to England. France never again crowned a monarch, and republican political elites in France and elsewhere were understandably reluctant to allow future presidents full autonomy from parliament.

Even de Gaulle in 1958 did not demand such autonomy. The upgraded presidency he sought (and for which he was able to win approval by referendum) represented what was called a "second executive." The French National Assembly would serve up to five years, while the president was to be separately elected to a fixed seven-year term. The president, the elected head of state, would select the premier, who, assuming he could assemble a parliamentary majority, would be confirmed as head of government. If the president's choice as premier proved unable to nail down a majority (or lost his majority mandate once he was a confirmed incumbent), the president would be free either to choose someone else or dissolve the legislative branch, triggering new elections for the National Assembly. The president's own seven-year term would continue to completion unaffected, unless he died or chose to resign, in which case an election for a new seven-year term would quickly be held. The Fifth Republic has no vice president, so a presidential vacancy was to be filled on an interim basis by the president of the senate, a relatively marginal body elected not by the people but by several thousand local officials.

De Gaulle won his first seven-year term in late 1958 by vote of an electoral college of notables, but in 1962 he won approval in a national referendum of direct popular election of the president, effective in 1965. If no one received a majority of the votes in the first round, a second election would be held between the two top finishers. (In the 1965 election, de Gaulle needed a second round to defeat Socialist candidate François Mitterand, 55 to 45 percent.) De Gaulle and his party did well in legislative elections, but he preferred to settle debates of paramount importance, such as his plan to end France's colonial war in Algeria, by referenda, which in the Fifth Republic the president has the right to call at any time; if approved, they have the force of law.

Another institutional change de Gaulle achieved was abolition of proportional representation, the elective system used in the Third and Fourth Republics and that the older democracies of Europe had overwhelmingly adopted (it's since been adopted for elections to the European Parliament as well). Historians tend to give it minimal attention in comparison with the Fifth Republic's independently elected presidency, but this reform was vital to de Gaulle's plan to end the chronic weakness and instability of the Third and Fourth Republics.

Taken at face value, proportional representation is the most pro-democratic of all voting systems: It attempts to match the exact voting strength of a political party with its representation in parliament. In reality, such a system keeps in existence minor parties (like the Free Democrats in Germany) that could get nowhere if they had to win actual elections in districts around the country. Such a system in practice makes it nearly impossible for any one party to win a majority of seats, and it invariably results in a system of brokered rule by national elites from multiple parties. Of all democratic systems, centralized rule by a parliament chosen by proportional representation puts the greatest number of barriers between voters and their leaders.

Just as de Gaulle attempted to make the French system more "American" by means of a strong, independently elected presidency, in replacing proportional representation with a system of direct voting for each district of the National Assembly, he was making France's parliamentary system far more like Britain's. The British election system, widely imitated by other English-speaking or British-influenced parliamentary democracies (including the world's largest democracy, India) is known as "first past the post"—a term from horse-racing that Americans translate as "winner take all."

De Gaulle's election reforms were successful in making French politics both more decisive and more responsive to changes in sentiment among the voters. Against the expectations of his critics, many of whom tended to assume that anything de Gaulle favored was a mere pretext to enhance his own status, these changes led to a marked decline in the dysfunctionality that had plagued the Third and Fourth Republics, not to mention European neighbors such as Italy and Germany that have continued to operate with parliaments chosen at least in part by proportional representation.

But it must also be said that a centralized French political culture so steeped in centuries of conflict politics aiming at unitary rule has had a hard time grasping the possibility, much less the desirability, of plural rule, a view of politics that sees multiple power centers as a good rather than an anomaly or an inconvenient impediment. For all its grandeur, the Fifth Republic presidency ultimately has limited ability to govern without the cooperation of France's parliament. On the two occasions when a Fifth Republic president of one party served for a time with a National Assembly and premier of a different party, it was dubbed "cohabitation"—a term implying illicit union.

When a president won an election and confronted a National Assembly in which his allies were in the minority, the new president's ultimate dependence on France's parliament made it natural for him to dissolve the National Assembly and try to prevail in new legislative elections, rather than attempt to work out a trans-partisan consensus on policy changes. This proved comparatively easy for a newly elected Fifth Republic president to pull off, given that he was fresh from winning a national mandate and was willing to tell voters that the makeup of parliament made his mandate impossible to carry out. In a presidential system in which the executive and legislative branches are truly independent of each other, emergence of such a pattern would be seen as a dangerous erosion of legislative independence. By enacting fixed and unalterable dates of election for both the legislative and executive branches, the American founders made sure that the earliest a newly elected president could seek to change Congress is toward the end of his second year.

By the time Gaullist president Jacques Chirac ran for reelection in 2002, he was seeking not a second seven-year term but a five-year term. Uncomfortable with the presidency's superior prestige with voters, French elites in 1990 had reduced the presidential term to make it no lengthier than the maximum duration of the republic's legislative branch. Equally striking, in 1986 proportional representation was restored for elections to the National Assembly. When the elections that year produced a conservative majority that brought on a two-year "cohabitation" between the right and Socialist president François Mitterand, the nation reverted to winner-take-all districts for the subsequent election. Yet no less than the reduction of the presidential term, this episode underlined that the reforms de Gaulle had set forth as essential could easily become expendable once he was gone from the scene. It also underlined the fact that centralized parliamentary constitutions are quite easy to amend by whoever at that moment has the legislative majority.

France's centuries of commitment to centralized, unitary rule—earlier by monarchs such as Louis XIV, more recently by elected legislative elites—had not fundamentally changed; nor is it clear that de Gaulle, for all his contrarian creativity, really wanted it to. In the last analysis, France and Western Europe continued to assume that the centering of power, if not in one man, at least in one elite political institution was the most sensible way to adapt the compelling new idea of political equality to the reality of human nature. In important respects, this made European parliamentary democracies similar to Renaissance monarchies enfolded by burgeoning court bureaucracies

De Gaulle's economic policy, centered on greater gold backing for France's currency and ending the Fourth Republic's chronic inflation via introduction of the New Franc, gave the French economy of the 1960s one of its most impressive periods of growth in recent history. Yet in spite of his many successes— and these most certainly included, in the eyes of millions of

French voters, his willingness to elevate France at the expense of the United States and Britain—de Gaulle proved to be the most visible European victim of the 1968 upheavals.

De Gaulle's Diagnosis of 1968

As argued earlier in this book, the social and political unrest of the 1960s originated in the United States in the midst of a high-profile victory for the Enlightenment vision of social and political equality: the 1964–1965 enactment of civil rights laws protecting American blacks. The explosion of left protest that came to be called the Movement later took on an antiwar coloration, but it is often forgotten or underemphasized that major student unrest *preceded* any protest against the Vietnam war. It began on elite college campuses, starting with the University of California at Berkeley in 1964, and the initial target was institutional restrictions on student freedom and behavior on the college campuses themselves. These issues included demands for free speech in public places and the existence of "parietals," a now nearly forgotten word describing various university-imposed restrictions, often concerning men's access to women's dormitories. To many observers at the time, the Movement's rage seemed centered not so much on the restrictions themselves as on the institutions imposing them.

Reinforcing this impression is the fact that early participants in the Movement, as well as its rapidly increasing brigade of sympathizers, were articulating no dissatisfaction with the civil rights movement or the civil rights legislative agenda Congress was then struggling to map out. Mario Savio, the Berkeley student who was the first effective leader of the Movement (which at the time consisted mainly of professors and other members of the intellectual elite) was himself a civil rights activist recently returned from organizing in the South.

Rather, intellectual elites seemed to experience a wave of doubt as to whether the kind of political equality belatedly extended to American blacks—the kind of equality set forth in the Declaration and by Lincoln at Gettysburg—would prove at all adequate to their needs. Would the kind of civil and voting equality that President Johnson was pushing through Congress turn out to be a virtually meaningless palliative in the face of the oppressive power exercised by American institutions? And even assuming the civil rights bills would prove more than a palliative, what of the many other inequalities—e.g., of Latinos, Native Americans, women—that American culture and its corrupt institutions were enforcing every day? A movement that began as a drive for student liberation from deans and their regulations had, somewhat surprisingly, morphed into an assault on virtually every American institution.

The unrest several years later in the France of 1968 also started on campus with issues of student liberation, at the University of Nanterre on the outskirts of Paris. The French movement's first and most vivid leader, Daniel Cohn-Bendit, was the son of a German Jewish couple who escaped Hitler by emigrating to France in the 1930s. Born in 1945, Cohn-Bendit was raised in France but opted for German citizenship because France had military conscription and West Germany did not.

In March 1968, "Danny the Red," as he came to be called, led a protest against his school's officials in which students occupied the administration offices and shut down the university for a day. Cohn-Bendit's main grievances had to do with sexual freedom on campus, in particular the ability of men to visit women in their dorms. By May, the protest had spread to another university, the fabled Sorbonne in Paris, expanding at warp speed into an across-the-board attack on French institutions. Even though the nation's powerful labor unions and its Communist Party, second to Italy's CP in the democratic world in terms of vote-getting, were baffled by the uprising and tried to remain in a stance of skeptical neutrality, eleven million workers were on strike by the second half of May, virtually shutting down the national economy. No one seemed to know why. Certainly no one had predicted it.

The ruling Gaullists internalized the magnitude of the crisis far more quickly than did France's old left. In particular, premier Georges Pompidou, a former academic who six years earlier had been raised from obscurity by President de Gaulle despite vehement objections from much of the political elite, grasped that the government's survival depended on separating the grievances of the striking workers from those of the radical, unpredictable student progenitors of the revolt. He negotiated a generous package of pay and benefit increases for labor but deployed police to crack down on the students and intellectuals. Pompidou talked de Gaulle into calling a snap election for the National Assembly only one year after the previous one, and the Gaullists and their conservative allies went from a thin majority to nearly three-fourths of the members. De Gaulle, at this point 78 years old with four years remaining in his second presidential term, now had a legislative majority big enough to pass nearly any package of reforms he cared to submit.

But even though de Gaulle in the short run made all the decisions he needed to regain the upper hand, he seemed to sense that what had taken place was more than a violent passing storm accidentally ignited by a handful of horny collegians. At one point during the lockdown of his country, he flew to Germany to confer with an old army friend who commanded the French forces still stationed there as a result of post–World War II occupation agreements. De Gaulle did this without telling his own head of government where he had gone. De Gaulle at first resisted Pompidou's push for new elections, arguing instead for a national referendum.

With the election returns in and simple math showing the Gaullists more dominant than ever, de Gaulle immediately fired Pompidou, the prime architect of his victory, and began formulating the referendum he would submit to the French electorate in April 1969. He made clear, as he always did with each of his referenda, that it would either win approval or he would resign the presidency. This time the electorate, perhaps having had its fill of melodrama from both the new left and de Gaulle, called his bluff and rejected his package of reforms, 52.4 percent to 47.6 percent. De Gaulle promptly resigned, Pompidou was overwhelmingly elected president later that year, and de Gaulle died a year later in 1970, just short of his 80th birthday.

Yet even in this final episode, when de Gaulle seemed to be needlessly inviting political oblivion, he was more focused than ever on the need for structural reform and expansion of French democracy. The theme of his campaign was "participation." The targets for enhanced popular self-government were the universities—the trigger of the 1968 crisis—the moribund French Senate, and the state and local governments. Regarding the latter, he proposed to significantly decentralize decision-making, an idea that had been almost totally absent in French politics since the 17th century.

Like most French leaders since the 1790s, de Gaulle was no friend of the conservative enlightenment, yet neither did he believe it was acceptable for the left to set the national agenda. More than any of his conservative allies, he sensed that while 1968 with its stunning signs of institutional breakdown may not have been an existential threat to the regime, it was in fact a grave warning sign for European civilization as a whole. His drive for increased popular participation and empowerment was brought to an abrupt halt by rejection of his 1969 reforms, but his sense of urgency turned out to be more in accord with reality than the attitude of leaders like Pompidou who more adroitly rode the storm in the short run.

The origin of the 1968 near-revolution in a campus drive for sexual liberation did not prove as odd or anomalous as appeared at the time. One of the best-known signs carried in the mass demonstrations, widely attributed to Danny Cohn-Bendit, could have been written by Rousseau: "It is forbidden to forbid."

During the de Gaulle presidency, France was by some measures more sexually conservative than the United States. The contraceptive pill, introduced in the United States in 1960, did not become legal in France until 1967. But as mentioned in Chapter 7, by 1974 a newly elected president allied with the Gaullists was pressing for permissive abortion laws and prevailing with little opposition. In the 1960s, a decade in which the divorce rate soared in the U.S. and Britain, it was relatively stable in France. But beginning in the 1970s, it took off.

Europe and the U.S. Part Ways

There are today a number of well-known economic and social divergences between Europe and the United States. Unemployment rates have been consistently higher in Europe. So are taxes and transfer payments (entitlements) as a share of GDP. Hours worked in a given week or year are significantly higher for workers in the United States than in Europe. So is weekly church attendance. So is the female fertility rate, the main factor in determining population growth or the lack thereof.

It is sometimes assumed that these differences date from 1945 or even earlier. In large part they do not. They date from around the mid-to-late-1960s. Until then, for example, Europe's democracies had notably *lower* unemployment rates than the United States did. Even church attendance, one of the most striking differences today, was not nearly as divergent in the 1960s.

Warning signs of the political dimension of Europe's new trajectory began to appear in the 1970s and 1980s. For all the embarrassment of the European left in missing the revolutionary moment of 1968, in these two subsequent decades, it achieved some of its best post–World War II showings at the polls. The Italian Communists peaked at 34 percent in the national election of 1976, and the French Communists became full election partners of the Socialist Party for the first time in the 1981 presidential runoff, helping François Mitterand oust incumbent Valery Giscard d'Estaing. Thus began the first left presidency in the 23rd year of the Fifth Republic, one that would last 14 years. Similarly, the West German Social Democrats (SPD), never having led a government since the beginning of the Federal Republic in 1948, held the chancellorship without a break from 1969 to 1982.

The European left at times acquired even greater momentum outside the framework of elections. In 1974, Marxist army officers overthrew a long-ruling civilian dictatorship in Portugal and came within an eyelash of rolling up NATO's southwestern flank. In the late 1970s and early 1980s, the nuclear-freeze movement turned out millions of people in the streets in opposition to deployment in Europe of American medium-range missiles, a deployment meant to counter a massive Soviet medium-range missile buildup that threatened to achieve stark Warsaw Pact nuclear dominance over NATO in any future crisis.

By then, however, Ronald Reagan and Margaret Thatcher were gaining power in the two countries most identified with the forces of the conservative enlightenment. Perhaps even more important from Europe's vantage point, a politically sophisticated Polish cardinal named Karol Woytila had been crowned Pope John Paul II in October 1978, breaking a centuries-long chain of Italian popes and thrusting deeply and unexpectedly into the heart of Soviet imperial unity.

Beginning in the early and mid-1980s, Western Europe's leaders, most emphatically including democratic socialists such as France's Mitterand and Helmut Schmidt of West Germany, answered the call of revived American leadership and overcame the powerful opposition of the nuclear-freeze movement, which at its peak extended to the streets of Britain and the United States and even won tacit endorsement by the national conference of U.S. Catholic bishops. But the tough, persistent leadership of an older generation of European politicians tended to obscure how eager Europe's emerging post-1968 elites were to decouple from American leadership in the climactic stages of the Cold War. It seems possible Europe's new left might well have succeeded in distancing itself from the U.S. had the Soviet empire itself not been in the midst of what proved to be its terminal crisis. The opening of the Berlin Wall on November 9, 1989, marked the irrevocable end of the Warsaw Pact and the division of Europe.

On December 25, 1989, Leonard Bernstein led a continent's celebration by conducting Beethoven's Ninth Symphony with a stupendous multinational orchestra and chorus in Berlin. The lyric of the climactic "Ode to Joy" was changed for the occasion to "Ode to Freedom." In the following year, a little too swiftly for the taste of either Prime Minister Thatcher or President George H. W. Bush, Christian Democratic chancellor Helmut Kohl engineered the reunification of Germany. Two years to the day after the Bernstein concert in Berlin, Soviet president and Communist Party chairman Mikhail Gorbachev ordered the flag of the Soviet Union lowered in the Kremlin for the last time.

The European Union and Elite Rule

In the 1990s, most of Europe wanted to be democratic; nation-states far removed from the North Atlantic lined up to join NATO, and *every* government seemed to want to be a member

228

of the European Union. The economic ground rules of the EU made this far from a simple task for countries emerging from top-down Marxist autocracy, yet winning EU permission at least to begin the process came to be seen as a sine qua non not simply of becoming good Europeans, but of qualifying for the freedom and affluence of modern life itself.

In the first years of the new millennium, a surge of admissions raised the number of EU member states from 15 to 25 in 2004. The ambitions implicit in the European Union's name seemed on the verge of being fulfilled. Europe's many centuries of oscillation between unity and division was to be resolved in decisive victory for freely chosen unity. It now seemed appropriate for Europe to ratify this decision by agreeing to a federal constitution.

When it came to drafting it, the elective elites of the member countries deferred to bureaucrats in Brussels, and they produced seventy thousand words—10 times the length of the American Constitution, which unlike Europe's had been hammered out from below, by delegates from each of the 13 states.

Disorder and squabbling had marked the Articles of Confederation, and it was therefore assumed in Philadelphia that ratification by states from diverse regions with sharply differing demographics would be difficult; the delegates accordingly fought hard for provisions needed to satisfy local electorates. Because the states found it far easier to agree on a few core principles than on a detailed blueprint, the Constitution was of necessity concise, and the new powers of the central government were limited and carefully defined.

Undoubtedly, the drafters two centuries later in Brussels thought they were exercising at least comparable foresight. They included many, many human rights beyond the basic ones in American constitutional law, and they were far more explicit in spelling out ways and means of administering them. But lacking more than a tenuous political connection to the governments involved, the drafters' method was to anticipate every significant potential problem and spell out a mechanism for dealing with it. Like most bureaucrats, they favored bureaucratic procedures.

These left room for very little democratic debate or decision-making by voters in the 25 member states. The elected European Parliament was not given a central role in making new laws. Laws were to be initiated by the Council of Ministers, subject in most cases to ratification by the Parliament. The Council (prior to the constitution known as the Commission) was to be chosen from among the heads of government of the member states. The Council was also to choose the cabinet and (after a lead time of a few years) the president of Europe for up to two terms of two and one-half years each, subject to approval by the Parliament.

So in a way, the unelected executive branch enjoyed a role reversal with the directly elected Parliament. The executive was to craft the legislation, subject only to a veto by the legislators, even though the legislators were the only people democratically elected for the purpose of governing Europe as a whole. On some issues, the Parliament would not even have a veto. All this was to come in the context of increased power for Brussels and reduced power in the 25 capitals.

The participating governments had delegated supervision of the drafting to a committee in 2001, and the text was ready for approval by the member states in 2004, the year the EU expanded from 15 countries to 25. In countries whose constitutions required ratification only by elected political elites, there was not so much as a close vote or serious debate. However, a few countries required direct ratification by voters. These included two of the strongest advocates of European unity, France and the Netherlands, both of which had been among the six founding members of the Coal and Steel Community a half century earlier. In late May and early June of 2005, French and Dutch voters rejected the constitution in referenda held within a few days of each other. Because unanimous consent of all EU members was required, the constitution became a legal nullity.

Except that it really wasn't. EU elites made virtually no changes in the rejected document but decided to submit it for ratification as a set of amendments to previous EU treaties instead of as a stand-alone constitution. This meant that no electorates on the continent would need to approve the "Treaty of Lisbon" for the European constitution to go into effect. Only Ireland has a constitutional requirement for voter approval of treaties, and Ireland had experienced an economic boom since its admission to the EU. Nonetheless, Ireland's voters rejected the treaty in June 2008, 53.4 percent to 46.6 percent.

Ireland is a republic with an intense commitment to self-determination developed over its centuries of contention with Great Britain. The preamble to its constitution invokes the trinitarian God of Christians and the first human right the document mentions is the right to self-determination. The only way to amend the Irish constitution is by a direct vote of the people, and even repackaging the European Constitution as a "treaty" did not remove the need for a referendum, according to well-established Irish supreme court decisions, and given the significant changes mandated in Irish governance should the treaty win approval.

To a far greater degree than in France or the Netherlands in 2005, Ireland's 2008 rejection of the constitution was powered by populist, pro-democratic resentment of the oligarchic shape of the new Europe. In fact the grassroots anti-constitutional campaign in Ireland, which prevailed over political elites from all three major parties, was consistent with the belief system of the conservative enlightenment. Given its antimonarchical history and constitution, Ireland is as close as any country in the EU to an explicit belief in a God-given birthright of political equality. In June 2008, Irish voters appeared as reluctant to surrender this heritage to bureaucrats in Brussels as to the King of England or the British parliament a century earlier.

According to the EU's ground rules for ratification, rejection by any one of the (now) 27 member states meant the constitution was rejected. Moreover, the Irish vote brought latent opposition in Eastern Europe into the open, particularly from the Czech Republic and its populist conservative president, Vaclav Klaus. But EU elites were no more disconcerted by this voter rejection than they had been in 2005 by the French and Dutch rejections, or (going back to 1992) rejection of the Maastricht Treaty by the voters of Denmark. With full cooperation from Irish political and business elites, and amid new assurances from Brussels that Ireland could retain its low corporate tax rates and prohibition of abortion, still another Irish referendum on the Lisbon Treaty was slated for October 2009.

By the time of this second vote, Ireland's decade-long economic boom had been sent abruptly into reverse by the global banking crisis, beginning in late 2007 with the U.S. real estate crash, which became a worldwide recession in the second half of 2008. The Ireland of spring 2008 was still confident of its economic future. The Ireland of fall 2009, with plunging home values and an unemployment rate of 12.6 percent, was not. In the second referendum, economic as well as political elites were far from shy about predicting even harder times should Ireland effectively sever its ties with the vast, integrated economy of mainland Europe. Sharply reversing its vote of little more than a year earlier, Ireland gave the Lisbon Treaty a landslide victory of 67 percent. A new European superstate, 27 nations strong, was well on its way to becoming reality.

The second Irish referendum took place almost exactly 20 years after the dismantling of the Berlin Wall, which effectively ended Europe's division into a democratic West and an autocratic East. It had been only 10 years since the fall of Serbian strongman

Slobodan Milosevic ended Europe's last mini-empire, spinning off seven independent states committed to democracy. Why, so soon after the seemingly definitive triumph of political equality in Europe, were more than two dozen independent countries, home to more than half a billion people, willing to give up not only much of their sovereignty, but also a large portion of their claim to democratic self-government?

Despite the intermittent tension between Europe's electorates and its political elites, the process of unifying Europe was in no sense characterized by political polarization. Because political elites of the left, right, and center were overwhelmingly in favor of political integration, there was little in the way of an articulate political debate, even in most of the countries where referenda took place. The debate that did happen was mainly economic, and because the economics of a single market had always invariably proven to be pro-growth dating back to the European Coal and Steel Community of the 1950s, advocates of further integration enjoyed a built-in advantage.

Post-1960s Europe and Relativism

Contrary to the expectation of many conservatives, the universally recognized role of Pope John Paul II as the catalyst for the breakup of the Warsaw Pact did not lead to a revival for religion in any significant precinct of Europe, with the possible exception of Poland itself. Moreover, at a time when Vatican II, greatly influenced by the American Jesuit thinker John Courtney Murray, had brought Roman Catholicism to a vision of democracy and human freedom—including freedom of religion—as moral imperatives consistent with innate human dignity, European elites after the 1960s were firmly moving toward the enshrinement of moral relativism. These elites welcomed the post–Cold War breakthrough to democracy, but now virtually all of them (in contrast to Adenauer and the other key architects of post-war Europe) rejected Christianity and natural law as democracy's moral underpinning. Casting a baleful eye over Europe's violent, predatory history between 1600 and 1945, they arrived at a consensus that intense belief was itself the chief culprit, and that tolerance must therefore become the supreme value of the new Europe.

But of its nature, systematic elevation of tolerance severely constricts political choice. In the American founding, social issues were assigned to the state and local communities who would have to live with the outcomes. The premise of today's European Union is that decentralized moral debate, and any resultant diversity of outcome as to community standards, is over time the chief threat to peace, and must therefore be removed as a possibility whenever possible. It's true that during the 2009 referendum, Irish voters were assured by EU elites that they would be permitted to maintain their restrictive policy on abortion, but there is nothing in the European constitution as written that backs up such assurances. Europe-wide criminal law and social standards are defined as supreme, overriding national preferences in the event of conflicts.

Europe's belief in tolerance as the underpinning of democracy constricted the subject matter open to debate, as well as the circle of permissible participants. In 2004, Rocco Buttiglione, an influential member of the Italian cabinet, was nominated to be an EU cabinet member (commissioner) with a portfolio of justice, freedom, and security. He was effectively turned down for the appointment by a committee of the European Parliament, on the grounds that as an orthodox Catholic he could not be trusted to enforce provisions (such as homosexual rights) with which he disagreed, despite his stated willingness to enforce such laws and a past record in Italy of having done so. In this instance, tolerance as the inviolable basis of European democracy produced a decision that looked remarkably like intolerance toward traditional Christian believers.

This was even more strikingly evident when John Paul II pressed for an acknowledgment of Europe's Christian roots to be included in the preamble to the European constitution during its 2001–2004 drafting phase. With minimal debate among European elites, the pope was firmly rebuffed. Including even a mention of Christianity in the seventy-thousand-word document, it was decided, would put at risk the tolerance needed to sustain modern democratic institutions.

Given that no one could seriously argue that Christianity was a non-factor in the shaping of Europe, it was quickly recognized that the decision to omit any mention of it was far more significant as a statement about Europe's future than its past. The political authorities of the emerging European superstate were attempting to exclude traditional Christian morality from any possible role or revival in public life by placing it explicitly outside normal politics. It was not an attempt to preclude the possibility of established religion, in the manner of the First Amendment adopted by the United States in 1789. It was an attempt to discourage civil strife and warfare by relativizing all moral beliefs, with the sole exception of tolerance itself.

In November 2009, the last holdout against ratification of the European constitution, President Vaclav Klaus of the Czech republic, became the 27th and decisive signer. Just days before he reluctantly signed, Klaus gave an interview to *National Review* in which he compared the new European Union to the old Warsaw Pact, with Soviet rule from Moscow giving way to faceless bureaucratic rule from Brussels.[*]

---

[*] "The World with Vaclav Klaus," Chapter 2, *National Review Online*, November 10, 2009 (interview by Peter Robinson).

As if to underline the point, the first EU president, elected unanimously following a series of closed-door meetings reminiscent of the Politburo, was Herman van Rompuy, who had been serving for less than a year as premier of Belgium and was virtually unknown elsewhere in Europe. An even more obscure British trade negotiator, Baroness Catherine Ashton, was chosen as High Representative of the Union for Foreign Affairs and Security Policy; she had never won or even sought elective office of any kind. Her best claim to experience in security issues was her role in the early 1980s as national treasurer of the Committee for Nuclear Disarmament, a British peace group that was later found to have accepted secret subsidies from the Soviet Union.

In choosing Rompuy, EU elites passed over one of the most successful and best-known politicians on the world stage, Tony Blair. Here was a gifted politician who had won parliamentary majorities in three British elections—more than any other Labour Party leader in history—and served as prime minister from 1997 to 2007. The EU rejected Blair in part because he was close to the Bush administration, particularly when it came to the 2003 invasion of Iraq, in which Blair became Bush's most influential foreign supporter. But it is also true that many members of the EU establishment feared that Blair might turn an undemocratically chosen presidency into an institution with a broader popular base. That, after all, was the genesis of the U.S. presidency: By the 1830s, under the leadership of a series of politically gifted, democratically inclined presidents from Jefferson to Jackson, the elitist electoral college of the republic's early years was transformed into a broad-based popular process.

But if the EU presidency has any potential to evolve in such a manner, the mind-set of today's EU elites does not encourage such hopes. A 2005 description by Vaclav Klaus still seems to apply: "In Europe we've witnessed the crowding out of democracy by post-democracy—a bureaucratic unification of the European continent that tilts government upwards to the level where there is no democratic accountability, and the decisions are made by politicians appointed by politicians, not elected by citizens in free elections."[*]

It thus appears that European elites have carried out a peaceful antidemocratic revolution that has to a considerable degree reversed the democratic revolutions that followed World War II and the Cold War. There was popular opposition to this top-down transformation, as indicated by the referenda in France and the Netherlands (2005), and particularly Ireland (2008). But when EU elites decided to change the rules of the game by enacting the constitution in the form of a "treaty," popular protest on the continent was negligible; and opposition in Great Britain and Ireland was similarly sporadic and transitory, despite these two countries' deeply rooted affinity with the pro-democratic spirit of the conservative enlightenment.

Political elites in formerly Communist countries in Central and Eastern Europe, particularly in Poland and the Czech Republic, did seem to have qualms about going along with a partial rollback of the democratic revolution from which they had so recently benefited. But the aura of modernization and affluence associated with the EU's successful history of economic integration seems to be overcoming such qualms in the ex-Marxist lands as well.

The ease of this transition from democratic to increasingly bureaucratic rule suggests that the crucial decision point for Europe was not the Communist collapse of 1989–1991 but the victory of the social-issue-centered left in the 1960s and 1970s. This is underlined by the fact that the decline of Europe's fertility, work effort, and religious observance—the demographic

---

[*] "The Intellectuals and Socialism: As Seen from a Post-Communist Country Situated in Predominantly Post-Democratic Europe," speech by Czech President Vaclav Klaus to the Mont Pelerin Society, Reykjavik, Iceland, August 22, 2005.

facts that most separate Europe from the United States today, as well as from an earlier Europe—date from the social and sexual revolutions that flattened all remaining political opposition in the Europe of the 1960s and 1970s.

The biggest recent surprise is the palpable connection between Rousseau-type social revolution—the march through the institutions first laid out nearly a century ago by Marxism's Frankfurt School—and the apparent willingness of the European public to let go of democracy itself. Part of the phenomenon lies in the fact that European democracy has almost always lacked mechanisms (party primaries, popular initiatives and referenda, etc.) that invite voters to take back control of political life from runaway elites. This absence is particularly evident in centralized parliamentary regimes in which becoming national nominee of a major party need never involve facing more than a small fragment of the national electorate. In such systems, the path to power is much more a function of winning the favor of political elites than of electorates, and power is almost by definition self-perpetuating. (This is the system de Gaulle detested as inbred and toxic and attempted to reform with his addition of an electorate-driven French presidency.)

Europe's Great Transition

But all this raises a further question: Why did Europe arrive at such elitist versions of democratic rule in the first place? Put another way, why did the apparent triumph of political equality—seen as a logical consequence of the Enlightenment in both 1848 (the year of Europe's multinational popular rebellion against blood elites) and in 1948 (ratification of the Universal Declaration of Human Rights)—add up to so little in the land of the original Enlightenment?

The short answer is that democracy, the real-time fulfillment of political equality, is not the most highly valued outcome in the eyes of Europe's triumphant left enlightenment. This should come as no surprise to anyone who accepts (as does this book) the continuity of the left from Rousseau and Robespierre to the present. The left, whether in its Marxist, pre-Marxist, or post-Marxist phase of today, has always been mainly about the crushing of traditional social institutions to pave the way for autonomous human freedom.

This core identity of the global left is today affirmed in China, the largest country where a Communist Party has managed to maintain a political monopoly through the upheavals of the 1960s and the collapse of European Communism in 1989–1991. Beginning in 1978, Chinese political elites shed their ideological commitment to a government-run Marxist economy. But when it comes to the Party's ongoing commitment to suppressing the independence of society's two most powerful social institutions, the traditional family and religion, they have remained rigidly loyal to their ideology.

In most of Europe, the left succeeded in neutering these institutions in a democratic context. In Central and Eastern Europe, post–World War II Marxism-Leninism seemingly did most of the job. In a single country, Poland, the marginalization of religion has not yet happened and democratic Poland has prohibited most abortions, but the continuation of a very low fertility rate suggests that the nuclear family has not found its way to a positive turning point in even this predominantly anti-left country.

Even if fertility did turn upward in Poland or in other European countries, the persistent demographic trends of Europe (as well as of Japan) are becoming more and more unforgiving. That is, even if Europe regained the fertility rate of 2.1 children per woman at which populations eventually stabilize, whichever generation of women returns to that birth rate will be far smaller than needed to avoid sharp population declines in the immediate decades ahead.

Even such a limited turning point seems unlikely, particularly in Western Europe, with its heavy taxation of families and cradle-to-grave entitlements increasingly unsupportable by a rapidly aging work force. The bureaucratic, elitist trend of EU political governance makes anything approaching a democratic debate on Europe's demographic plight very difficult to imagine. Indeed, the emphasis in climate-change policy on sharply reducing industrial-related emissions casts a kind of virtuous backlight on Europe's demographic and economic decline.

A retrospective look at 15 centuries of European history suggests that, contrary to the expectations of Tocqueville and so many others, the idea of political equality never gained a solid foothold in continental Europe (the British Isles are a somewhat distinct case). Europe has never overcome its origin in post–Roman Empire tribal politics. The politically competitive civilizations—Confucian China and the various Islamic caliphates—were considerably more successful in subordinating tribal and racial factors to an overarching idea, whether religious or social.

Previous chapters have discussed the role of European blood elites—the institutions of monarchy and aristocracy—as stubborn and effective opponents of political equality. Their strength traces back to the powerful tribal invasions of the Roman Empire, as well as to the chaotic aftermath of those invasions and the rise of western European feudalism, which acted as a barrier against the persistent continent-wide military threat posed by the devastating raids of the Vikings.

When it comes to the subsequent fate of equality, two features of feudalism stand out: the militarily necessary top-down social structure, which emerged as local and blood-determined; and the multiplicity of authority, exemplified by the initial weakness of national monarchies, the number of independent political jurisdictions, and (perhaps most distinctively) the attempt to fashion a division of power between the political and religious spheres, including but not limited to the many centuries of tension between emperors and popes.

The hierarchical coloration of European politics persisted long after feudalism's end. This partly explains the success of the left enlightenment in France, the western European country in which top-down centralized monarchy had achieved its most thoroughgoing triumph a century earlier in the reign of Louis XIV. Despite the vehement antimonarchical, pro-equality strain in the French Revolution, at no phase of the upheavals that wracked France and Europe between 1789 and 1815 was there a widespread questioning of Europe's bias in favor of top-down government, either in France or in the European countries that resisted the French revolutionary and Napoleonic bid for hegemony.

Feudalism's second relevant feature, multiplicity of authority, did not prove nearly as durable. To many of Europe's rapidly multiplying late-medieval and Renaissance elites, shared rule was messy and unattractive—even though it had fostered the key conditions that allowed them to emerge and grow with a dynamic independence denied to comparable elites in the Islamic world and China.

The revolution in political philosophy ignited by the writings of Niccolo Machiavelli (1469–1527) was particularly pivotal. In the wake of Machiavelli, as Leo Strauss and his followers have often pointed out, political philosophy's two-thousand-year quest for justice largely gave way to emphasis on the gaining and wielding of power. This focus on desirable ends rather than moral means as the heart of politics paved the way for the rise of the left and other forms of utopianism (however much that might have surprised Machiavelli).

Even apart from utopianism, Machiavelli's emphasis on political *goals* led also to a certain impatience with the slowness of systems whose hallmark is diffusion and restraint of power. Even the subsequent Western thinkers who set forth increased democracy as a goal, such as Princeton political scientist Woodrow Wilson, placed far greater emphasis on tangible, this-world accomplishments, to be achieved if possible within a political leader's active career.

With the elevation of definable goals, political players now largely welcomed conflict (or at least accepted it) as the most efficient, real-world avenue of progress toward the kind of government considered effective. Conflict was no longer the sad but necessary side effect of institutionalized diversity of power. In fact, Machiavelli's school of power politics was utterly in sync with the drive to unitary government associated with the national monarchs of the Renaissance, although "Divine Right of Kings" might not have been the Florentine republican's first choice of slogan.

As noted earlier, by 1600, political thought on the continent was committed to the quest for unitary government, with conflicting bids for power accepted as the predominant means of getting there. By 1700, this was true not only of predominantly royalist Europe but also (as outlined in Chapter 8) Britain, which after two civil wars arrived at de facto unitary rule by Parliament. Continental Europe's battle between political equality and monarchy was undecided, but plurality of rule (an important tenet both of medieval politics and of the conservative enlightenment), was left without a strong ideological foothold either in Europe or in the emerging parliament-centered British system.

Europe's Democratic Exceptions

Even Europe's few exceptions bring home the point. After a decades-long rebellion, the federated Dutch Republic won its independence from Spain in the 1580s and became a naval and commercial power with global reach in the 17th century. In the 18th century, constantly pressured by the French monarchy, it went into an extended decline and lost its independence in 1795. Its conqueror, France's First Republic, forced the Dutch to suppress their provincial power centers and adopt a centralized, unitary form of government, presiding over a country now renamed the Batavian Republic. When Napoleon rose to power, he declared this French satellite a kingdom, to be ruled by his brother and later his five-year-old nephew. When the Dutch regained their independence from Napoleonic France, the hereditary Prince of Orange became king of the Netherlands, confirmed in 1815 by the Congress of Vienna.

In a very different way, Switzerland provides another instance of the marginalizing of plural rule and limited government in Europe. Beset by civil strife between Protestants and Catholics, Switzerland had a brief civil war in 1847. Immediately thereafter, between 1848 and 1874, it developed a federal system with a radically democratic constitution. It then became, by almost any measure, the most affluent and best-governed country in European history. Beneath a façade of parliamentary government, the voters of Switzerland or of any of its cantons can overturn the handiwork of the elected legislators, and they frequently do, nearly always to good effect. Three sizable ethnic groups with a history of religious strife inhabit the continent's least promising topography; despite potential for recurring conflict, Switzerland has built a successful model of democratic self-government in the heart of Europe. In pure institutional terms, it is at least the equal of the United States among adherents of the conservative enlightenment.

Yet at no phase of the tumultuous European history of the past century and a half has Switzerland's success in achieving prosperity and social peace spurred other European countries to emulate its constitution. This is further indication that to European political elites, many of whom are veterans of unitary parliamentary systems, adoption of formal democracy has seldom been about the securing of an inalienable right to popular rule.

This is all the more striking because by adopting direct and decentralized democracy, the Swiss successfully resolved not only their religious split, but also their version of Europe's much longer preoccupation with race. The once volatile division in Switzerland among Germans, French, and Italians has been so completely tamed that critics of democracy sometimes argue (with unintended irony) that the Swiss success is inapplicable elsewhere by virtue of Switzerland's well-known history of social peace.

If there was ever a moment when political equality in Europe was destined to come to the fore, it was the aftermath of World War I, which brought rule by Europe's hereditary blood elites to a decisive end. To a degree this did happen, in the form of a debate between Marxism-Leninism and the democratic left; conservative-enlightenment advocates (still with some strength, especially in the British Isles) looked on as interested spectators who leaned toward the left democrats.

Resilience of Europe's Tribal Roots

The debate about the nature of equality was quickly dwarfed by the rise of outright enemies of equality in Italy, Germany, and elsewhere. The rise of Fascism traces back to the 19th century, when

European blood elites' self-interested opposition to equality was energized by a new ideological racism whose most prestigious figure was composer Richard Wagner. A rising conflict-driven, nationalistic imperialism, which had zero interest in equality or any other transnational ideal, further buoyed the blood elites' anti-equality stance. This aggressive, powerful nationalism, influenced by Machiavelli and subsequent German thinkers, all of whom subscribed to conflict theory, was pursued most successfully by the architect of the Second Reich, Count Bismarck. But we can also understand all these seemingly new anti-equality currents as throwbacks to Europe's pre-Christian tribal and pagan roots. And after 1914, it turned out that the centrality of blood in European politics easily proved strong enough to survive the banishment of monarchy and aristocracy from politics.

In fact, the urge to return to primordial roots was made much more explicit by the eclipse of the nominally Christian hereditary elites. Nazism in particular was anti-Christian and fascinated with the atavistic paganism of the Norse gods. It was in the 1930s and 1940s, when Europe's Christians played the most minimal political role imaginable, that Europe's two-thousand-year-old entanglement with race wrought its greatest destruction.

Following the defeat in World War II of Europe's virulent anti-equality forces—ideological racism and the hypernationalism known as Fascism—European politics swung back toward its pursuit of shared values. For a time, this pursuit put the universal vision of the conservative enlightenment back into play against the left enlightenment, which itself remained divided between democratic and Marxist-Leninist versions.

But the seminal post–World War II politicians of the conservative enlightenment—Adenauer, De Gasperi, and Schuman—each proved to be pretty much one of a kind in the postwar politics of Germany, Italy, and France, the three most populous countries of a now predominantly democratic Western Europe.

245

Their failure to generate political imitators may not have been inevitable, but it was understandable, given the earlier political course of European Christians and conservatives.

The strength of the blood elites and the antireligious, anti-family tendencies of the revolutionary left had driven Christians and conservatives toward alliance with monarchy and aristocracy before 1914—and more than a few toward collaboration with Fascism as the most viable alternative to Communism between the wars. In Catholic countries, this phenomenon was sometimes described as "Throne and Altar" conservatism, and its practical result was that much of European conservatism took on an anti-democratic tinge.

For besieged European Christians, collaboration with anti-democratic forces may have aided short-term survival; but in practice, "establishment" of a church invariably meant its subordination to the state, accompanied by the loss of vitality this nearly always entails. The resultant weakness of Christian churches was undoubtedly a factor in the ability of the democratic social left to turn traditional social and sexual morality upside down with so little serious opposition in the Europe of the 1960s and 1970s.

But even the lack of conservative and Christian resistance doesn't fully explain why the inversion of sexual morality was so swift and unexpected. After all, for all the feebleness of Europe's state churches, the 1940s and 1950s had, perhaps in revulsion at the horrors of Nazism, seen a revival of European interest in absolute moral standards, exemplified by the Universal Declaration of Human Rights and the strongly Christian orientation of the founders of the Common Market. Moreover, the brutality of Stalin's suppression of Eastern Europe had significantly dampened the charisma of the European left. In the United States, the 1940s and 1950s saw a rise in churchgoing and a sharp increase in the birth rate that became known as the Postwar Baby Boom.

The Overpopulation Narrative

In retrospect, it is clear that a single narrative swept all before it and laid down the conditions for the social left's breakthrough in Europe and North America in the 1960s. This narrative was the purported global crisis of overpopulation.

The core premise of the narrative is pessimism about humanity's ability to support a growing population, and it recalls the dire predictions of starvation by the 19th-century English theoretician Thomas Malthus, the classical economist most influenced by conflict theory. A particular target is the fertility of marriages. The more children nuclear families have, this logic says, the greater the chance that the world will run out of food and other resources. By the late 1950s, belief in the population crisis was nearly universal, especially in Euro-American elite opinion.

The birth rate did not collapse all at once, even with introduction of the highly efficient contraceptive pill in the United States in 1960. But surprisingly quickly, families' sense of self-esteem became inverted. In 1950, having and raising a big family was widely believed to be unselfish. By 1960, more and more couples believed that limiting themselves to a small family was unselfish. So birth control became something of a universal social norm in North America, Europe, Japan, and the Communist world in the 1960s and 1970s. More than any possible frontal attack, this diluted the prestige of a social institution viscerally disliked by Rousseau, Marx, the Frankfurt School, and other widely separated adherents of the left enlightenment: the nuclear family centered on monogamous marriage.

Once acceptance of contraception as a *moral* necessity took hold even in the context of marriage, the key predicate of the sexual revolution was laid down. This involves the maximum feasible separation of sexual intercourse from the idea of having children. In cultural terms, it implies the social elevation, in popular entertainment and elsewhere, of recreational sex as qualitatively preferable to procreative sex, as well as dilution of society's previous bias in favor of marital sex. As argued in Chapter 7, the left's success in allying the sexual revolution with adversarial feminism was its greatest post-1960s political breakthrough. This alliance took hold in the United States even before it did in Western Europe and soon spread to one degree or another to much of the world.

In the wake of such seismic moral and social realignment, no breakthrough concerning matters such as food production—e.g., the development of "miracle wheat" that won a Nobel Prize for American agronomist Norman Borlaug—was likely to have much effect on the overpopulation storyline. Later elite narratives, such as human-caused "climate change," have reinforced the overpopulation narrative, delaying or obscuring serious debate over depopulation and the economic stagnation expected to result from the rapid aging of work forces across the developed world. Instead, elites in Western governments and foreign-aid bureaucracies continue to offer condoms and other contraceptives to the Third World as a cornerstone or even condition of development aid.

Resistance to the global left's potent moral attack on family autonomy has had episodic political success not only in the United States, with the rise of social conservatism, but also in the Third World. For example, mass opposition to semi-coercive new birth control strictures played a critical role in unraveling prime minister Indira Gandhi's attempt to suspend democracy and impose one-party rule in the India of the 1970s.

But invariably, when such resistance has appeared in Europe— for example, mass street protests against enactment of same-sex marriage laws by Spain's socialist government in 2004 and 2005— conservative elites vote no in parliament but announce they will not make rollback an issue in subsequent elections. For Europe, unpolarized politics means that the issue-by-issue triumph of the Rousseau-style social left is always a matter not of whether, but when.

After two thousand years of oscillation between unity and particularity, Europe has successfully contained its racial and religious divisions and is inexorably uniting behind the universal vision of the left enlightenment. But when one recalls the Europe described by William H. McNeill as poised to achieve global pre-eminence in 1500—a dynamic Europe characterized by political division but also by its depth of popular participation and by receptivity to the best ideas of competing civilizations—today's bureaucratic, stagnant, aging Europe scarcely seems European at all.

Through all its changes in the last two centuries, Europe's left enlightenment has always forwarded an ambitious vision of human fulfillment by means of self-liberation, verging on self-reinvention. Did its advocates ever suspect that their political mastery, once achieved, would coincide with a cultural and demographic decline verging on suicide? Such fatalism is foreign to Rousseau and Marx. If anything, it seems more typical of the egalitarian left's most implacable 19th-century enemies, men such as Nietzsche and Wagner. But if the coming end of Europe is giving the heirs of the left enlightenment any second thoughts, they've disguised such misgivings very well indeed.

10

THE GLOBAL FUTURE OF SOCIAL CONSERVATISM

The question of social conservatism's global viability at first glance seems an odd one to raise. After all, as defined in this book, it exists in only one country, the United States. And even here, it has minimal support in elite opinion, and its political victories have been too few and too unacknowledged for it to acquire much momentum or prestige.

Yet as a surviving mass-based descendant of the conservative enlightenment, American social conservatism represents one of only three surviving political belief systems making a claim to universality in our age of accelerating globalism. If social conservatism isn't sustainable in the United States, the odds are that its parent, the conservative enlightenment, will not soon make a sustainable appearance anywhere else.

The other two political visions that aspire to universality are the left enlightenment and a universal religion that is also a political ideology, Islam. The divergence of Europe from the United States is now so great that the latter two belief systems, rather than the conservative enlightenment, have become the main contenders for Europe's future.

If these prove to be the only two exportable ideas in near-term politics, the world has some bleak, bureaucracy-blighted decades ahead. Neither the left nor Islam has much optimism about ordinary people's ability to make good decisions in politics, economics, or anything else. They are both paternalistic.

As one consequence, neither vision in its contemporary form lends itself to technical innovation or economic dynamism, and neither seems likely to change anytime soon if dependent on internally generated reform. They have that in common. Another thing the left and Islam have in common is fear and dislike of the United States, particularly when it is led by believers in "American exceptionalism"—which in reality (and contrary to this oft-used label) is a competing political belief system that, if true, has universal applicability.

If the global outcome of today's three universal political visions were dependent on Western society's elites, including the elites of the United States, the three-sided conflict would soon be over. American social conservatism would be obliterated, and the last surviving traces of the optimistic, natural-law-centered conservative enlightenment would disappear from this portion of history. Fortunately for social conservatives, one of the characteristics of the massive social upheavals of the last two centuries is that elites no longer have the kind of sway they enjoyed as recently as 1800 or even 1900.

Two social changes, changes so pervasive that they are often taken for granted, have been particularly important in the declining power of society's elites. One is that as a result of a painful, extended transformation culminating in the 20th century's two world wars—the first of which ended European ruling monarchy and the second of which defeated European-derived ideological racism—blood is no longer the main measure of status in human affairs. As Tocqueville anticipated nearly two centuries ago, some version of belief in social equality is nearly universal, and blood has largely given way, as a standard or even as a means of self-identification, to personal and professional merit. This sea change finally includes Europe, though apparently not in a form allowing Europe to endure as a center of human creativity or military power.

First Predictive Indicator: Immigration

The emergence of equality when combined with technological progress has led to the second big change: vastly enhanced mobility for individual human beings. Much of this modern movement involves urbanization, a long-term, economically driven relocation from farms to metropolitan centers, often within a single country or region. But the average nonelite person also has far more ability and inclination to migrate great distances, including the ability to cross national lines, without the leadership or consent of elites.

The most impressive attempt by modern elites to suppress this kind of migration was the Berlin Wall, which was erected on the orders of left oligarchs in 1961 and operated with considerable success until 1989. The most impressive current effort is the immigration policy of the Japanese government, which severely restricts immigration into their wealthy, technically advanced island nation in an era when more and more Japanese families are not raising children.

In the roughly five thousand years of recorded history, there have been two prominent variables that rely mainly on human decision-making: the progress of ideas and the movement of peoples. Much of this book has been an attempt to analyze the playing out in politics of the most recent big idea, the European Enlightenment of the 17th and 18th centuries. An interesting question: How might the future be affected—or even predicted—by the changing patterns of human migration and settlement?

Most historic migrations of any size and distance have been collective in nature. They were organized and led by political (often tribal) elites, acting from a variety of motives. These motives, while often predatory, frequently had to do with a people's loss of viability in its former location, due to famine and drought, or fear of subjugation or annihilation by other peoples. Particularly in the latter instance, a multiplying chain reaction sometimes occurred.

The biggest such movements came in extended waves that lasted centuries and that were usually followed by even longer periods of consolidation and relative stability, as the recent migrants put down roots in their new locations. Historians sometimes refer to each such protracted mass movement as *volkerwanderung*, a German word that means a wandering of the peoples. Notable examples include the far-flung Aryan invasions of the second millennium BC and the predominantly German push into Europe that pressured and eventually destroyed the western Roman Empire in the first centuries AD.

Mass collective displacements still happen, but usually as a result of state-sponsored ethnic cleansing. Notorious recent examples include Stalin's mass relocations of ethnic minorities from one part of the Soviet Union to another, and Kemal Ataturk's ejection of millions of Turkish Greeks in the 1920s from an Asia Minor their ancestors had inhabited for three thousand years.

Mass immigration to the United States, which began not long after our founding, has been different. Unlike the nations of Europe, almost all of which are essentially ethnic in origin, the United States is a country founded on an idea. It was an idea—

innate human equality—that very quickly became known and, from the beginning, exerted a magnetic pull on nonelite people looking for a better life. What could be called the era of micro-immigration had begun.

Micro-immigration as defined here is immigration undertaken by individual decision-makers and through individual exertion, rather than a "macro" or collective movement of tribes and nations making their way in large bodies. In the 19th century, the sea voyages required of most micro-immigrants to the United States were demanding and life-threatening. Millions came anyway because of where they wanted to be. They wanted to be in the New World.

Given the increasing affordability of travel, if micro-immigrants had arrived in the United States and found that this country was not the New World they sought, they could have returned to their countries of origin. Even more, their "word of mouth," in the 19th century mainly taking the form of letters to relatives and friends, might have greatly reduced future micro-immigration from the countries of origin.

Although poor word of mouth undoubtedly discouraged migration in individual instances, immigrants overall have never of their own choice stopped relocating to the United States. Only disruptive events such as world wars and sporadic anti-immigrant crackdowns in the United States have ever deterred immigrants. Why?

Certainly in recent decades, America's popularity as a destination did not emerge as a reflection of elite opinion in the countries of origin. At least since the late 1960s, foreign elites have in large part depicted the United States as the world's foremost pillar of political reaction and economic inequality.

In those same few decades, the U.S. culture exported via movies, music, and the like has at best been a mixed bag. Hollywood has vividly shown American wealth, which is undeniably attractive to many, but it has also depicted a level of violence and social dissolution that would, if taken literally, turn away many if not most prospective immigrants.

Nor have recent decades been a time when immigrants could expect Middle America to welcome them with open arms. As a consequence of rigid restrictions on legal immigration, the heavily Latin American wave of the last three-plus decades has included millions of illegal entrants. Naturally, immigrants working "off the books" are likely, at least initially, to be limited to low-wage jobs, and most micro-immigrants are well aware of this even before starting out. And although Latin Americans have constituted the majority of recent immigrants, inhabitants of very different population centers, including East Asia, the Indian subcontinent, the Muslim world, and sub-Saharan Africa, all seem to agree that the United States is a desirable place to live.

So in the eyes of masses of nonelite people, and often against the grain of the outspoken views of global elites, the United States after more than 230 years of independence is still the closest thing to a New World—that is, a society able to adapt itself to modern trends and conditions in a way that makes it the most attractive place for a great many people to live.

Immigration and the American Founding

Many things have changed in the two centuries or so since the United States gained this reputation. One thing that has changed less than most is the influence of our founding principles on the nature of what foreigners hope to find, and to a considerable degree do find, when they arrive.

In particular, immigrants are encouraged when they learn that the rights they will enjoy if they become Americans are defined as "unalienable." Just about anywhere else, such rights are defined as coming from government, and thus by implication political elites can always suspend or revoke them. In the United States, this is far less likely, because the rights of the people are defined as coming from God-made, unchangeable moral law.

Moreover, because our first and most politically important "self-evident truth" is that we are all "created equal," there is far less threat than in their countries of origin that social elites will erect barriers to immigrants' success. By virtue of the equal possession of unalienable rights, recently settled nonelites have an open path to advancement here, and most perceive the U.S. as a country where individuals and their families can freely engage in the "pursuit of happiness."

Most of the world's political elites do not believe nonelite people are ready to walk down such an unimpeded path. The rights they emphasize have more to do with the right to government protections from economic misfortune than with freedom to advance on one's own terms. In most of Latin America, it is extremely difficult for an ordinary person to open a legal business without connections to the government. In much of Europe, the level of unemployment and welfare benefits ensures that workers lose a relatively small portion of their income should they lose their job. In Japan and China, it is possible for a bank to make bad loans that leave it with a stupendously negative balance sheet, while it uses taxpayer subsidies to continue to operate long-term as if it were a normal business.

The United States is by no means the only wealthy country that receives today's immigrants. During the micro-immigration of recent decades, the wealthy but demographically declining countries of Western Europe have accepted millions of foreigners, many of whom are Muslims from Africa, the Middle East, and South Asia.

The policies of France, Germany, Britain, and other European states differ widely in openness to citizenship for these immigrants. But in none is there a significant effort to assimilate them into French, German, or British culture, which today includes the relativist, sexually permissive values of the social left. Nor does there seem to be much desire on the part of most Muslim immigrants to interact with this host culture. On the outskirts of Paris, the grimy working-class suburbs that a generation ago voted Communist are today heavily Muslim. During periodic episodes of violent unrest, French police officers are reportedly hard to locate in these neighborhoods.

Immigrants to the United States are far more likely to want to become like other Americans. This is not seen as a matter of having to abandon religious or ethnic identity, given that the popular definition of an American, unlike self-definition in most European nations, has little or no racial content and that Americans have always enjoyed religious diversity. The United States remains today a country founded on an idea rather than blood, and most immigrants to the U.S. are intrigued by that idea and the conditions and opportunities it creates. It's not much easier to become a legal resident of the U.S. than a resident of most European countries; our immigrants, however, including most of those who are Muslim, continue to be far more interested in assimilation than are immigrants elsewhere.

The history of European nationalism does not make the idea of assimilation easy. In 1648, the Treaty of Westphalia achieved the marginalization of Europe's most powerful multinational empire, the Holy Roman Empire of the Habsburgs, and ushered in the era of domination by ethnically and religiously homogeneous nation-states. When the Enlightenment spawned the movement for political equality, bringing an overwhelmingly royalist Europe to the brink of multistate republican revolution in 1848, European blood elites countered by retracting even further into single-nationality ideologies and configurations. It was in this spirit that modern Italy and modern Germany were founded within a short space of time in the early 1870s. Shortly after creating the Second Reich, Bismarck, an observant Lutheran from overwhelmingly Protestant Prussia, deepened German national- ism's commitment to ethno-religious conformity by campaigning to deny the Catholic Church its status as a public religion via the Kulturkampf. When ruling monarchy after World War I was succeeded in some countries by Fascism and other forms of dic- tatorship, the mainly European phenomenon of racially defined nationalism became even more pervasive and far more predatory, whether toward foreign countries or their own minorities.

In the first decade or two after World War II, immigration to Europe was a minor issue, except as one of the more limited legacies of the liquidation of Europe's overseas empires. When broader-based micro-immigration to Europe began in the 1970s, the social left was completing its march through the institutions. The big jump in immigration coincided roughly, in Europe as in the U.S., with the crash of fertility rates in the wake of legalized abortion.

In principle it would seem that the triumph in Europe of the left enlightenment, a political ideology that is antiracist and makes universal claims, might have led to a pattern of success- ful assimilation of the growing numbers of Third World immi- grants. But it has not.

Much earlier than the victory of the left enlightenment in Europe, which did not become definitive until the upheavals of the 1960s and their aftermath, Europe had shed its medieval com- mitment to separation of powers, whether of church and state or the analogous separation of legislative and executive. As noted in earlier chapters, the key momentum-changer was the Renais- sance monarchs' drive to establish the Divine Right of Kings, always including subordination of the church; this went hand in hand with Machiavelli's redirection of European political thought toward conflict theory. By no later than 1648 in most of Europe and 1688 in Britain, elites saw plural power centers as, at most, an unfortunate if necessary stage of conflict on the road to unitary power within the state and in society as a whole.

This meant that when the left won the day, Europe would be conditioned to see room for only one ideology in the European polis. This was Rousseau-style moral liberation, facilitated by a relativism that abhors any form of Western exceptionalism, whether in the religious sphere (Christianity or Judaism) or the political (the Natural Law–centered conservative enlightenment, embodied in post–World War II Europe by only a handful of impressive but isolated "retro" figures such as Adenauer).

Multiculturalism vs. Pluralism

Europe's unitary turn of mind thus facilitated acceptance of the social left as the unchallenged moral authority in the age of globalization, which for Europe is deeply intertwined with the elite drive toward political integration via the European Union. But an ideology founded on relativism—no moral absolutes except tolerance of non-Western belief systems—was unlikely to demand that Islamic immigrants fold themselves into a culture of sexual liberation and declining fertility, even assuming relativistic ideology had the slightest chance of persuading recently arrived Muslims to do this. So the branch of left-enlightenment relativism that turns its face toward Third World immigrants to Europe made its appearance under the rubric of "multiculturalism."

Multiculturalism is a Euro-American term that is rivaled on the left only by "progressive" as a substitute for "liberal" and "socialist," descriptive words of earlier generations that acquired negative connotations for many voters in Europe and North America. Multiculturalism, which is also a theme in school curricula formulated by the left, is at root a misnomer. Multiculturalism deals only occasionally with multiple cultures; its main focus is traditional Western culture, which it assails by means of selective narrative and premises that are thoroughly relativist. The prefix "multi" is front and center not to praise or even to say much of anything about non-Western cultures, but to serve as a backdrop for the systematic deconstruction of Western culture.

As it relates to immigration policy, it's important to note that multiculturalism is not a new word for pluralism, but more like its polar opposite. Pluralism, shaped by the idea of unalienable personal equality, is a code of respect for neighbors of different religious or socioeconomic backgrounds. In keeping with innate equality, which is about affirming human dignity as a birthright, pluralism actively discourages religious, ethnic, or class prejudice. The idea of pluralism, not surprisingly, is far more likely to take hold in societies such as the United States that value separation of powers and plural autonomy of rule, including most especially autonomy in matters of faith and religious practice. Pluralism values diversity of cultural background but aims for unity behind common principles of a more political cast. In the case of the United States, pluralism respects who you are and where you (or your ancestors) come from but believes in assimilation to the ideas of the founding and fidelity to the civic and social ground rules they imply. This is the content of a phrase inscribed on American coins: "e pluribus unum."

Multiculturalism rejects the idea of assimilation. It believes attempts at cultural integration, which it often labels "chauvinism," endanger the rich diversity that a host country should welcome from its immigrants. In contrast to "e pluribus unum," multiculturalism tends to perpetuate cultural separateness, which in some cases includes dissent over core civic values. Some (mainly non-American) advocates of multiculturalism have even raised the possibility of Muslim immigrants maintaining their own Sharia law, separate from the laws of the host nation.

On the economic plane, American-style assimilation coupled with pluralism opens the door to faster advancement for immigrants and greater economic benefit to the host nation. By contrast, European-style multiculturalism, for all its rhetoric of accommodation, seems often in practice to relegate immigrants to economic backwardness, perpetuation of language barriers, residential segregation, and alienation from the political and civic values of the host society. In the post-2001 context of Muslims living in majority non-Muslim countries, domestic terrorism has usually posed more of a threat under multicultural societies than under pluralist ones.

So in this era of mass micro-immigration and of cultural encounter on a global scale, the pluralist coloration of the conservative enlightenment, rather than the multiculturalism preferred by the left, appears better adapted to rapidly changing demographic realities. In this important sense, it is more modern, and American society retains its global aura as the New World.

Second Predictive Indicator: Thriving in a Global Economy

A second and related phenomenon in which the conservative enlightenment appears more adaptive than the left or Islam is the globalization of economics. Great Britain, the most powerful adherent of the conservative enlightenment between 1815 and the fall of the final Gladstone ministry in 1894, brought to life the idea of global free trade when it repealed the Corn Laws in 1846. Internal deregulation and rapid, politically backed private-sector development elevated Britain as the worldwide exemplar of middle-class urbanization and the Industrial Revolution. In 1816, the Coinage Act for the first time established gold as the only metallic standard for convertible bank notes and non-gold coins; and in the second half of the 19th century, the most economically advanced nations of the world joined, one by one, what had developed into international recognition of gold as the final money of the world. It is a truism among economic historians even today that the world economy never integrated more rapidly than in the several decades before it was shattered into pieces by World War I.

When Britain's democratic left gained the upper hand as domestic agenda-setter in the first two decades of the 20th century, the United States succeeded its mother country as both the preeminent adherent of the conservative enlightenment and the world's economic cutting edge. Its inventors and engineers multiplied the mobility of human beings and their products, on the ground and through the air. American-style personal property rights, which unlike those of Europe reach deep into the soil, created incentives for massive continent-wide drilling and the invention of the petroleum economy. Commercial electricity found dozens of applications and sparked an unprecedented leap in living standards to virtually every corner of North America, no matter how isolated or primitive.

By the early 1940s, with Britain engaged in a new world war and struggling for survival, the American dollar decisively replaced the British pound as the most important world currency. In 1944, it was President Franklin Roosevelt who called emissaries of the soon-to-be victorious powers of World War II to Bretton Woods, New Hampshire, for the purpose of setting up a new economic regime formally linked to gold but in reality revolving around decisions by U.S. economic policymakers.

The Bretton Woods monetary system proved to be deeply flawed in comparison with the pre-1914 gold standard started in 1816 by Parliament and centered on the Bank of England. Still, the U.S. after 1945 presided over a new generation of tariff-cutting and economic integration fashioned and led by the Democratic Party but supported on a bipartisan basis.

The political and social upheaval of the 1960s, generated and led by the worldwide left, seriously threatened all these economic achievements. By the end of the 1970s, the left had ended any chance for the conservative enlightenment to remain a significant force in non-Communist Europe. All over the world, it had called into question the structure and purpose of the traditional family and put into serious doubt survival of the globalizing, private-capital-driven growth economy of the 19th and 20th centuries. At the tail end of the 1970s, the American dollar was in such imminent danger of worldwide collapse that President Jimmy Carter pushed aside his own appointee as chairman of the Federal Reserve and appointed iron-willed inflation hawk Paul Volcker to administer harsh medicine to the U.S. and world economy in order to save the dollar and the tottering global system it anchored.

In 1974, a newly appointed professor of economics at Columbia University named Robert Mundell, himself a Canadian, was quoted in the *Wall Street Journal* by one of its editorial writers, Jude Wanniski, as stating that the United States should adopt an economic policy mix of tight money and sharply lower taxes. This was an exact inversion of the policy both Republicans and Democrats followed at the time. Virtually no one in his profession publicly seconded Mundell. But in 1981, under Ronald Reagan, this became the economic policy of the United States. By the end of the 1980s, just 10 years after the near collapse of the dollar, the U.S. had emerged more strongly than ever as the institutional center and cutting edge of the world economy (though the bulk of the American economics profession denied this status to Reaganomics, awarding it instead to Japan).

It was in the latter part of 1982, after Fed chairman Volcker relaxed his high-interest-rate policy, that the global economy began to respond to the stimulative effects of Reagan's tax and regulatory policies. The U.S. pulled out of a severe recession and led the world economy to a 25-year era of wealth creation that (among other accomplishments) raised literally billions of people in the Third World from subsistence poverty to the middle class.

Even Al Qaeda's shocking and damaging attack on the American homeland in 2001 caused only a brief recession, and it did not bring the quarter century of worldwide growth to an end.

That generation-long expansion was built on American high-tech leadership, a nearly universal movement to lower income tax rates, and an explosion of debt-financed investment and acquisition. Due to the successful disinflation engineered in the 1980s and 1990s by two Fed chairmen, Volcker and Alan Greenspan, short- and long-term interest rates steadily declined. Most borrowers felt this as a boon, but in particular it enhanced the ability of sophisticated investment managers to achieve huge, leverage-driven gains in their portfolios. In the last decade or so of the 25-year boom, a series of financial bubbles grew and burst: the Asian and Russian default crises, Long-Term Capital Management, and the internet-telecom equity bubble that popped in 2000.

None of the bursting bubbles of the late 1990s seriously threatened American preeminence in the world economy. But after the Internet bubble burst, Fed chairman Greenspan over-reacted to fears of deflation and depression. Greenspan's response was influenced at least in part by Princeton professor Ben Bernanke. An early George W. Bush appointee as Fed governor, Bernanke was an academic expert on the Great Depression, and he was determined not to see it repeated on his watch via a failure to combat deflation. The Fed reduced its federal funds rate target to 1 percent and kept an easy-money policy in place even after it became evident that the 2001 and 2003 Bush tax cuts had returned the U.S. economy to healthy growth. This meant that the next "hot money" bubble, the one built on U.S. residential real estate and its financial derivatives, assumed gigantic proportions, spreading abroad and intertwining deeply with virtually every banking system in the world.

When the U.S. residential market went suddenly into reverse in 2007, the subsequent financial crisis hit hard worldwide, and in a manner that made the U.S. look as baffled and unprepared as anyone. U.S. unemployment doubled in little more than a year, hitting the low double digits that had for decades been a feature not of the U.S. economy, but of Western Europe. Furthermore, the anti-incumbent wave among American voters brought to power Barack Obama, who as president soon made clear his belief that the U.S. should be satisfied with a much more modest profile, both in foreign policy and in terms of economic leadership. If anything, Obama's domestic agenda in his first year suggested that far from setting the pace, the U.S. should focus on playing catch-up to Western Europe's level of bureaucratic and regulatory paternalism, including a far higher level of entitlement spending in health care and other areas.

Political success for Obama's economic agenda thus implied an end to the two-centuries-long status of the countries most influenced by the conservative enlightenment, first Britain and then the U.S., as global leaders of modernization. Another way of stating it is that if Obama became a transformative president, he would very likely succeed in breaking the remaining influence of conservative-enlightenment ideas on American economic policy, instead making our economic policy far more like that of the left enlightenment that holds sway in Western Europe. On the "micro" level, this implied a far more restrictive and regulatory approach to bottom-up business enterprise.

Rise of the Tea Party

On taking office, Obama was extremely popular yet increasingly frank in making clear he wanted to fundamentally alter the trajectory of the U.S. economy in a leftward direction. In his first months in office in early 2009, it seemed at least plausible that Americans' fear of the continuing financial meltdown would

266

enable the president and the now heavily Democratic Congress to enact a transformative agenda with at most minimal opposition. Newly installed White House Chief of Staff Rahm Emanuel, a sophisticated veteran of both the Democratic congressional leadership and the Clinton White House, captured the mood when he remarked: "You never want a serious crisis to go to waste. And what I mean by that is the opportunity to do things you think you could not do before."

But strong opposition to Obama's agenda arrived far earlier than almost anyone expected. Some of it involved an intensely negative reaction among social conservatives—a Gallup survey found the only early Obama policy to trigger majority opposition was an executive order restoring abortion funding to U.S. foreign-aid programs—but most of it did not.

On February 19, 2009, less than a month after Obama's inauguration, Rick Santelli, a 56-year-old business reporter for the financial news network CNBC, delivered a live four-minute rant on the floor of the Chicago Mercantile Exchange against the administration's proposed relief for defaulting home-mortgage holders. Expanding into a broader attack on bailouts backed by the president and Congress, Santelli called for a modern-day "tea party"—a reference to the anti-tax, anti-British riot in 1773 in the Boston Harbor—to protest the Obama spending programs.

Santelli's tirade was posted on the Drudge Report, a popular conservative Internet site, and within hours it became a widely watched posting on YouTube. Within days, "tea parties" were being announced and scheduled all over the country. The quickly blossoming movement met initial skepticism from Republican elites, for it broke all political rules concerning presidential honeymoons—specifically, the widely held belief that any incoming administration deserves a grace period free from criticism.

The Tea Party movement transformed the early opposition to Obama. Resistance became bolder and far more ideological, yet at the same time less clearly Republican, because it was skeptical of Republicans in Congress (many of whom had supported various bailouts) and had nothing good to say of the Bush administration, which had initiated most of the bailouts.

In particular, the Tea Party movement was instrumental in making opposition to Obama's domestic centerpiece, his plan for centrally administered universal health coverage, an essential component of an across-the-board, vehement opposition to the "transformative" aspects of the president's agenda. We might fairly sum up this agenda as making the United States look much more like Europe with respect to entitlements, the degree of centralized economic regulation, and a virtually dissent-free devotion to the social values of the left enlightenment.

Because the Tea Party movement was centered on resistance to Big Government, it was possible to see it as an emerging rival to social conservatism, when it came to defining agendas and rallying the conservative base. But in operational terms, there was little tension between the two movements. During most of the fight over Obamacare, pro-life Democrats in the House maintained their opposition to federally funded abortion. As leader of this group, Michigan's Bart Stupak ultimately capitulated to party leaders only hours before the decisive vote on March 21, 2010. Nonetheless, the Democratic pro-life opposition proved the single biggest obstacle to Obama and House Speaker Nancy Pelosi as they struggled to mobilize the overwhelming congressional majorities their party enjoyed. Some Republican elites and conservative talk show hosts tended to downplay the importance of pro-life social conservatives in the congressional struggle over Obamacare, but grassroots Tea Party activists expressed no noticeable resentment. They may well have had different reasons for wanting to stop the Obama program, but they welcomed any political impetus toward achieving that result.

Without question, some Tea Party activists were socially liberal, just as a few social conservatives are economically liberal. But the salient aspect of the conservative uprising against Obama in 2009 was its potential for reuniting popular voting blocs that had been far more ambivalent about the moderately conservative Republican nominees George W. Bush and John McCain than they had been about Ronald Reagan.

This seemed to open the possibility that the road to the next cycle of Republican success might be a more ideologically comprehensive and radical one, the road of Reagan rather than of Nixon or the Bushes. In a context of increased political polarization, emergence of a more integrated and consistent Republican agenda that is far more militant on economic *and* social issues would be no great surprise—particularly in the wake of the analogous Democratic transition from the strategically eclectic, tactically nimble "triangulation" of Bill Clinton to the ideologically consistent left agenda of post-Clinton candidates such as Howard Dean and Barack Obama.

There is a further intriguing question about the Tea Party movement, one that at this writing must remain largely unanswered. A central premise of this book is that American social conservatism is the only mass movement in American or European politics that carries forward core tenets of the conservative enlightenment, tenets most fully captured in the ideas of the American founding. Is it possible that the Tea Party is emerging as a second such mass movement?

As with social conservatism, there is no movement remotely similar to the Tea Party in Europe or Japan. The very name Tea Party suggests an affinity with the politics of the American founding, particularly those aspects of revolutionary America that were not a phenomenon of elite opinion. We can also discern an affinity in reports that more than a few Tea Party activists have been observed consulting pocket copies of the Declaration and the Constitution, mass-produced and disseminated without charge in recent years by the libertarian Cato Institute and other right-of-center organizations.

The Tea Party also resembles social conservatism in its agenda-driven militancy. A key test of the movement's significance will be whether a good portion of this militancy on issues persists when (or if) the economy returns to a more normal growth path, regardless of which party predominates in national politics when this occurs. If most left analysts are right, the sudden prominence of the Tea Party in 2009 and 2010 is almost wholly a function of the weak economy of these years. If such analysis proves wrong, the Tea Partiers will join social conservatives as a mass voting bloc capable of generating party and ideological realignment in the years ahead.

But the Tea Party movement's most palpable common ground with social conservatism is that it seems quite comfortable with the idea of American exceptionalism, which as we have seen is not really exceptionalism at all but a belief in the universal truth of the ideas of the founding. Whether the Tea Party embraces, or later in its development will come to embrace, the implications of this universality is open to question. But it does seem certain that any Obama-style appeal for America to become as "advanced" as Europe could fall on no deafer ears than those of the Tea Party.

Indeed, avoiding Europe's fate became a subtext of the popular rebellion against the expansionist federal agenda that absorbed much of President Obama's first two years in office. It was a line of attack that, at least potentially, neatly divided much if not most of the left from everyone else in the electorate. The American left, particularly its elites, would be hard-pressed to name a policy or cultural characteristic of the Netherlands or Germany that it would *not* regard as an improvement over the present situation in the United States.

As President Obama in his first year successfully pressed forward with a nearly unprecedented expansion of federal spending and a European-style takeover of the health insurance system, a growing question among American conservatives, and not only social conservatives, was whether a significant expansion of entitlement spending and the enhanced paternalism of our central government would lead America to European results. In particular, are we headed toward Europe's demographic collapse?

In his book *Redeeming Economics*, social-conservative economist John Mueller examined 50 countries, accounting for two-thirds of the world's population, for which adequate demographic and predictive data are available. He found that at present four factors explain a remarkable 80 percent of the variation in national birth rates. The birth rate of a country is inversely proportional to (first) the level of per-capita entitlement spending and (second) per-capita national saving. Both of these factors roughly measure a society's provision for individuals' current and future well-being (as opposed to having and raising children).

A third factor is whether a country has a recent history of totalitarian government, which by itself reduces the birth rate by about six-tenths of one child per couple, not only in currently totalitarian governments such as China and Vietnam, but also in the formerly Marxist-Leninist countries of Eastern Europe including Russia. Confirming the fears of conservative critics of Obama's policies, Mueller projected a decline in the U.S. birth rate from its recent (roughly replacement-level) fertility rate of 2.1 to about 1.6 in the next few decades due to scheduled increases in federal entitlement spending. Moreover, he made this calculation *before* he could include the effect of health reform and other Obama-backed expansions of entitlement spending in the projection.

271

The fourth factor in fertility, Mueller found, was a striking correlation between a couple's propensity to weekly worship and the number of children they will have. In Mueller's words: "Those who devote scarce resources like time and money to worship also devote such resources to children for the children's sake. The world over, weekly worshipers have about 2.1 more children per couple than those who don't worship, with relatively little variation by religion or denomination."[*]

In this regard Western Europe and affluent East Asian countries such as Japan and Singapore are truly canaries in the coal mine. Their mass cultures are the only ones in today's world in which allegiance to traditional religion has shrunk to minimal levels (with the exception of Europe's recent Islamic arrivals), and they are also the ones whose demographic suicide appears difficult if not impossible to reverse.

Third Predictive Indicator: Religious Independence

If it is true that the need for purpose—in particular, for regular worship—is an important factor in human survival and flourishing, this raises a third broad area in which the conservative enlightenment seems to possess superior tools for survival than competing universalisms. That is the relationship between religion and the state.

At first glance, adding this criterion might seem to undermine the very words *social conservatism*. Many critics of social conservatism, as well as a few of its sympathizers, believe "social conservatism" is a euphemism or placeholder for bringing religion back into a favored role in politics and government.

---

[*] John D. Mueller, *Redeeming Economics: Rediscovering the Missing Element* (Wilmington, Del.: ISI Books, 2010).

But as noted in earlier chapters, social conservatives familiar with recent history suspect that a reversion to "Throne and Altar" government is the last thing traditional believers or well-wishers of religion should desire, because (especially in the modern West) "established" religion is a formula for its marginalization and decay. As a corollary, the century-long hope of Europe's Christian Democrats to reinforce traditional morality by giving religion an official or quasi-official role in government has also proven to be an exercise in futility.

Even Islam, a universal faith whose texts argue the superiority of a state that fully integrates Islam into its laws and government, shows some sign of suffering from state entanglement in today's world of mass micro-immigration. Many officially Islamic countries, including Iran, have seen their birth rates plummet in recent decades, while birth rates of Muslim immigrants and descendants of Muslim immigrants in countries with a non-Muslim majority appear to have held steady.

In *The New Shape of World Christianity*, Evangelical scholar Mark A. Noll, a professor of history at Notre Dame, argues that beginning in the late 18th century, a new, more entrepreneurial approach to faith took shape in the United States. "Then," he argues, "over the course of the twentieth century what had become standard American religious practice grew increasingly representative of what was taking place around the world."

Some of this happened because of the influence of American missionaries, but a great deal more, argues Noll, because the kind of grassroots religious organization pioneered in North America was far more adaptive and effective. "In North America, the older pattern of European state churches was set aside and Christian faith advanced (or declined) and flourished (or decayed) as believers took the initiative to do the work themselves." As recently as 1900, 70 percent of the Christians in the world lived in Europe.

Today, Noll notes that more people go to church in Kenya than in Canada, the number of practicing Christians in China may be approaching the number in the United States, and India is home to the world's largest chapter of the Jesuit order of Roman Catholic priests.

There are very few European missionaries to send abroad, but 10,000 foreign Christian workers are ministering in Britain, France, Germany, and Italy. Another 35,000 are doing so in the United States. No less than capitalism, by Noll's account, this more populist version of Christianity is putting down roots in many non-European cultures in the context of globalization, with at least as many opportunities as strains and dislocations.[*]

Many assume that the explosion of Christianity and Islam in the Third World in recent decades is merely a function of the relative poverty of the Third World. But the continued strength of religion in the United States, the most economically sophisticated nation in human history, suggests a more complicated causality. So does the vigor of religion in the big economic-growth success stories of the late 20th and early 21st centuries: India, China, and South Korea. It seems plausible that it is not wealth, but the centuries-long subjugation of religion to political elites characteristic of both Europe and Japan, that is the true harbinger of religion's marginalization in the modern world.

And the disappearance of worship, where and when it occurs, coincides with the disappearance of the next generation. The correlation found by Mueller is so exact that cause and effect matter little in practical terms: If a modern country or culture experiences one, it is likely before too long to get the other.

---

[*] Mark A. Noll, *The New Shape of World Christianity: How American Experience Reflects Global Faith* (Downers Grove, Ill.: InterVarsity Press, 2009), 9–14.

The Superiority of the Conservative Enlightenment

To summarize, in each of these three forward-leaning areas—attractiveness to immigrants; economic dynamism in an era of globalization; and separate, autonomous realms for religion and government—the conservative enlightenment has enjoyed a more consistently robust performance than the left or Islam. The United States, still significantly influenced though no longer dominated by the conservative enlightenment, remains the New World in terms of its ability to attract immigrants, thrive in the integrating world economy, and live with purpose in a world changing with dizzying rapidity.

These strengths are not fundamentally different from the qualities William H. McNeill singled out in the Europe of 1500. In 2012, the belief of the conservative enlightenment in innate human equality works better than its two rival belief systems in encouraging broadly based, effective activity in the spiritual, economic, and political spheres. In a world of accelerating cultural and institutional complexity, the idea of self-government—in the moral and economic spheres no less than the political—seems more and more attractive when compared with direction by elites (political, economic, clerical, and cultural) as envisioned by the social left and Islam.

That does not mean the conservative enlightenment will prevail or even survive. Almost all of today's global elites reject as naive the notion of God-given equality and have particular contempt for those American social conservatives who still believe in it. In the three-way struggle among the surviving political creeds that make universal claims—the two enlightenments and Islam—the view of women is strikingly different, and perhaps therefore pivotal to future outcomes, given the relationship of female fertility to the future of any society.

Women and the Future of Civilization

With the discrediting of empirically based claims of male superiority, the position of women is increasingly a function of political power and ideology. In traditional Islam, men remain firmly on top. The vigorous survival of Muslim honor killings of women in countries with non-Islamic majorities is striking evidence of the tenacious hold of ideology. Acceptance of such male supremacism is reinforced by multiculturalism, both in nations dominated by the social left and in international forums; among left elites, allegiance to multiculturalism nearly always trumps support for liberation of women.

Multiculturalism's temptation to argue that Islamic women have a cultural or ideological preference for subjugation by men is reminiscent of the insistence of many American segregationists as recently as the 1960s that black people prefer white paternalism to the possibility of freedom. In our age of equality, a similar assessment of Islamic women deserves roughly the same respect. The left is more believable when it frankly admits that it endorses cultural relativism even when doing so means, as it often does, accepting that the culture denies equality to half of its people.

Such tolerance by the left enlightenment of the Islamic view of women is rewarded and reciprocated, not verbally but where the democratic rubber meets the road: voting. In democratic Europe and North America, Muslims have joined adversarial feminists as core constituents of the ideologically left parties. Even though the left has frequently accused social conservatives of affinity with militant Islamists—going back a generation to Walter Mondale's description of Ronald Reagan as an "ayatollah" in 1984—such alleged resemblances seldom seem to lead to Islamic votes for conservative candidates on Election Day. While sharing some moral beliefs with Islam, social conservatives in recent times have also been demographically the most important supporters of morality in American foreign policy, U.S. military intervention against Islamic rogue states, and the U.S. alliance with Israel. With the possible exception of Israeli Jews, American social conservatives appear to be the least favorite people of today's resurgent Islamists.

At the other extreme from Islam in its view of women is the adversarial feminism that still firmly prevails on the left. As argued in earlier chapters, the left's most impressive breakthrough since the 1960s was its ability to convince the bulk of the feminist movement that the sexual revolution is in the interest of women. The left did not accomplish this by trying to make feminist role models of *Playboy* founder Hugh Hefner and other depicters of women as sex objects. A foundation was laid, first, by the increasingly fashionable devaluation of procreative sex in the wake of the overpopulation scare beginning in the 1950s, a downgrading that the Pill helped make operational.

At least equally important is the continued sway of conflict theory on the left, even after the 1989–1991 demise of Marxism-Leninism, the best-known left version of conflict theory. Class conflict may have declined amid the economic successes of capitalism, but tensions between men and women presented new opportunities for the left, especially at a time when fear of overpopulation had raised new questions about the social desirability of childbearing.

The thought that women's fulfillment is in tension with traditional marriage and with childbearing has not been an obscure one on the revolutionary left. A key member of the Frankfurt School, Herbert Marcuse (1898–1979), in a 1974 lecture at Stanford called for replacing "male domination" with "the legendary idea of androgynism" and cited liberalized sexual standards and birth control as key preconditions for the liberation of women.

An advocate of the sexual revolution since the 1930s, Marcuse in his influential 1955 book *Eros and Civilization* advocated "polymorphous perversity" as his preferred form of sexuality in the ideal left society. He explicitly repudiated Freud's belief that psychic repression is the necessary building block of civilization, arguing instead for a Rousseau-style substitution of Eros for work as the key to happiness.[*]

Antonio Gramsci (1891–1937), the Italian Communist leader discussed earlier who spent most of the last decade of his life as a political prisoner of Mussolini, is increasingly analyzed as a precursor of adversarial feminism. Like Marcuse, he explicitly downplayed Marx's economic determinism, having come to the belief that workers' advances into the middle class—a success of capitalism—had rendered class conflict unpromising as a trigger for revolution.

Gramsci also believed that the continued grip of religion, particularly Catholicism, on the European masses of his time was another barrier to revolution, but one that Communists could more successfully attack by mobilizing Renaissance and Protestant critiques of the church. In a striking confirmation of the continual influence of conflict theory throughout Europe's modern era, Gramsci took Machiavelli's advice on achieving power, originally given to "the prince," and redirected it to modern revolutionary parties. Very much in the spirit of Rousseau, Gramsci's rejection of Marxian economic determinism challenged the left to find ingenious new pathways—specifically, via social conflict—for attacking traditional institutions like the church and the "patriarchal" family.

The left psychoanalytic writer Erich Fromm, an off-and-on adherent of the Frankfurt School, was even more explicit in a 1975 interview in Italy: "One cannot understand the psychology

---

[*] Herbert Marcuse, *Eros and Civilization* (Boston, Mass.: Beacon, 1955).

278

of women . . . if one does not consider that there has been a war between the sexes going on in the last six thousand years. This war is a guerrilla war. Women have been defeated by patriarchalism six thousand years ago and society has been built on the domination of men. Women were possessions and had to be grateful for every new concession that men made to them. But there is no domination of one part of mankind over another, of a social class, of a nation or of a sex over another, unless there is underneath rebellion, fury, hate and wish for revenge in those who are oppressed and exploited and fear and insecurity in those who do the exploiting and repressing."*

The first important work by a full-fledged adversarial feminist was published in France in 1949: *The Second Sex*, by Simone de Beauvoir (1908–1986). Like her lover of 51 years, Jean-Paul Sartre, Beauvoir was an existentialist philosopher, a Marxist-Leninist, and a prize-winning writer of fiction, much of it semi-autobiographical and intensely sexual. Beauvoir wrote that throughout history, women had been stereotyped and defined by men for the benefit of men. Her philosophic belief that existence trumps essence led her to argue that gender is a product of social hierarchy, that women are therefore mostly "made" rather than born. Her historical analysis of women as the wholly Other, defined exclusively by men, is a conscious extension of Hegelian conflict theory from class (master vs. slave) to gender (male vs. female).

In the United States, Betty Friedan (1921–2006) in her 1963 bestseller *The Feminine Mystique* was the key figure in popularizing adversarial feminism in the United States, from which it spread worldwide. She argued that American housewives had lost their chance for self-fulfillment by devoting themselves to

---

* Quoted in Douglas Kellner, "Erich Fromm, Feminism, and the Frankfurt School," paper delivered at an International Interdisciplinary Symposium on Erich Fromm and the Frankfurt School in Stuttgart-Hohenheim, May 31–June 2, 1991.

their husbands and children. A member of Smith College's class of 1942, Friedan spent the first part of her career as a propagandist for the left end of the American labor movement, and she was alive to the potential of adversarial feminism as a potent new weapon in the left's arsenal. Friedan later became the most influential figure in making legalized abortion a central goal of the feminist movement, and she led a blistering and effectively suppressive counterattack on anti-pornography crusaders among 1970s feminists, on the ground that any restriction of pornography would violate the First Amendment.

The Gender Gap

The success of Friedan and others in connecting American feminism with the liberationist left changed the narrative about women, particularly in elite opinion. From being a force for stability and family values, women's image became that of an oppressed out group, analogous to blacks and the homeless. The "gender gap"—Democrats doing better among women voters than men—appeared in the elections of the 1980s and has fluctuated up and down ever since. A look inside the numbers reveals that the main source of the gender gap is a marriage gap: Married women are about as Republican as the electorate as a whole if not more so. Women who are single, particularly the divorced and never-married, are significantly more Democratic.

The gender gap is real, but it is interesting to note that it tends to be greatest in years of above-average overall *Republican* performance. More than a few Democratic students of public opinion have concluded (not very vocally) that for their party, the gender gap is more correctly seen as a recurrent Democratic weakness among male voters. Moreover, the gap appears driven more by the support of single women for government-aid programs, rather than by women having become significantly more liberal than men on social issues. On abortion, an issue adversarial feminists always classify as a "women's issue," most polling finds no significant divergence between women and men on the desirability of legalized abortion.

Where there has been a difference, large and unarguable, is among female elites. Of the 535 members of the 111th Congress, the one elected with Barack Obama in 2008, there were 72 female Democrats and only 21 female Republicans. Even in the meager ranks of 17 Republican women in the U.S. House, 7 were members of the Main Street Partnership, a publicly disclosed 38-member caucus of the GOP's moderate-to-liberal wing. This meant that Republican congresswomen were more than twice as likely to define themselves as moderate-to-liberal as their male Republican colleagues were. There is no similarly public caucus that classifies U.S. senators, but all 4 of the female Republicans in the Senate in 2009 listed themselves as pro-choice on abortion, as did all 13 Democratic female senators.

The disproportionate dominance of the feminist left among women who have risen to elite professional status has not been limited to politicians. Adversarial feminism has achieved a virtual monopoly on university faculties, particularly in the liberal arts. Because university tenure is the closest thing in American life to a self-perpetuating oligarchy, women who have achieved high status in the liberal arts at elite universities have most often done so by building a body of writing that "deconstructs" the bulk of history and literature into an unbroken saga of male oppression and female dejection.

Adversarial Feminism Meets Sarah Palin

It's hard to avoid the conclusion that the nearly comparable left feminist consensus among successful women in the mass media helped shape the extraordinary reaction to the vice presidential nomination of Sarah Palin. The ridicule and venom directed at Palin from the instant McCain announced her selection on August 29, 2008—at a moment when the only details most elites knew about her was that she was a popular pro-life governor in an intact marriage and the mother of five children, including a Down syndrome baby that she knowingly carried to term at the age of 44—suggest that this combination of facts was widely and instantaneously seen by many elite American women as an implicit rebuke of the left feminist narrative.

The core of adversarial feminism, in terms of women's basic life choices, implies that there is a binary choice between happiness as a "traditional" wife and mother of a large family, on the one hand, and professional achievement in elite society in competition with men, on the other. A successful woman in elite media could be married, of course, and the mother of one or perhaps even two children—but not five, and not a high-maintenance Down syndrome baby added to the family in one's 40s.

The apparent happiness and professional success of Sarah Palin as a conservative pro-life governor, wife, and mother of five had to be false *by definition*, and a cottage industry sprang up in the mass media to prove it false, or at the very least to prove she was an empty-headed fraud. At this writing in 2011, more than three years after her selection to the Republican national ticket, this relentless journalistic onslaught shows no sign of coming to an end. In fact, it still appears lavishly financed at a time when most other line items in elite media budgets are sharply contracting.

Does all this suggest the possible emergence of a distinct social-conservative view of women? The quick take of the movement's critics would probably be that the social-conservative view of women is no different from the conventional male view of women in Victorian England or North America.

But the social conservatism analyzed in this book did not exist in Victorian England or Victorian North America. It is a political movement unique (at least so far) to the United States. It is considerably less than 50 years old, and it came into being here because it provided the only mass-based vehicle for the belief system of the conservative enlightenment, which was in the process of being dismantled or marginalized by the triumph of the liberationist left in Europe and anywhere else the left was breaking through with its two-century-old anti-institutional ideology. Beginning around 1900 and intensifying in the 1960s, the conservative enlightenment came under withering assault in the United States as well, but it survived here because millions of Americans still believed, as did virtually all of our founders, that equality is given at birth by God, not by government officials or anyone else.

So like its parent the conservative enlightenment, American social conservatism as a movement is not at all about patriarchy, but revolves around a firm commitment to innate human equality, a purer equality than that affirmed by the left, which favors elite management toward future equality.

It is possible for believers in both kinds of equality to view the heart of American history as a struggle to bring social and political equality to more and more people not included in American electorates of the late 18th century. And it is a fact that most black male ex-slaves obtained the right to vote decades before most American women of any race did so.

Why did achievement of the franchise happen in this order? The answer of most adversarial feminists would be simple and clear: Wretched as the condition of black slaves in 1860 undoubtedly was, the oppression of women by men was even worse; therefore, men's resistance to female liberation was even more stubborn and intense than the resistance of slaveholding Southerners to ending slavery, a resistance that led to a devastating civil war.

The response of most social conservatives goes to the heart of that movement's nature, even of its name. While not denying the importance of injustice toward women, social conservatives believe we cannot assess the condition of women (or of men) without taking into account the condition of marriage and the family. We cannot seek our human freedom or even analyze it in isolation from the freedom and dignity of other persons—that is, from its *social* context—and assuredly not in isolation from members of one's own family.

Social conservatives emphatically reject the autonomous freedom advocated by Rousseau and his successors, who clearly include such founders of adversarial feminism as Simone de Beauvoir and Betty Friedan. Earlier American feminists—and a solid majority of the feminists who fought for and won the right of women to vote in the early 20th century—were pro-marriage and pro-children, if not as often pro-husband. In the same era when these feminists were escalating their demands for the right to vote, many were also involved in the successful multistate movement in the second half of the 19th century to pass antiabortion laws in the states. These feminists viewed legal abortion, as well as male alcoholism, as a direct threat to the dignity of women.

Women and the Urban Revolution

Only a few decades earlier, in the late 18th and early 19th centuries, humanity was beginning its economically driven transition from farm to metropolis that in much of the world is far from complete even today. The phenomenon of mass urbanization was first noticeable and first chronicled in Great Britain, which also happened to be the first territorially extensive nation-state that had decisively shed the institution of ruling monarchy and, more than any other, nurtured the egalitarian ideas of the conservative enlightenment.

In the subsistence farming that supported most families in most of the five thousand years of recorded human history, the work of men and women was not greatly differentiated. Then as now, men tended to handle tasks requiring greater physical strength and women's work patterns were affected by childbirth during their fertile years. But men and women (as well as their children) worked in close proximity and were producing the same things.

Urbanization brought work differentiation and physical separation to men and women during the family's work day. Men left the house, and women stayed home with the children, who became less and less likely to be forced into child labor. For children in countries such as Britain and the United States, few historians would dispute that in time, urbanization added up to a form of liberation, accompanied as it was by the rise of mass childhood education.

For society as a whole, and for most families, urbanization brought a sharp growth in wealth. Any given metropolitan woman was likely to have a higher standard of living than her rural counterpart. Yet it was also true that workday separation of men from women made husbands more publicly prominent in relation to their wives than had been the case on farms. In the urbanizing Britain and North America of the 19th century, which increasingly coincided with early mass democracy, man the breadwinner became also man the voter.

But in the same decades when women were being left behind as voters, they were gaining operational power within the nuclear family. Far more clearly than on subsistence farms, women became the nurturers and shapers of the next generation. And because of the increased complexity and division of labor inherent in urban life, this was a far bigger challenge than raising the next generation of subsistence farmers.

How did all this sort out in terms of the status of women? For adversarial feminists such as Simone de Beauvoir and Betty Friedan, the answer is unambiguous: The role of housewife in urbanized society, for all its affluence and greater responsibility for the future of children, represented a trap. Not only did it involve a position inferior to the men who were gaining social and political power in the transition to democracy; it effectively closed off the path to a fulfilling professional life that, in the eyes of many feminists, alone translates to human happiness in modern society. Many adversarial feminists would question, as Beauvoir and Friedan explicitly did, the *possibility* of happiness or true fulfillment as a wife and mother.

While acknowledging women's left-behind status in the civil sphere of early British and American democracy, social conservatives would give considerable weight to the new challenges families faced in a rapidly changing economy, and the centrality of women in grappling competently with these challenges. Moreover, when combined with the inexorable progress of equality, this very competence helped set the stage for women's attainment of equal property rights, mass admission into higher education, their breakthrough into medicine and other restricted professions, as well as the right to vote. Sarah Palin, who often describes herself as a "frontier feminist," notes that supposedly less sophisticated women from the western states preceded their eastern sisters in gaining the franchise, which until ratification of the 19th Amendment in 1920 was strictly a state-by-state decision.

But social conservatives are repelled above all by adversarial feminism's negative view of marriage and the family. To denigrate the possibility of mutual love between husband and wife, the complementarity rather than interchangeability of mother and father, the joy involved in the birth and nurturing of children—to many women and not only those who are socially conservative, that is a recipe for the impoverishment of human life, not to mention the decline and eventual marginalization of the human race.

In the last few decades, the ideological descendants of Rousseau have succeeded in putting enormous pressure on the institution of marriage. Left social historians have even convinced much of elite opinion that monogamous marriage as we have known it is a relatively recent invention, or at most an optional feature of human society.

Elizabeth Fox-Genovese (1941–2007), an Emory University scholar and pioneer in the field of women's studies who became a social conservative, came to a different conclusion in *Marriage: The Dream That Refuses to Die*: "At first glance the history of marriage and the family may appear to offer a wondrous array of diversity, but that first glance, like others, is more deceptive than trustworthy. For, on closer inspection, history teaches that civilization has always been accompanied by—indeed grounded in—an ideal of marriage and the family that attempts to join the biological difference of men and women in the common project of responsibility for the next generation."*

Relation vs. Autonomy

Coming back to the three-way struggle for the future—and putting aside the handful of women who, if given a true choice, might see their role in traditional Islam as something other than involuntary subservience to men—women will decide which of the two enlightenments is right about the nature of humanity. Is human fulfillment primarily about relation or about autonomy? Rousseau would not (and did not) disagree that most of history depicts man as a social animal, which may be why his autonomous "natural man" had to be posited in prehistory.

Rousseau's greatest ideological breakthrough in history itself, and potentially the most consequential breakthrough achieved by the global left that fashioned itself from his ideas, is the sexual

---

* Elizabeth Fox-Genovese, *Marriage: The Dream That Refuses to Die* (Wilmington, Del.: ISI Books, 2008), 127.

revolution. Now that the sexual revolution has had several decades to influence society, it seems reasonable to ask how it is working out for women, the custodians of humanity's future.

If there is a central imperative that defines the sexual revolution, it is the drive to separate sex and procreation. The aim was to take the psychic stress out of sex and free it to be completely recreational, available to both unmarried and married couples. With efficient contraception—and nearly always with legal abortion understood as the fail-safe backup—sex could now be treated more casually, without the portentous backdrop of the possibility of bringing a new human life into the world, together with all the responsibilities this implies.

When the Pill came into wide use in the 1960s, many pictured abortion as becoming quite rare—a sort of necessary evil to be mobilized in those rare instances when the new and more efficient means of contraception failed. It turns out that in the United States, adding together births and recorded abortions yields a number well above replacement rates, though not as high as the fertility rates of the baby boom. That is, if one were to count legal abortions as pregnancies carried to term, the fertility rate would be nearly 3 children per woman rather than the present 2.1.

This suggests that in this country (and to varying degrees in other countries where abortion was legalized), abortion is doing much if not most of the work in reducing birth rates. Modern methods of contraception, while undoubtedly preventing many pregnancies, proved to be a far from sufficient means of preventing a high level of births. This suggests, in turn, that the key to the sharp reduction in birth rates was not simply contraception, but the contraceptive ethic: systematic separation of the sexual act from procreation. For many people, internalizing this mental separation legitimated abortion (perhaps as a byproduct making use of the Pill, with its strong side effects on the female body, less obligatory in the eyes of women who take part in recreational sex).

One of the most far-reaching results affecting American women is the near disappearance of the "shotgun wedding"— a once widely accepted practice whereby the father of a pregnant single woman pressured the prospective father to marry his expectant daughter before the birth of the child. In a landmark 1996 essay in the *Quarterly Journal of Economics*, liberal scholars George Akerlof, Janet Yellen, and Michael Katz demonstrated that the availability of legal abortion and improved contraception has directly led to the surge in out-of-wedlock pregnancies. For millions of women, the binary choice of an earlier era—rushed marriage vs. unwed motherhood—has morphed into a binary choice between single motherhood and abortion.[*] For women, most of whom are by now aware that single motherhood suppresses family income and increases the likelihood of behavioral problems for the child, this may not have the feel of an uptick in female status.

For similar reasons, neither does the "no fault" (unilateral) divorce that the forces of liberation rammed through state legislatures with minimal opposition in the 1970s. After less than a decade, Lenore Weitzman in *The Divorce Revolution* (1985) had found a sharp decline in income for divorced women, nearly all of whom wound up responsible for raising the children. Studies showing behavioral and psychological problems for the children of divorce—problems also borne disproportionately by the divorced mothers—came somewhat later, but these have proven equally unambiguous.

---

[*] George A. Akerlof, Janet L. Yellen, and Michael L. Katz, "An Analysis of Out-of-Wedlock Childbearing in the United States" in *Quarterly Journal of Economics* (May 1996: 277–317).

Gender-Based Abortion

The spread of legalized abortion to much of the Third World beginning in the 1970s, in conjunction with the dissemination of ultrasound imaging, caused a sharp increase in sex-selection abortions of girl babies. If adversarial feminists were uncomfortable about this extremely widespread and well-known consequence of unlimited abortion on demand, particularly prevalent in Asian cultures, their discomfort has been restrained. And (as in the case of Betty Friedan's defense of pornographers' right to depict women as sex objects) such restraint is clearly due to ideology: In the larger left cause of autonomous freedom, millions of girl babies have no standing compared with the "choices" of their mothers—or even (perhaps more typically) compared with the preferences of the mostly male relatives who pressure Asian women to abort their daughters.

Now, more than a generation after the advent of ultrasound triggered the era of mass asymmetric abortion of girls, a typical year in China sees 120 boys born for every 100 girls. It might seem plausible that the desire of most young men for marriage would put this less numerous cohort of women on a pedestal, or at least in a position to be highly selective in relation to their multiple suitors.

But instead, the scarcity of young women in China has "fostered a brisk trade of women sold into marriage or slavery, as well as a flourishing prostitution industry," according to Phillip Longman, senior fellow at the liberal New American Foundation and author of *The Empty Cradle*. "This in turn has led to a pandemic of venereal disease, including mounting incidence of HIV/AIDS and Chlamydia, which causes infertility in about 8 percent of women who contract it. . . . In some major provinces, such as Hainan and Guangdong, the surplus of male over female infants exceeds 30 percent. By 2020, the number of unattached young men in China could reach 33 million. The few other examples in history of societies in which sex ratios become unbalanced in this way—third-century Rome, for example, or the American Western frontier in the mid-nineteenth century—tended to be highly volatile and violent."*

The cover of the March 6–12, 2010, issue of *The Economist* was titled in huge letters "GENDERCIDE: What Happened to 100 million baby girls?" And the pro-choice magazine's multi-article update provided few grounds for optimism: "The destruction is worst in China but has spread far beyond. Other East Asian countries, including Taiwan and Singapore, former [C]ommunist states in the western Balkans and the Caucasus, and even sections of America's population (Chinese- and Japanese-Americans, for example): [A]ll these have distorted sex ratios. Gendercide exists on almost every continent. It affects rich and poor; educated and illiterate; Hindu, Muslim, Confucian and Christian alike."

Although the abortion of girls is in some respects a carryover from the female infanticide of more primitive eras, legal abortion has brought with it male-female birth discrepancies that dwarf those recorded in earlier times. Moreover, *The Economist* found it is the more affluent provinces of China and India that tend to have the highest boy-over-girl asymmetries. One reason is that China enforces its one-child policy much more strictly in the (far more affluent) cities than it does in the countryside, but that can't be the reason for strikingly high levels of sex selection in economically dynamic northern India, which has no coercive one-child policy. The pattern points instead to the ideological strength of the sexual revolution among budding economic elites. Of all the dozens of countries where a high level of male birth predominance appeared in recent decades, only increasingly

---

* Phillip Longman, *The Empty Cradle: How Falling Birthrates Threaten World Prosperity and What to Do About It* (New York, N.Y.: Basic Books, 2004), 54.

Christian South Korea has seen a retracing of gender asymmetry back to near parity.

How are things panning out in the country characterized by the deepest and most extended pattern of sex-selection abortion of female babies? According to *The Economist*, the "crime rate has almost doubled in China during the past 20 years of rising sex ratios, with stories abounding of bride abduction, the trafficking of women, rape and prostitution." A study commissioned by the Bonn-based Institute for the Study of Labor concluded that these phenomena are intimately connected to each other—and above all to the accelerating decline of women as a percentage of China's population.

Sexual Liberation and Human Trafficking

Another clear consequence of the sexual revolution, and specifically its raising up of a global mass market of sexually liberated male consumers, is the worldwide explosion in sex trafficking of women, many of whom are below the age of consent when they fall into this life. Trafficking is a confusing term, implying that transportation of the victims is the core of the activity. It is true that moving women and children to an unfamiliar locale is a frequent component of sex trafficking, but more salient is the condition of the victims once they've been moved. That condition is a form of involuntary servitude bordering on slavery.

To be fair, most modern feminists believe sex trafficking and prostitution are very bad for women (although few make the obvious connection between the rise of sex trafficking and the triumphs of the sexual revolution). But a surprising number of left feminist groups fighting the exploitation of women believe that the solution for many prostitutes and trafficking victims is not rescue or escape, but organization as "sex workers," with innovative new labor unions displacing the pimps and madams of less enlightened times. Here the adversarial feminist ideal of women gaining autonomous control of their bodies is pushed toward an ultimate logic of women commodifying their bodies to market them to male consumers. For such feminists, even what might look to some like primordial sex bondage can morph into a benign new form of economic liberation.

One could also argue that at least some of these impacts of the sexual revolution on women, however unfortunate, are necessary accompaniments of the larger feminist project of liberation. Adversarial feminists, in particular, still seem certain that rendering sex mainly recreational is the only way for women to achieve a measure of independence from the nemeses of their self-fulfillment: husbands and children.

The harvest, many believe, is the remarkable and growing success of women in the professional life of the United States and other affluent countries. This is a rise toward parity and even beyond. Particularly striking is the fact that women now constitute close to 60 percent of all American undergraduates.

Such advances, evaluated in themselves, are consistent with the core agenda of the conservative enlightenment, which is about continuing the implementation of innate human equality in a non-monarchical culture still at a comparatively early stage of development in the context of five thousand years of recorded history. To the extent American social conservatives have reservations about the emergence of female equality, it is a fear that the cost will be a further weakening of the institution of monogamous marriage. This decline is hard to miss, chronicled as it is by left-of-center establishment journalists with scarcely concealed satisfaction, often in the context of promoting same-sex marriage as the next logical step along the path of equality, newly redefined. Another way of looking at it is that more than

293

a few social conservatives fear that the central premise of adversarial feminism—that women's advancement depends *by definition* on the decline of monogamous childbearing marriage—is proving correct.

Childbearing as a Goal of Women

But fear that a social decline is irreversibly connected to a widely supported economic advance can lay the groundwork for ceasing to fight such a decline. A number of surveys suggest that American women, precursors of female opinion nearly everywhere else, are far from seeing husbands and children as the chief impediments to their fulfillment or happiness.

Phillip Longman cites a number of polls suggesting that increasing numbers of women (as well as most men) hope to get married and have children.[*] He also notes that couples are overly optimistic about how adversely the trend toward postponing marriage and children affects their lifetime fertility, and in practice they wind up giving birth to fewer children than they would have liked.[†] Furthermore, contrary to stereotypes, more American women express a desire to quit or cut back on paying jobs to be at home with their young children than was the case a decade or so ago.

Yet year after year, American marriages seem to result in fewer children. The most recent fertility rate is less than 1.3 children per marriage (with the remainder of 0.8 children now being born to unmarried women). And marriages show no sign of witnessing a reduction in the average number of hours a wife works for pay outside the home. The trend continues to be strikingly and overwhelmingly in the other direction.

---

[*] Ibid., 79–81, 83, 85–86.
[†] Ibid., 83.

Between 1950 and 2000, the number of American adults participating in the labor market (that is, working for pay or unemployed—defined as looking for paid work outside the home) rose from 59 percent to 67 percent. But within this historic increase, the participation of women in the labor market rose from 34 to 60 percent, while the participation of men *declined* from 86 to 74 percent. Early indications are that the 2007–2009 recession, which as to be expected reduced employment and labor-force participation among both men and women, set back men significantly more than it did women. Definitive numbers are not available at this writing, but labor-force participation among men probably dropped to a range of between 62 and 64 percent, while women maintained levels of around 53 or 54 percent. So the male paid-employment lead of 86 to 34 percent of 1950—a 52-percentage-point asymmetry—has shrunk to a gap of 10 points or so amid the high unemployment period beginning in 2009, according to most estimates. Why?

One's answer to this question is a rather important one, given the relationship between married women's ability and willingness to take some time off paid work and their ability and willingness to have additional children. Is their desire to withdraw at least partially from paid work and have more children—consistently expressed to pollsters and social researchers—a sham, masking a fervent desire to continue working outside the home at the expense of having a second or third child? Or is some other dynamic at work?

Entitlements and the Feminization of Work

In *Redeeming Economics*, John Mueller undertakes an in-depth econometric analysis of the impact of federal entitlement spending. He demonstrates that the surge in transfer payments of recent decades has increased unemployment and significantly reduced take-home pay for workers by reducing the potential for after-tax income while simultaneously increasing employers' labor expenses.

Moreover, the taxation of labor, the method usually chosen to pay for entitlements, lessens the number of hours worked and, as a consequence, overall national output. In *The Impact of Labor Taxes on Labor Supply*, Arizona State professor Richard Rogerson looks at 50 years of time-series data from the United States and 14 other affluent countries. He found that a 10 percent increase in the tax rate on labor leads to a 10 to 15 percent decline in hours worked. Rogerson notes that in this regard so-called consumption taxes such as the Value Added Tax (VAT), adopted by most industrialized countries in recent decades beginning in the 1960s but not by the U.S., operate identically to overt taxes on labor. Whatever they are called, increasing such taxes puts mounting pressure on working families with children—the families most likely to have defined spending needs.*

Such supply-side studies have quantified broad economic effects long suspected by conservatives. More startling is Mueller's finding that, depending on the type of entitlement, there is an enormous difference in the net impact on male vs. female participation in the paid-labor market. Transfer payments that go to people in the labor market—such as unemployment insurance and welfare that goes to the able-bodied, including a big portion of the mammoth food-stamp program—reduce male and female pay and employment roughly equally. However, the most rapidly growing portion of American entitlement spending consists of transfer payments to people completely outside the labor market—mainly the retired and those who are inac-

---

* Richard Rogerson, *The Impact of Labor Taxes on Labor Supply* (Washington, D.C.: AEI Press, 2010).

tive for medical reasons. Because the structure of most marriages still leaves men greatly exceeding women in lifetime work
income, and because women are eligible for fewer of the non-
labor-market entitlements during their years of prime earning
potential, increasing transfer payments to people outside the
labor market causes a sharp increase in labor-market participation by women while at the same time lessening labor-market
participation by men.

What this means is that national tax and entitlement policy in
the U.S. and most other affluent nations, taken alone and quite
apart from underlying cultural trends, is resulting in growing
feminization of paid-work incentives. President Obama's chief
economic adviser, Lawrence Summers, lamented the outcome as
it relates to male employment in an April 2010 interview with
The Hill: "The best way to put it is this: Forty years ago, one in
20 men [ages] 25 to 54, in America, was not working at a given
point in time. Today, the number is not one in 20. It's one in five.
And a good guess, based on extrapolation of trends in this area, is
that when the economy recovers, five years from now, assuming
we return to normal cyclical conditions, one in six men who are
25 to 54 will not be working at any point in time."

What if all government transfer payments were to disappear?
Mueller estimates that labor-market employment of men would
rise to 89 percent while labor-market employment of women
would fall to 25 percent. These are male and female participation
rates comparable with those of 1950, when federal entitlements
were quite low as a share of national income.

Mueller does not argue, even in the context of such an
unlikely collapse in entitlements, that the massive entry into the
work force of American women would all be undone, or even that
it should be undone. The average job of 2010 is less physically
demanding than the average job of 1950, and far more women are

obtaining the college credentials that provide entry to the bulk of new jobs in a modern information economy.[*]

But it does suggest that a large number of those married women who express the desire to sacrifice some or all of their paid work to have additional children would in fact do so, if economic conditions and incentives changed in a pro-family direction. It also suggests that recent fertility declines and the resultant aging of the work force are not a preordained result of greater affluence—the American economy was never more dynamic than during the post–World War II baby boom—but of the nature and growth of modern welfare states, especially when these intersect with legalization of abortion and the rest of the sexual revolution.

Bismarck and the Entitlement State

As I have argued throughout this book, the sexual revolution is integral to the origin and nature of the left since the left's inception in the Paris of the 1790s, and the sexual revolution's transformative success in the past four decades is therefore the global left's greatest political triumph. But perhaps surprisingly, the left did not invent the modern entitlement-driven welfare state. It was formulated and enacted in Germany in the 1880s by that newly united country's first chancellor, Otto von Bismarck, the 19th century's most powerful monarchist and most effective opponent of political equality.

Bismarck hated and feared the left. In the years immediately prior to his social legislation, he accused German socialists (probably inaccurately) of two unsuccessful attempts on the life of the emperor, and he won approval of legislation outlawing the Social-

---

[*] Mueller, op. cit.

ist Party (whose leaders promptly gained seats in the Reichstag by running as independents).

Bismarck was usually either opaque or deceptive about the motives behind his political actions, but most contemporary German political elites believed his enactment of health insurance (1883), accident insurance (1884), and old-age and disability insurance (1889) added up to a concerted move to neuter the left. The Second Reich's conferral of unexpected benefits on the masses was designed, most German politicians believed, to dull the cutting edge of socialism's revolutionary fervor. How urgent is violent or even electoral revolution if the state is now committed to generous aid for the working class?

The German left understood this line of attack as well as Bismarck, but despite growing legislative strength in the Reichstag, there was little they could do about it. In the first decade or two after Bismarck inaugurated the world's first welfare state, it's fair to say that the German left and their most implacable foes, the monarchists, shared a second order of agreement: Bismarck's design had worked. The working masses had been bought off, and the German left lost its chance to gain the upper hand. Even in the chaos that followed Germany's defeat in World War I, the German left, once militant and dynamic, never gained the critical momentum it was soon to enjoy in other European countries, including France and even Britain.

But in the longer run, the welfare state is of course proving a threat not only to the chances for socialist revolution, but to the conservative enlightenment as well. This became true in the 1960s and afterward, when American and (particularly) European political elites utilized the sustained economic growth of the post–World War II era to vastly expand the size of transfer payments and social entitlements as a share of their national incomes.

Bismarck would have been dismayed had he lived to see the fall of ruling monarchy in the aftermath of World War I, but his invention's negative impact on the democratically oriented conservative enlightenment would have provided him great satisfaction. In Bismarck's time in power, 1862 to 1890, the left had not yet gained firm political power in a single European country. But the conservative enlightenment had a strong foothold in Britain, particularly in the second half of the century when William Gladstone came to dominate Britain's reform agenda, first as a cabinet member and later as prime minister. And Bismarck's loathing of Gladstone and his democratic reformism was so intense (according to his English biographer Edward Crankshaw) that he could barely mention the British leader's name without losing his composure.* To the iron chancellor, Gladstone was the epitome of everything that was threatening in the modern world. And Gladstone strongly resisted not only predatory empire-building but also the Bismarck-invented paternalistic welfare state, believing as he did that economic dynamism and the independence it brought were integral to the electorate's growing ability to self-govern.

Like the bulk of the European blood elites he led to such a remarkable political comeback in the second half of his century, Bismarck despised both kinds of equality put forward by the enlightenment—the God-given, democratic-leaning innate equality favored by the conservative enlightenment no less than the elite-managed social and economic equality, with its ultimate goal of moral liberation, favored by the left enlightenment. In line with its actual origin, one could argue that the entitlement-driven welfare state at root is about neither kind of equality, but the kind of paternalism European blood elites clung to in resisting universal equality. It's a form of paternalism that, at least stylistically, made a seamless transition to its post-monarchical version, egalitarian elitism, which has proven particularly attractive to the nominally anti-aristocratic bureaucratic elites who

* Edward Crankshaw, *Bismarck* (New York, N.Y.: The Viking Press, 1981), 377–378, 397.

issue their deadening summonses to conformity from Brussels and Strasbourg.

*****

So what does all this say about the global future of social conservatism? The outcome of today's three-way ideological struggle is no more predictable to me today than was the decades-long, worldwide upheaval that erupted a short time after I became a college freshman in 1961. But I'm confident of the importance of several factors in this clash.

Because it is based on the natural law believed in by our founders, American social conservatism has a universal application. As Abraham Lincoln and Ronald Reagan both understood, American exceptionalism has global power because, like its rivals the left and Islam, it is either universal or it is of no permanent consequence. There is no middle ground. A universal politics cannot turn its back on the rest of the world without conceding its own irrelevance, a reality that American social conservatives—the most powerful demographic base for such things as alliance with Israel, morality in foreign policy, and universal human rights—increasingly accept.

Because of the now unavoidable collision of the entitlement-driven, overtaxing welfare state, on the one hand, and restoration of sustainable human fertility, on the other, social conservatism and economic conservatism must end the fiction that they are operating in separate, fundamentally unrelated realms of human affairs. The rise of the economic-centered Tea Party movement, as well as its affinity and operational alliance with social conservatism during the 2010 election cycle, suggests this may be starting to happen. In the years ahead, analysts such as Jack Kemp's long-time chief economist John Mueller will either be permitted to provide the economic and demographic underpinning for this budding alliance, or conservatives will find it impossible to over-come the unified, unceasing, fully integrated assault of an elitist global left whose mix of social and economic policies has proven itself capable of bringing on a worldwide demographic collapse.

While it remains true that social conservatism only exists in explicit form in the United States, any success it has here will not go unnoticed or remain unimitated in other countries and regions. The power—which includes the staying power—of the founding vision of the United States is so compelling that, as long as this vision is capable of domestic victory, the world's electorates will sense they have an open path to the future that represents an attractive alternative to the paternalistic creeds on offer from Islam and the left. And Lincoln was surely right when he said: "America will never be destroyed from the outside. If we falter and lose our freedoms, it will be because we destroyed ourselves." Our idea of a nation, our nation of an idea, can perish only through an internal process of self-amputation that still looks like the most un-American outcome of all.

INDEX

Bush, George W.: attempts to ease polarization, 101–103, 123; Department of Homeland Security and, 73–74, 107; economic and taxation issues, 103, 113–116, 121–122; election of 2000 and, 45–49; faith-based initiatives of, 61–65, 103–107, 121; Iraq War and, 66–67, 74–78, 120–121; same-sex marriage and, 71, 79–97, 108–109, 121; September 11 attacks and move to moralism from realism in foreign policy, 65–71; and social issues, generally, 61–65; Social Security reform and, 116–120; stem cell research and, 64, 80, 113; Supreme Court nominees, 109–113, 120

Bush, Jeb, 93

Buttiglione, Rocco, 234

Calvinists, rejection of subordination of church to state, 183–184

Campbell, Tom, 4

Campbell-Bannerman, Henry, 194

Canning, George, 179

CARE Act, 105–106

Carter, Jimmy, 23, 24, 25–26, 29, 67, 115, 264

Casey, Robert, 37

Casey, William, 140

Castle, Michael, 4

Castlereagh, Lord, 179

Cato Institute, 270

Chamberlain, Houston Stewart, 185

Charlemagne, 172

Charles I, King of England, 157

Charles II, King of England, 157

Charles V, Holy Roman Emperor, 173

Cheney, Dick, 66–67

Cheney, Mary, 86, 96

child tax credit, 114

childbearing: discouraged by feminism, 248, 277–287; as goal of women, 293–295

China: business climate in, 257; Confucian, 169, 240; Cultural Revolution in, 133–134, 142; one-child policy, 143, 239, 290–291; religion in, 146, 274; unrest in 1960s, 133

Chirac, Jacques, 220–221

Christian Democratic Union (CDU), in Germany, 210–213

civil rights movement, 131–132

Clark, William, 140

Cleveland, Grover, 201

Clifford, Clark, 136–137

Climate change, 248

Gore, Al, 19, 45–49, 62, 71, 104, 117

Gramsci, Antonio, 58, 141, 278

Great Awakening, 146

Great Britain: free trade and, 262–263; Muslims and lack of assimilation, 257–258; political equality in, 165–167, 176–179; rejection of conflict-driven nationalism, 187, 191–199; role of religion and, 147; supply-side economics and, 52–53

Greece, 179

Greenspan, Alan, 265

Gregory, Dick, 138

Hastert, Dennis, 117

Hegel, Georg Wilhelm Friedrich, 187–189

Helms, Jesse, 68

Henry, Patrick, 166

Henry the Navigator, Prince of Portugal, 169

higher education: political correctness and, 142, 145; women and, 286

Hitler, Adolf, 203–204

Hofstadter, Richard, 29

Homeland Security, Department of, 73–74, 107

Hoover, Herbert, 28

Horton, Willie, 19

human trafficking, 292–293

Humphrey, Hubert, 138–139

Hussein, Saddam. *See* Iraq War

hyper-nationalism, fascism as, 204, 245

immigration: historical, 253–254; micro-immigration to U.S. and, 254–257, 258; multiculturalism, Europe's moral liberation, and rejection of assimilation, 257–262

Impact of Labor Taxes on Labor Supply, The (Rogerson), 296

India, 146, 219, 248, 274

Indonesia, 146

Internal Revenue Service, 26

Iowa, 97

Iran, 273

Iran-Contra investigation, 78

Iraq War, 51, 66–67, 69, 74–78, 99, 120–121

Ireland: economic issues, 6, 231–232; European Union and, 231–232, 234, 237; self-government issues, 191–192, 195–198

Islam: birth rates and, 273; as conflicting belief system to social conservatism, 251–252, 301–302; Islamic caliphates and Ottoman Empire, 169, 172–173, 179, 240; in Third World, 274; women and, 276

unitary rule: conflict theory and
regression to, 168, 180–191; by
parliaments, 217; power and,
158; religion and, 150–154;
tension between political
diversity and 167–180
United Nations, 207
United States: conflict theory
and rise of the left in, 199–201;
Europe's decoupling from,
226–228; financial "crisis"
in, 265–266; globalization
and, 263–265; left's assault
on institutions in, 131–132;
micro-immigration to,
254–257; in 1960s, 130–145;
political equality in, 165–167;
realignment of elite opinion
to left and popular opinion
to right, 138–140, 209–210;
rejection of conflict-driven
nationalism, 191–199; religion's
role in, 146–149; religion's
role in, and rise of secularism,
152–154; religion's vitality
in, 215–216, 246; strength
of independent branches of
government, 220
Universal Declaration of Human
Rights, 207, 238, 246
urbanization, role of women and,
284–287

Value Added Tax (VAT), 296
Vietnam war, 132, 136–137
Volcker, Paul, 115, 264–265
volkenwanderung (wandering of
peoples), 254
Voting Rights Act of 1965,
131–132

Wagner, Richard, 185, 203, 245,
249
Walker, Vaughn, 2–3
Walsh, Lawrence, 78
Wanniski, Jude, 264
Washington, George, 166
Washington Post, 139
Washington State, 90
Webster v. Reproductive Services,
33–35, 36, 39, 42, 69
Weekly Standard, 1
Weitzman, Lenore, 289
Wellington, Arthur Wellesley,
Duke of, 176, 185
Western Europe. *See* Europe;
European Union; *specific
countries*
Westphalia, Treaty of, 151, 174,
179, 180, 258
Wilberforce, William, 179
Wilder, Douglas, 34
Wilhelm II, Kaiser, 186, 190
Will, George, 19
William of Orange, 147, 158

Wilson, Woodrow, 200–201, 242
women: childbearing and, 293–
295; conflict theory and, 277–
278; entitlements and, 295–
301; feminism and denigration
of marriage and childbearing,
277–280; gender gap and, 280–
282; gender-based abortion,
290–292; human trafficking
and, 292–293; Islam and,
276; sexual revolution, birth
rates, and divorce, 287–289;
urbanization and, 280–282
World War I, 202
World War II, 203–205

"Year of the Woman" (1992
election), 36–37, 39, 42
Yellen, Janet, 289

ACKNOWLEDGMENTS

I would like to thank the Ethics and Public Policy Center in Washington, D.C., and its president, Edward Whelan, for making me a Visiting Fellow during the research and writing of this book beginning in 2007. Without EPPC's encouragement and generous financial help, completing it would not have been possible. In particular I would like to thank Mr. Whelan and EPPC's Hertog Fellow, Yuval Levin, for their moral support and sage advice.

My longtime business partner and mentor, Frank Cannon, urged me to write this book and greatly influenced the topics it dealt with. Professor Robert George, holder of the McCormick Chair at Princeton University and a founder of the American Principles Project, where I work as Policy Director, was instrumental in shaping the subject matter and helping me obtain backing for the project. The support and advice I received from Ralph

Benko, Merrick Carey, Keith Fimian, Mary Jo Joyce, Lewis Lehrman, James McLaughlin, the late Robert Novak, Robert Odle, Allan Ryskind, Craig Shirley, David Smick, Walter Stingle, and Kenneth Tomlinson were irreplaceable. Likewise for the shrewd suggestions of Roger Kimball and the superb editing and design by his team at Encounter Books.

Finally, I am thankful for my wife, Rosalie, and our four children, who put up with odd hours and eccentric behavior from a husband and father whose production of prose flows anything but smoothly.